COMMON WISDOM TO PROPER UNDERSTANDING

The Simplicity
of Wisdom
for Practical Living:
My Posted Sermons 2015

Pastor
Stephen Kyeyune

authorHOUSE®

AuthorHouse™
1663 Liberty Drive
Bloomington, IN 47403
www.authorhouse.com
Phone: 1 (800) 839-8640

Published by AuthorHouse 04/21/2016

ISBN: 978-1-5246-0501-8(sc)
ISBN: 978-1-5246-0500-1 (e)

Library of Congress Control Number: 2016906699

Print information available on the last page.

Any people depicted in stock imagery provided by Thinkstock are models, and such images are being used for illustrative purposes only. Certain stock imagery © Thinkstock.

This book is printed on acid-free paper.

Contents

About the Author

Pastor Stephen Kyeyune is currently the senior pastor of the Multicultural Family Fellowship Church at South Bend Indiana, USA. He is the author of several books including The New Generation of Worshipers; The Spirit is the Crown of the heart; The Acts of the Holy Spirit; When God Calls a Man; The Legacy of a Hero; A Miracle at Prairie Avenue; Devotional Journal Living; A series of books> Shaping the Society.

You may contact me on the address below:
Pastor Stephen Kyeyune
2029 South Michigan Street
South Bend Indiana 466613
<stephkyeyu@hotmail.com>

From my Desk

It is wise to acknowledge that we are different. One main reason is because our God is the God of variety. He created us different but equally beautiful in His eyes. We look different and our desires are different. Most probably because we grow up in different environments, and we learn how to solve the puzzles of life in different ways. Nature has a way of turning things around. Nature puts things at the top for a period and replaces them with others. Nature has tremendous impact on our habits too. Also, the impact of culture cannot be underestimated. Some things which are embraced by one culture are a reproach to others. The Church is bigger, older, and more important than any nation or culture. The Church is the cradle of a civilized culture. Then the fact that we are not exposed to the same opportunities. For example, some are born in wealthy families whereas others in relatively poor families. Knowledge increases with opportunities. In spite of our differences, we are all equally loved and valued by God. We all stand at the same level beneath the cross. None is alleviated above the other. The Bible encourages us to seek knowledge and understanding. In this book, I have managed to come up with some nuggets of wisdom for practical living.

Identifying a problem is the key to finding a solution. Then seeking godly wisdom to solve it. It is possible to make art a philosophy, and philosophy an art but the puzzles of life cannot be solved philosophically. The reason is because life is neither a mere mode of fiction nor a myth. God did not throw us into the troubled waters, in the pool of this world, without giving us the life jacket (blueprint) to help us to swim ashore. God is the source of life; He regulated life with some physical and moral laws that we may ignore at our peril. A life lived apart from God ends in disaster.

In this book, I have summed up everything you need in an epigram to your satisfaction. This book unveils nuggets of wisdom strategically one must stake if he or she is seeking success. It is my pleasure to introduce to you Christ-like characters. Those of you who are already in the sheep fold of the Chief Shepherd you will be strengthened, and those thinking about entering or have just entered you will be encouraged. Those thinking about leaving will think again and return to the sheep fold because that is where the future belongs. We have seen what happens to those who walk outside the sheep fold of Christ.

I always stand on this biblical truth that I can do all things through Christ who strengthens me (Philippians 4:13). But God blesses me in the context of family and friends like you. I want specifically to address my friends on social media: I made the right choice to have you and you made the right choice to accept me. I will cherish this forever. My doctrine is that, 'if you want friends be friendly.'

It is staggering for me to have so many friends on Facebook. Within such a short time the chain of friendship between us has tautened and blossomed. I never dreamed of having more than five hundred friends in a year!

With modern technology, it is easy to find friends. Social media has denied many to shine anonymously. Once you sign up on Twitter, LinkedIn or Skype, which are the playgrounds for every Tom, Dick, Harry and Harriet, you cease to be discreet. People can find you whenever they want. At the click of the mouse, Google will bring up your name or photograph.

To me, building up a network with key, knowledgeable and most importantly, trusted friends is paramount. Not just numerically but establishing and creating relationships that add value to my life and your lives. In pursuit of my objectives, I make sure that I send a personalized messages (inbox) to every friend of mine whenever there is a need. I don't mean one of those terrible copy and paste messages where you just change the name but a fresh email, with content aimed at establishing effective communication and maintaining relationships with my current friends. Also, I take a giant step to know your friends and befriend them too.

We may not necessarily ever met but we have come to know each other to a reasonable depth. You are in my heart and I am in your hearts. Indeed, the safest place where you can be is in the heart of those who loves you, where no one can hurt you.

Great things do come in small packages; once we were strangers, but now we are acquainted. You mean a lot me! We are not friends coincidentally. We were marched by divine appointment, and we expect to continue to be that way. Let us continue building a friendship circle that cannot be infiltrated by any adversity. I know there are going to be ups and downs but whenever we are weaned from our timidity, suddenly in the flush of love's light we dare to be brave. Remember that love is the strongest bond because love costs all we are and we will ever be phenomenally.

Special thanks go to those friends who constantly commented on my daily postings. At times my postings are challenging but cheers and special thanks to each and everyone who believed and still believes in me even in those moments when my life seems not to be promising and predictable. You give me a reason and courage to push on. I like this comment that was posted by one of my friends: "Tolerance is the password! And living and let live too! Facebook friends will take for granted even the most annoying thing about a friend, look at it, move on and accept each other as they are."

I acknowledge that we are different people genetically, culturally, mentally and we have different interests socially. As Aidan Jones says, "With social media playing a much greater role in how we network, the age of who knows you is becoming ever more important, and with this comes the responsibility of monitoring what you want people to know about you."

Mutual friendship depends on mutual trust. We shall continue like this, no retrogression, and no slowing down. Most probably in many cases what it takes to forge a long-lasting friendship is when our beliefs and ideals align. We can ignore some of the negative quirks in a friend's character as long as what brought us together stays intact.

Friends on social media are friends not out of pledge or any written document but it is friendship based on value and trust registered at the hearts. It is heart to heart trust; no penalties, no compromises. Just pure goodwill and love. In real life, people befriend those whom they agree with. But it is not the case with social media. Most of our friends are people we do not know well. Some of them are consumed with erratic behaviors contrary to our values. Facebook defies logic because in real life people judge your character by observing the characters of your closest companions. On social media, we have all kinds of people, and it is not logic to over-analyze the whole history and character of an individual by examining their associates.

I want to talk directly to my friends on Facebook. We are friends and mutual friends. We may not necessarily know each other well because I have never had any physical contact with most of you but we have many things in common that bind us together. That is why we are together on this platform. I can daily feel the love oozing from the pages of your postings. Our friendship is inked in incentive intimacy. It is sufficient that friends like you, on the social media, are ever there to offer moral and emotional support whenever there is a need. I can count on your shoulder to lean on in times of need.

I want to thank my Facebook friends in advance. I am humbled by your educative postings and comments on my postings. Ironically, once you post something on the social media, you open it up for everybody to share it; you no longer have a right to it. I like most of your postings but whenever I scroll through your posting, I am tempted to share only those postings which I feel might be substantially helpful to somebody out there. For my part, I do not read to please myself and do not like only what suits my taste. I look beyond entertaining to educating and much more to winning a soul to Christ and to strengthen those who are already saved. Taking into account the fact that to be born again does not mean ceasing to sin. It means exchanging our weaknesses with the strength of Christ that works in us teaching us to obey by the grace of God. Our new born nature does not eliminate the old nature but simply weakens it terribly. That is why even after we are born again we need to repent recurrently, not to be reborn again, but to sustain our communication with God that is already in place.

We have different weaknesses, and we should be careful to accommodate others weaknesses. We should avoid becoming snares leading to the fall of others. Yes, there are things posted which might not suit our tastes but it does not mean that they are completely useless to others. Given the fact, it is important to put others interests above ours. For example, I hate to watch bloodshed. Partly because of the trauma I went through during Idi Amin's times. Recently, I was greatly disturbed by the images posted during the weeks of xenophobic violence in the port city of Durban (South Africa), but for the sake of others, I reserved my comments. On the other side, one young man who happened to be one of my close associates benefited from the posted images. This young man who happened to be a Black American was obsessed with an ethnic stereotype labelling all White people to be racist. I had previously tried in vain to convince him that racism is an attitude of the heart as opposed to the color of the skin. But after watching the violence of Black Africans against Black Africans he was never the same; he believed me. Let us not rush into judgment when commenting on the postings of others. "The devil is happy when the critics run you off."

Social media defies nature. The more we are geographically separated, the closer we become friends by regularly communicating and sharing information. I have friends from all corners of the continents. Social media allows us to interact in spite of our differences. Social media has demystified the notion that some people in their own social set up are more important than others. The debate on recalcitrant and the social walls dividing us is gradually drying up. Somehow people are no longer willing to engage in bitter and entrenched biases on social media anymore. Social media helps us to eradicate stereotypes and explains who we are to others better. Of course, we still have a lot of bigotry and wrong stereotypes, but the bitterness and ignorance are slowly getting eroded.

Social media bridged the generation gap. We can spontaneously interact with people of all ages. Social media has liberated many social groups especially groups that were hitherto barred from expressing themselves on sensitive issues such as love. I think women, young and old, know exactly what I mean.

In this era of technology, the internet is the window to the world. I am thrilled whenever the photos of my Facebook friends flash on my screen. I am radically passionate to click 'Like' on each one of the photos posted, when I don't, it is because I am turned off by the appearance of the posted image, in particular when the dressing code contradicts my values. A picture is worth a thousand words. Likewise, Uncensored Revealing Photos paint a thousand words without any vowels. In everything we do there is a need to acknowledge that we are not the center of this universe but God is. Let us, therefore, bring values to Facebook while we are aware that we are accountable to the Supreme God for our actions in spite of the freedom of speech and expression. "Righteousness exalts a nation: but sin is a reproach to any people" (Proverbs 14:34).

I want to discuss the importance of reading. The fact is, most Americans just don't make reading a priority. According to the Pew Research Center, only three in four American adults ages 18 and older claim to have read at least one book in the last year—which means 25 percent haven't. Twenty-eight percent say they read an e-book while half listened to an audio book.

Somebody said that the safest place to hide your dollar bill is in a book. The reason he gave is that even if you leave it anywhere in the public place, you are most likely to find it as you left it with your money inside. Since few people are interested in reading, your money is safe in the book because nobody is likely to temper with it. No wonder we have low literacy levels. Stand warned that reading can seriously damage your ignorance. No wonder C.S. Lewis said, "You can never get a cup of tea large enough or a book long enough to suit me."

Charity begins at home. Reading should take a sizable portion of the family value time. Do you have young kids? Well, get a glass of iced tea, take them out to the porch or the couch and read to them! John Stonestreet says that there's an interesting discipline called bibliotherapy that addresses psychological and emotional issues via reading. Instead of "Take two aspirin and call me in the morning," it's "Take these books and put your problems in perspective."

Reading is the key to understanding. But you must know good books to read I order to be well informed. As one columnist insinuated. "A well-informed person his spirit yearns constantly for new experiences that will broaden his horizons; he wishes "to follow knowledge like a sinking star beyond the utmost bound of human thought." and forever grow in wisdom and in learning."

Despite the likely challenges encompassing the low literacy levels, we still have the capacity to improve or upgrade at different levels. Writers provide opportunities to retrace our steps from where the rain started. When it comes to prioritizing writers are in a premier league in transforming societies.

Writing is not just a hobby; it is in my blood. I would scrape and sell every little thing I have in order to write and publish a book. As you probably know, I'm a writer by trade but do not write to earn a living but to keep you informed. Somebody said that "It is with writing that we conceal our true intentions." Friends like you have inspired me to write. Every time I am exposed to an interesting article, it becomes like the hot coal in my bosom, such that I would gladly let it go, by sharing it. I am in particular thrilled and attracted to researching faith-inspiring stories involving the Church.

True, none of us was born a writer. It's not a crime if you're not born as one. However, the crime is ignoring your potential capability to write. There is always something interesting to write about. As one writer said that, "Knowledge tormented me to tears, because I couldn't attain the heights of all things that make beautiful the universe. Doing nothing about it enslaves me further into more torture and distress." It is from the same prospective that I decided to pen down what I see and sense.

Facebook presents to us golden opportunities to write our stories and to read other people's stories. This is an exhilarating way to start on your career as an author. We cheat civilization if we don't write our stories. Writing an autobiographical work is not presumptuous. All of us have skeletons in our closets. It occurred to me that it was time to set the record straight. When you write your story don't let anyone else hold the pen; do it yourself and be yourself. I am the author of my life story and reserves the copyright to it. If you wish to edit anything, I am sorry nothing can be edited.

Every person has a story to tell. We are encouraged by reading other people's stories. There is the depth to every story. A story is not just limited to accessing information but includes other things like extending imaginations, facing our fears, discovering and planning our future lives. We have diversities of weaknesses and fears. Reading gets us acquainted with other people's fears and their triumph. The bottom line to the life stories is that God never forsakes us but goes with us through our trials.

We are encouraged by reading posted messages on the social media. In the most trying times of life, it is crucial to speak positive words for your words are containers that bring us out of where we are to where we wish to go. Let us continue that way while eluding inadvertently or foolishly any attempt to maliciously demoralize each other.

According to Titus Kakembo, blogging and social media is a replica of African oral literature, where the narrative instantly gets the audience laughing, crying or rebuking a given post. "If I want to have a hearty laugh on super prose and original imagery, I simply log on or post something for criticism." Ikhelea confided, "There, one's morals are checked. Compliments are showered where they are due. And barbs of criticism are not spared a negative post."

A published author, poet, and columnist Mukhoma Ngugi said the current topics of a blogger today are different from the topics handled by the likes of Chinua Achebe, Okot P'Bitek and others back in the 1960s. "Social media is a response to reinvent traditional literature which was replaced by African Writers Series duplicated from the Western world. But this stereotype of publishers has been replaced by Twitter, Facebook, and blogs."

Social media is journalism at its best. Addressed in the mentioned social media platforms are values like; the plight of social culture, migrants abroad like family break up, non-acceptance by the host communities and unrealized great expectations. Fiction, humor, and satirical stories are common postings on social media which is not the case with good journalism. Professional journalists are critical of satirical writing. They say that it may be the social media's specialty but it is antiquated and definitely of no consequence to the vast majority of people. It is like ghettoizing the noble profession of journalism. Michela Wrong is critical of fiction stories: "In journalism, facts are the foundations of any good story. In fiction, I have to lift real life characters, places, and circumstances. Surprisingly I have been approached by several personalities claiming to be the people in the stories."

Uganda Author's blogger Nyana Kakoma tipped a gathering of hopeful social media fans that the print media platform cannot exist without the other in this generation. Society has an agenda. But ask yourself why the Premier League or The Oscar Awards are so popular. It is because they have successfully branded themselves. People want to know what the other movie, football, and music stars are doing. He summed it all up by saying: "Brand your blog to boost traffic on it. Adverts will follow in a long queue – in the long run."

There are three players in this tragic comedy: the proprietors of the non-paying media outlets who get rich off the wealth of a creative class; the writers who often cling to romantic ideals about what journalism is and deny the realities of a business model; and finally the tragic readers who are left with articles written by those with vested interests.

Fiction sells because most people are interested in reading fiction. I'm not opposed to writing fiction but I am opposed to manipulating others into believing that the fiction tale is factual. All of us have been guilty of posting on social media stories which we thought were true, only to find out later that they were false. Most of these false stories disguise as coming from trusted sources when in reality they are not. Some stories may be true but they are spiced with serious exaggerations and outdated information. So how do we resist the temptation to spread the fake news? Here's what Stetzer suggests: First, when you see a story so shocking you can't believe it—don't. Stop yourself from reflexively sharing it because you think it will outrage all of your friends. "It is YOUR job," writes Stetzer, "yes YOURS—to check the facts. [These websites] are more concerned with gaining your page view than growing your credibility." Second, if you've already been suckered, he suggests posting a retraction for your friends to read. Tell them you're sorry for sharing a false or misleading story and warn them not to do the same. And finally, if you can't confirm that a story is true, just don't post it! Wait a while and see if anyone verifies it. "As Christians," concludes Stetzer, "we have a higher standard than even the journalist. We aren't protecting the reputation of an organization or a website, we bear the name of our King." Yes we do—and this King is the source and standard of all truth and He commands us to hope—not alarmism.

Technology has been used to its uttermost in the area of communication. It's surprising how quickly people get acquainted with the digital progression. Successful people have foresight and flexibility to adjust and adapt to the ever-changing market and technology. The impact of the social media on communication cannot be underestimated. High-speed Internet has become part of our social activities as people keep their smartphones on and with them at all times. The Pew Research Center found 77 percent of Americans polled felt it was acceptable to use a smartphone while strolling down the street. Three-fourths also said it was OK on public transit or while waiting in line at the store.

America, mobile Internet traffic is dominated by YouTube and Facebook. YouTube accounts for nearly 20 percent of all mobile traffic, and Facebook tops 16 percent. Facebook on July 30th said it is ready to begin test flights of a high-altitude drone designed to provide Internet access to remote locations of the world. The Aquila drone has a wingspan on par with that of a Boeing 737 jet; weighs less than a small car; can remain aloft for three months or so, and will beam Internet service to the ground from altitudes ranging from 60,000 to 90,000 feet (18,000 to 27,000 meters).

My country, Uganda, is now one of the top ten countries in the world, where people turn to Internet usage for personal communication, business dealings, politics and passing on of information or simply looking for it. In 2001, Uganda had only 40,000 people connected to the internet, today the figure is approaching 9 million users. It is estimated also that over 75 percent of Ugandans at the level of secondary school education and higher, operate a Facebook account. Even those with no internet connected devices are active on the social media platforms through using internet cafes, workplaces, family or friends' devices.

Nigeria has come on the global scene in the information communication technology sector, as 9-year-old Jomiloju Tunde-Oladipo joined the community of achievers when he became one of the world's youngest 2013 certified Microsoft Office specialists for Office Word 2010. The examination report showed Jomiloju scored 769 points, 69 points higher than the required 700 to be recognized as a Microsoft Office Specialist.

The Global alliance has been successful due to social media. Mark Zuckerberg the founder of Facebook says that "Today, we're taking the next step with Internet.org by enabling anyone to build free basic internet services to help connect the world." He insinuated that "We'll make faster progress towards connecting everyone if we all work together and give people even greater choice of services. Giving people these free services is the right thing to do." Facebook boasted of a new benchmark Thursday in its seemingly inexorable march to Internet ubiquity: a billion people used the social network in a single day. 1 in 7 people on Earth used Facebook to connect with their friends and family. Increasing consumers is the priority without allowing Internet companies to exploit them.

Today, most successful businesses around the world achieve the high level of productivity and customer support by implementing network-based communications technology. Success depends on updating communication processes rapidly, in a way that supports future growth. Yael Maguire, the engineering director of the project, told journalists the team had "achieved a significant milestone" with laser communications for high-speed data connections that are faster than most current speeds. Using the solar-powered drone could mean "quickly bringing connectivity to an area that needs it," he said at a presentation at Facebook's California headquarters.

President Obama insinuated that the internet is not a luxury, it is a necessity. Obama has plans to make broadband internet cheaper and affordable for residents of low income areas and public housing. Smartphones have opened a new chapter to the monopoly of internet use globally. The majority of people cannot wait to jump on the bandwagon of owning a smartphone. Telecom companies are trying to outsmart each other and lure more customers to their data services. The companies dangle all sorts of baits – many of them centering around internet speeds - to entice undecided customers to choose them. There is craving for new devices appearing on the market transitory. Instead of focusing on what we actually need, we have an unfortunate tendency to focus on what other people have.

In the coming years, we are going to see more people connected to the internet because the majority of the phones that are coming are internet-enabled. The good part of it is that the social media has created a united voice for advocacy to enhance the youth entrepreneurship. The social media has been instrumental in curbing the alienation of young people from contributing to programs and projects at the community level. The social media has engaged young people's participation in global social activities allowing them to be part of the solution instead of the problem or seeing them as the perpetrators.

Younger adults between the ages of 18 and 29 are most tolerant of public mobile smartphones. They have for the most part effectively used the social media to their advantage. And this is the age group that constitutes the majority of the population, and they are the very people, currently being targeted by all political groups in their political struggles. The majority of the young folks are equipped with mobile devices. You know when you see young folks these days with their heads tilted down, glued to their mobile devices.

But 88 percent said a family dinner was not an appropriate place for phone use and most said the same about a meeting (94 percent), the movie theater (95 percent) and a place of worship (96 percent). Eighty-nine percent said they used their phone during a social gathering -- 61 percent to read a text message or email, 58 percent to take a photo or video, 52 percent to receive a call, and 25 percent to surf the web, for example. On a typical day, it is estimated that

98% of Millennials use smartphones. 81% of Millennials own a smartphone. They do it late at night when their parents are asleep. They do it in restaurants and while crossing busy streets. They do it in the classroom with their hands behind their back. They do it so much their thumbs hurt. No wonder Whats App is currently the biggest messaging social network.

One of the advantages of the internet is that it provides a platform to engage our youth and other stakeholders in enhancing the entrepreneurship qualities which really benefit young entrepreneurs. Social media can be a significant muscle to push the youth to love to work. Taking into account the fact that the youth make up the majority of the world population but yet they are either unemployed or engaged in disguised employment and consequently they are unable to produce and generate income. Therefore, they are unable to contribute to GDP.

Young folks are mentors to each other whereas old folks have no mentors. The old generation are a bit slow to use social media to the full capacity, partly because of our cultural upbringing and the structure of social media that favors youth. The good news is that you don't have to go to college in order to learn to operate these new devices. Every person knows something and teaches the other. One expert on social media asked that, "Are you afraid that the digital migration may find you before you actually migrate? If you need technical advice on what decoder to invest in inbox me and you will get you connected."

Whether you're new to computers or just new to Windows, it's important to learn the basics of using your computer. If it all seems a little overwhelming right now, don't worry! Contact somebody that knows, and he will take you through it step by step and show you some of the most fundamental things you'll need to know, such as how to work with the desktop, how to open and close windows, and how to turn off your computer.

Texting can be an enormous tool. The technology is open for all of us. It is the responsibility for each and every one us to become players rather than spectators objectively to work towards a life we deserve. I call upon all people of good will to dominate the social media network in anticipation to enhance and nature the morality of the young generation through character formation and mentorship.

Before Twitter was a multi-billion dollar tech juggernaut, it was a small short-form messaging service designed to allow users to update their social status with their phone. Twitter limits Tweet length to 140 characters making the definition of a "character" and how they are counted central to any Twitter application. Twitter's already dropped such limits from private messages; it has also introduced a change to the retweet feature, which gives users more space to comment on the tweets they share.

Facebook has become an increasingly important source of news, with 30 percent of adults in the U.S. consuming news on the world's largest social network, according to a 2013 study by the Pew Research Center.

People are increasingly not trusting the newspapers because they are biased. Although journalists still have the upper hand for their professionalism and researches. They rarely report other people's researches. There is a difference between a journalist and a person whose work is to reproduce what has been said. As Mr. Ron Nixon said concerning good journalism: "We are not stenographers but journalists."

Social media is a new phenomenon and it is unstoppable. It is not good news for dictators that are used to regulate media or to sweep some information under the carpet. More people are resorting to social media as their reliable source of information. Pope Francis's willingness to utilize technology has undoubtedly enhanced his popularity, allowing him to connect directly with Catholics and non-Catholics alike. He has called the internet "a gift from God," has held virtual audiences with people from all over the world, and is an avid Twitter user. According to the site Il Sismografo, the pope pulled in 29,000 new followers each day during his recent eight-day trip to South America, versus his already impressive average of 20,000. Pope Francis surpassed 22 million Twitter followers Wednesday on his multiple accounts, joining the ranks of tech-savvy entertainers and world leaders who command tens of millions of eyeballs on social media.

Businesses are booming on social media. We need to reflect on the widespread changes that the social media and the digital revolution have provided us and our businesses. "When you have a social media strategy, you get to know what your customers like and what they don't like, you get new followers hence increasing you target audience," Namara added.

Our day to day activities are highlighted by occasional social turmoil. Protest and activism have become a tool for cheap popularity, recreation and public relations for our celebrities and power thirsty youth. Yet, nothing is exaggerated when reporting in newspapers like Church matters. The world system holds prejudiced views against the Church. Eventually, it has created a dilemma between telling the truth and adhering to the sensibilities of morality. I encourage pastors to use the social media as a platform to reach out to the lost world. Truly the voice of the people is the voice of God. You have the voice, you have the power, you have the muscle and clout to shout and speak on behalf of God and for the people. You have the divine mandate to steer the world in the right direction. Social media provides us the platform to active our objectives. Unfortunately, my experience is that pastors tend to be more committed, resilient and less involved in social media.

The influence of social media cannot be underestimated. Twitter and Facebook are popular in particular because they are easy. It's easy to update a Facebook page with frequency and engage with users there. It's easy to share great links in Twitter that get Re-tweeted and leverage it as a CRM tool. Even easier to set them up. No wonder some significant political figures today opt for the social media platforms in unveiling their candidatures. It is advantageous to launch on social media where they are not limited by sanctions and where there is no wary of the likelihood of the state cracking down on a public launch event. Unlike the media, governments have no control over what is published on social media. It has been proved true that campaigning on social media avails politicians' mileage.

Social media is no man's land. People have freedom to comment as they see things without being pressured. After all, Facebook is not equipped with a tool, whose plug-in verifies the identity of those who post comments or even requiring people to use their real names. Perhaps the nightmare and embarrassing moment is discovering unwanted postings on your home page. Perhaps the nightmare and embarrassing moment is discovering unwanted postings on your home page. It is a disturbing trend. Strange that some people choose to tag others on porn materials without someone's consent. This is bad and I will be glad that I am completely kept out of such posts. To all my friends who have seen this please note that I am a victim of circumstance beyond my own making and I can't in any way be associated with such posts.

Roses have thorns too. In the same manner, the social media has some impediments. Some people abuse the same freedom by going to the extremity. The Internet was supposed to facilitate better exchange between the public and news media. But vile and hateful comments changed all that. In the face of rising vitriol -- attacks, bigotry, and general nastiness -- news organizations are increasingly throwing in the towel on online comments. The fabricated and defaming stories often posted illustrate [the] vileness of the dark forces of disinformation and proclivity of others to readily embrace the negative narrative on others. We can root out this menace by minimizing selfishness and ego. Eternal vigilance is the price worth paying. I am my brothers' and sisters' keeper! I watch their backs and they too reciprocate.

True, the social media is easy to use but easy is not necessarily better unless it leads to outcomes. There are reasons that more robust platforms like blogging are less focused on. It's a blank slate and requires creativity, critical thinking and planning. Not forgetting to mention that Twitter and Facebook (and even LinkedIn) are not opt-in at the source as they are configured as real-time streams. They are designed for you to miss things and focus on just what's new, now.

There are many cyber-crimes cases reported to police. Some people have lost millions of shillings while others are related to threats and acts intended to destabilize the communities. Recently, the president of Uganda twice warned users of social media platforms to stop inciting hatred and tribalism. His warnings followed an audio exchange on Whats-app social media platform between people suspected to be of two ethnic communities from western Uganda each calling the other names.

According to the Prime Minister of Uganda, Ruhakana Rugunda, the issue of cyber security; it is no longer an issue of the computer alone but rather a threat to national security, government, businesses and individuals among others. There are some elements who have been sharing information on social media, Whats-app, and Facebook, something that is not only a threat to Uganda alone but it's a global concern. It can be used in terrorism, some can be conned off through it. The question is "How do you deal with this without compromising the whole issue?" He said that UCC, the regulator is working with security to tackle issues of cyberbullying without compromising our freedom, our mandate and so forth.

Immorality and crime have been recently high rocketing in particular among the youth because of Internet. Given the fact, social media provides ample opportunities to us to fight crime. I came across such websites: Instant Checkmate aggregates hundreds of millions of publicly available criminal, traffic, and arrest records and posts them online so they can easily be searched by anyone. Members of the site can literally begin searching within seconds, and are able to check as many records as they like (think: friends, family, neighbors, etc. etc.). Some opponents of the website say this seems like an invasion of privacy, to advertise people's "previous addresses, phone numbers and birth dates," seems a little excessive. They say that one could easily stalk you with this info if they are good. However, many people have been helped to know well about the people that enter their lives and surroundings. It is a win-win situation!

Another problem is the gradual reduction in physical contacts between people. Researches indicate that abstainers from social media have a richer social life and fewer difficulties in concentrating. Despite the booming of virtual platforms, Skype, Google hangouts, Whats-app, telephone, the fact is that there is no substitute for a face-to-face interaction. Paul Zake insinuated that "I realized mentoring is all about relationships and about 50 percent of communication is non-verbal." As much as texting is good, there is a need to stimulate physical contacts.

January: Month for Preparation to prosper

There is a reason for all of us to thank God for 2015. For those of you who lost deals, achievements and material stuff in the year ending, there is still room to thank God because you are still alive. Remember that life is a precious thing, and in even its humblest form it is superior to death. A living ant is better than a dead lion. This is eminently true in spiritual matters. It is better to be the least in the kingdom of heaven than the greatest out of it. The lowest degree of grace is superior to the noblest development of unregenerate nature. Life is the badge of nobility in the realm of spiritual things, and men without it are only coarser or finer specimens of the same lifeless material, needing to be made alive, for they are dead in trespasses and sins. Think about it!

****

The year is coming to an end in spite of many unfulfilled dreams. Success will certainly come if God promised it to you. Never despair in case you pleaded for something for the past twelve months without manifestation of tangible evidence. Stand assured that God will not turn a deaf ear when His people are serious about a matter that concerns His glory. Remember Jesus asked us to forgive seventy times seven or endlessly (Matthew 18:22). Likewise, we must not dream of unbelief but to hold on to our faith endlessly (seventy times seven). Faith restores expectant hope in a hopeless situation and resists the possibility for you to be crushed by repeated frustrations. "Faith is quickened in order for you to plead more fervently with her God. She is humbled but not crushed: Her groans are deeper, and her sighings more vehement, but she never relaxes her hold or stays her hand."

****

End of the year means ushering in of the New Year. We are about to replace our old calendars with new ones. Old in this case means expired, and new means update. The past year is gone never to resurface. We can't recycle the past time into present. But we can redeem the past by investing wisely in the present. As the year changes make a resolution to change with it. It is far more difficult however to change yourself than turn the calendar to a new page. New Year should be a time for new beginnings and learning experiences. A new beginning can be forged from the shards of the past experiences. Past is experience, Present is experiment, Future is expectation. Use your experience in your experiments to get your expectations. Above all, focus on God who is source of life and the author of time (past, present & future). Plan everything in accordance to His purpose and schedule. Of course, questions about purpose can only be answered by the One who purposed us. Wishing you a happy new year!

****

Time is either the school in which we learn or the fire in which we burn to ashes. The fact that you are still breathing is proof that you survived the flames of the past year. As 2015 slams its door behind us, 2016 swings its door wide open for us. What one always requires at the start of a new adventure is motivations and boosting of morale, along with things to ponder upon. Use your past as lessons of life to begin anew. Be a man and a woman of substance, and seize this opportunity to make a positive move, like a butterfly tearing its cocoon! Remember that a good beginning often determines a good end.

****

End of the year means ushering in of the New Year. We are about to replace our old calendars with new ones. Old in this case means expired, and new means different of its kind as opposed to new of the same kind. The past year is gone, and never to resurface. We can't recycle the past time into present. But we can redeem the past by investing wisely into the present. Make a resolution to change with time. Time is divided into the past, present and future. Past is experience, Present is experiment, Future is expectation. Use your experience in your experiments to get your expectations. A new beginning can be forged from the shards of the past experiences. I know it is grimmer to change yourself than to turn the calendar to a new page. But you have the potentiality to change. Begin by seeking the divine purpose for you in 2016. Of course, questions about purpose can only be answered by the One who purposed us. Wishing you a happy new year!

****

"As you logout of 2015, browse the 2016 domain, double-click GOOD HEALTH, download SUCCESS and install PROSPERITY; while shutting down FAILURE."

****

"As the New Year blossoms, may the journey of your life be fragrant with new opportunities, your days be bright with new hopes and your heart be happy with love! Welcome to 2016." Happy New Year.

************** **********************************

New Year for refreshing. I am refreshed wherever my source is El Shaddai. We plan but we must let God direct our steps. At times, the directives of God are seen by the world as weird. Never be swayed; if it is from God, go for it! Keep away from small people who try to belittle your ambitions. Swim against the tides, and sail to a higher ground. Put your convictions into actions with less worry of the outcome. Find strength in positive vibes. Remember that big dreams are reserved for big dreamers. Discouragement has no place in ambitious people. Ambition is neither a gift nor a privilege for few lucky ones. It is for those who choose to find a purpose and a reason big enough to go after! 2016 is your year of favor.

****

2016 is your year. "Be a voice, not an echo". Just because there is a formula out there for blogging success, doesn't mean you need to echo it to achieve your own success. Be your own voice, let others echo you. Remember that you are complete in Christ. When God is the largest portion of your very being there is nothing outside Him you need. A vision involves trusting in something bigger than you, and in this case, God. Decide that failing is not an option. You are not a failure until you give up. Hope is the precious jewel of faith.

****

Make resolutions but don't share the details of your future plans with people who have no intentions of helping you to implement it! Avoid moving in circles by kicking out of your circles the negative people. Negative people are like a car without gas and engine. You can sit in it, but will take you nowhere!

****

There is beauty in every small detail of life, and we can find it only when we take time to enjoy every moment of it without worrying or fussing. Your biggest asset is the people. Engage them cautiously. Be slow but sure to implementing any idea. Take one step at a time with confidence. Remember that even a snail will eventually reach its destination. Life is beautiful for those who take time to live in the moments that it offers whether positive or negative. Have a blissful New Year!

****

"The best way to predict the future is to create it." I think anything is possible if you have the mindset and the will and desire to do it and invest time in it. Of course remember that without God your efforts will not have lasting results.

****

"Life can only be understood backwards; but it must be lived forwards." May the good times, benevolences and treasures of the past and present become the golden memories of tomorrow. Wishing you a blissful New Year!

****

This year trust in the God of the impossibilities. He plants His footsteps in the sea and rides upon the storm. He can turn your disabilities into abilities.

****

Our mistrust of the future makes it hard to give up the past. Enter the New Year when unburdened of the failures of the past year. Sometimes burning bridges isn't a bad thing, it prevents you from going back to a place you should never have been in the first place to begin with.

****

Past is experience, Present is experiment. Future is expectation! Use your experience in your experiments to get your expectations. Wishing you a happy new year! ~ Albert Mucunguzi

****

Your mission for next year should be not merely to survive, but to thrive and to do everything with passion. Not forgetting to engage some compassion, some humor, and style because life is going to give you what you put in it. Be devoted to putting your whole heart into everything you do. Then pray and wait for God to blossom the works of your hands.

****

The New Year is your year. Your time is coming. You've waited and hoped for a long time. It's right around the corner. You are on the brink. It's time to roll up your sleeves, push on and work harder than ever. Don't allow discouragement to infiltrate your thoughts. Stay positive, stay focused and stay determined. The greatest resistance comes just before the biggest moments of your life. Stay the course. In a moment of time things will change to be in your favor.

****

Start this New Year with enthusiasm. Life is about doing things that we do not necessarily want to do but which we have to do. If God called you to do something do it. Don't do things to impress God because God cannot be impressed. The bottom line is that God is pleased by our faith and faith alone.

****

Missed your promise in the past year? God is never late. He is always on time. God's timing is the perfect timing. Faith is waiting patiently, waiting expectantly and waiting steadily when rooted in the Scriptures. It is believing that God has put a name on something you want. Therefore, no circumstance will swat God's plan to deliver what He promised to do.

****

Your life is your time. How you spend your time determines your life. God is the source of life; plan everything in accordance to His schedule. Of course, questions about purpose can only be answered by the One who purposed us.

****

"You have made us for yourself, O God, and our hearts are restless until they find their rest in you" ~ Augustine

****

Life has twists and turns but God's hand is at the center of the wheel of your life. This reminds me of the story of Joseph. His brothers had a nasty plan for him but God had even a giant plan for his life that could not be swatted. The pit you are in today is the means of your triumph tomorrow.

****

The law of nature states that every object remains at rest until an external force is applied to it. Start with what you have otherwise your dreams will remain elusive. Be expectant and do something in anticipation to win. Put your hands on something and ask God to bless the works of your hands.

****

Catch the vision larger than you. Having a vision is discovering the divine purpose for your life that is much bigger than you. In order to be ready for tomorrow trust in the God of tomorrow. No one is less ready for tomorrow than a person that trusts in their own abilities to change the future.

****

Proverbs 29:18 - "Where there is no vision, the people perish". A vision is about serving others. Christianity cannot be separated from the concept of serving. The only valid vision is about improving the lives of others. This is what it means loving your neighbor as you love yourself (Matthew 22:39). It is searching for Jesus within the lives of others. Jesus said that when you did it to these little ones you did it to me (Matthew 25:40). The vision gives you a purpose to live, a road map for your plans and a glimpse into the future accomplishment. A wise man grabs concepts from the future and places them in now. This is not just a matter of creativity but spiritual impartation. It overlaps the warming glow of rote religiosity and perfunctory performance and draws deep from the blazing rivers of God's eternal purpose.

****

Philippians 4:9 - "The things you have both learned and received, both heard and seen in me, these things do, and the God of peace will be with you." Knowledge brings accountability

****

You can turn the useless into usefulness because God did not create a useless person. "There is a plan and a purpose, a value to every life, no matter what its location, age, gender or disability" ~ Sharron Angle

****

There are a variety of ways in which our brains are fundamentally wired, and they shape how we think and function, right down to our careers and strategies. All of us are gifted to do something. God did not create a useless person. It is not a matter of whether you are gifted but how you are gifted. Don't just do something just because it's a trendy idea and will make you a lot of money. Do something that you are gifted to do. I mean something that you are passionate about and really believe in, and it will carry you through. God gifted you to be everything you have ever dreamed to be. Your gift is not beyond you, it is deep at the center of your being, requiring to be exploited. "Take charge of your life! The tides do not command the ship. The sailor does." Remember that idleness is a risky venture, because it justifies incompetence. You can do better than staying home hunting the squirrels and killing the snakes in the village!

****

A copyist becomes a victim of inconsistency; he is useful to others except to himself. Other people make him useful for themselves.

****

Your thoughts are the seeds. You can grow flowers, or you can grow weeds. Your destination is your decision.

****

Young people need to espouse and cultivate a value system based on love of work. If you do not have a target, you hit it. Never expect to harvest when you did not sow. The young folks of today's generation have lost the moral compass and integrity due to idleness. Building morals is like building a house. Once there is a crack in your morals, you cannot undo it unless you go back and demolish the part that has a crack and rebuilds it all the way from the foundation.

****

Hope you had a great New Year's holiday. Get ready to go back to work but with precaution. Track every single thing you do with such firm awareness that abundance health is better than abundance wealth. Never let your job Jeopardize your health. Happiness is better than money because you cannot keep money in your pocket when your overall health is shriveled and deteriorated. Think about it!

****

You have not danced as yet as long as you can still watch your steps. Real dancing is to step and sway and swerve in musical cadences without conscious calculation of your steps. For a dancer to rise above mediocrity must be a pantomimist. Dance like no one is watching. Work like you don't have to. Give like you don't have a need. Love like you've never been hurt. "A spiral with rhythms of progress and retrogression are mighty and sublime".

****

If a plan doesn't work change the plan but never the goal.

****

Be the change you want to see in the world.

****

The secret to change is to focus all your energy not fighting the old; but on building the new.

****

The lens through which you view the world shapes your reality, if you can change it you can change your reality ~ Jack Nyaga

****

Making mistakes is better than faking perfections

****

Never be afraid to fail. Being defeated is often a temporary condition. Giving up is what makes it permanent.

****

Procrastination is the grave in which opportunities are buried.

****

Two things rob people of their blessings: Failure to start/Failure to finish (unfinished works)

****

You can make all you can as longer as you are giving as much as you can.

****

Appreciate the little you have, and never be afraid of the little you can offer. "To whom little is nothing, nothing is enough."

****

Patience is the virtue that keeps your faith active while waiting for the promises of God. Patience eradicates negative emotions like frustration.

****

Sometimes God finds His heroes in the most unlikely places. God can meet you in your messed up life where you don't expect Him to meet you.

****

Opportunity is a given moment extended to you to do something. Opportunities come and go. Never miss an opportunity to do something because there might be just one of its kind to change your destiny.

****

The greatest pleasure in life is being able to do what someone else convinced you not to do out of fear of failing. I am a strong enough person to accept failure, but I'm not strong enough to handle not trying.

****

Dream big time. Without dreams we reach nothing. Remember that people associate themselves with high achievers.

****

There is so much untapped potential – ranging from designing, trade, agriculture etc. – in the economy. "Your brains are boiling with

ideas." Do not weep because you have no job, create jobs instead." ~ Nigerian billionaire Tony Elumela

****

"It's not about how much you do, but how much love you put into what you do that counts" ~ Mother Teresa

****

The future belongs to those who believe in the beauty of their dreams. Your dreams can be a reality if you passionately pursue them. When things are shaky, hold tight; don't give up. It could be a transition to another level. Even when they crush your hopes, keep dreaming. Even when they let you down, keep dreaming. Even when they shut you down, keep dreaming.

****

"Don't be discouraged by what people see in you! Be encouraged by what God sees in you! Never underrate the person next to you because you never know what the Lord has deposited in that person" ~ Kyeyune Floryn Florence

****

A butterfly passes through stages to reach the beautiful stage. The pupa stage is ugly and not admired by many. But it doesn't remain in that ugly state forever. It is a transit to the adulthood beautiful stage of a butterfly that is admired by all. Don't worry about your current horrid stage because it is a transit to God's final stage glittering with beauty. Rest assured, your destiny was predetermined by God. The heart of Him who has justified you beats with infinite love toward you. Lift your eyes up: God is at work bringing good out of evil, light out of darkness, corrupt out of the incorruptible through His indescribable grace freely demonstrated most supremely in Jesus Christ.

****

Be positive and stay positive by avoiding negativity. Norman Vincent Peale says, "Watch your manner of speech if you wish to develop a peaceful state of mind. Start each day by affirming peaceful, contented and happy attitudes and your days will tend to be pleasant and successful." Set aside some quiet 'me time' for reflection and create a set of deep truths about you that you can speak to yourself every morning. Daily affirmations will prepare you for the tough times in the day.

****

The Journey of life involves many twists and turns, but with faith and courage, no obstacle can stop you from reaching your goals. Remember that, "Smooth seas do not make skillful sailors."

****

You can't get to the top of a ladder without going through the steps of the ladder. Success takes a process.

****

Don't do things to impress others. "When one sets sail to do something great in the hope that he will be applauded at the destination, that motivation and hunger for man's approval becomes a distraction."

****

Never quit because of challenges. See challenges as opportunities to excel. "Stay the course, my friend. Bend but don't break. You were born with a high capacity decoupling capacitor that gives you unimaginable resilience and suppresses life's high-voltage situations. Use it" ~ Julius Lukwago

****

Little things can basically yield to great achievements. Sometimes, great things are done by series of small things brought together. It may sound simplistic, but it works.

****

When you get into a tight place and everything goes against you, never give up then, for that is just the time that the tide will turn ~ Harriet Beecher Stowe

****

When everything seems to be going against you, remember that airplane takes off against the winds, not with it.

****

Entrepreneurship is living a few years of your life like most people won't so that you can spend the rest of your life like most people can't. "Don't compromise yourself. You are all you've got" ~ Janis Joplin

****

It doesn't matter how much resources you have if you do not know how to use them, they will never be enough. Remember that the most important resource at your fingertips is not money on your bank account but people on board.

****

Insecure people are never successful even if they seem to be at the top. They always look down to step on the heads of those who are trying to climb the ladder to the top. A successful person is driven by the desire to see others join him on the same platform through his generosity and positive attitude ~ Godfrey Nsubuga.

****

Most people succeed because they are determined to. The Pain you get is temporary compared to quitting which lasts forever. If you remain static and wait for success to come to you it will certainly not happen. Set yourself into motion; don't wait lest you find the age of the great epics is past.

****

If you want to excel be creative. "You never change something by fighting the existing reality, but you change it by building a new model that will make the existing model obsolete".

****

God never leads us where He cannot sustain us. His grace is ever sufficient for us in all circumstances and conditions of life.

****

If God didn't mean it for you, you have no business with it. But if God meant it for you pursue it with all your mighty. Don't settle for a life of quiet desperation, when you were born for greatness.

****

Life is an echo. What you send out, comes back. What you sow, you reap. What you give, you get. What you see in others, exists in you ~ Zig Ziglar

****

Surrendering to Jesus is giving up everything and follow Him. Sometimes it takes losing everything you have to finally grow and find yourself. All David had were his faith and a rock and he defeated the giant. All you need is faith in the Rock (Jesus) to defeat your giants (Psalms 18:2).

****

It is pointless to ask God for direction if you are not willing to move your feet in the same direction. Every breakthrough and every success story is the combination of the divine power and the human response to embrace His guidance.

****

Disappointment is most likely to come from other people towards you. Discouragement is when you allow other people's disappointments to discourage you. Share your aspirations only with those who will support you, not those who will respond with criticism, doubt or lack of interest to discourage you.

****

Satisfaction in life doesn't jump on you, you work for it; you earn it. You will not sit in a place, fold your hands and expect to be satisfied with life.

****

A beautiful life does not just happen, it is built daily, in prayer and in sacrifice. Delight in your limitations. Never quit and leave the difficult task in search for the easy ones. "When you feel like quitting, remember why you started."

****

Courage rather than analysis dictates the truly important rules for identifying priorities. Choose your own direction rather than climbing on any cruising bandwagon aimlessly. Aim for something that will make a difference rather than for something that is safe and easy to do.

****

God created us autonomous but dependents too. Autonomous means not subject to the rule or control of another. We need each other but we naturally resist to be controlled by others. The only person you were created to control is You. Self-control brings on board the wisdom of discerning. You can strategically choose which battle to fight and which to ignore. You know when to walk away and have the guts and courage to do it with integrity.

****

High achievers are most likely to gain most out of the situations where the probability of success is relatively low and success is a challenge. A low achiever may see losing in such a scenario as a shame and shun away from a project. "The truth of the matter is that you always know the right thing to do. The hard part is doing it" - Norman Schwarzkopf

****

Design a brilliant strategy that is focused on working smarter instead of harder. Remember that smart people are never broke.

****

Nothing is permanent in this world, not even our troubles and challenges. Be expectant and have a new beginning in Christ. A catalyst is an agent of change. God's grace is the catalyst of change that can bring about hope in a hopeless situation. "Fallen flowers can't grow back on the tree, but if the root is strong new flowers certainly can."

****

Good choosing involves prioritizing. A choice is not really choosing what you want but rather getting attracted & narrowing down options of what is important. Opportunities follow those with no alternative choices.

****

People are remembered for two things – the problems that they created and the problems they solved. What people called problems yesterday are the very things that became breakthroughs for others. Every problem has embedded in it the capacity to become a turning point for greatness.

****

"You are more than what you do. Being and doing are different. You are blessed even if you do the work you don't like. You are favored even if you do what you never wanted. You are a success in the making even if you do a failure in outlook" ~ S. A. Bakutana

Success

Whether life is going well for you or it is collapsing before your eye, all of us want to succeed be better. We want more prosperous lives, happiness, wealth, love, family and etc. Success is the process of doing better. The key to living your life to full potential is to embrace the divine purpose for your life.

Success is a journey as opposed to a destiny. In spite of great achievements in life, my life is still very much a work in progress. Remember, success is not cash in the bank or degrees on the wall or material prosperity; it is living out your life's purpose. It is being all you can be in accordance to the sovereign divine plan.

I believe that we were not all called to do the same things but each one of us is born with a purpose in this life. Identifying, acknowledging and honoring this purpose is perhaps the most important action which successful people embrace. They take the time to study the situation and understand what they are here for and then they pursue it with passion and enthusiasm.

Pray about everything and worry about nothing. In Christ, you have everything you will ever need. The grace of God finds those who seek Christ. What the grace of God can offer cannot be fabricated by the world. Jesus said that "Look at the birds flying about! They neither plant nor harvest, nor do they gather food into barns; yet your heavenly Father feeds them. Aren't you worth more than they are?" (Matthew 6:26).

****

True hunger can only be filled with the divine encounter. You can never be truly satisfied in life until you know God, and have a divine encounter with Him. "Encounter with God is the breeding ground, benchmark for uncommon satisfaction, uncommon achievement, and supernatural placement in life..." ~ Jasper Nwokoye

****

Psalm 127:1- "Unless the LORD builds the house, the builders labor in vain. Unless the LORD watches over the city, the guards stand watch in vain." Life is like a structure built by many builders specialists in their fields of endeavor. The architecture and the plan of the building are essentially the expressed values of any given structure. The same is applicable to life. God is the Architect of our life with the definite plan regarding how it functions. Except we know God's plan for our lives & allow Him to guide us to follow His plan, we let our lives patterned by builders without a definite plan. Then life is reduced to mere existence as opposed to living. It's much better to embrace the divine rules in place, then have some obligation and some discipline restraining you than having no rules or even building on your own rules. I am just suggesting; you may ignore implementing my suggestion at your peril!

****

"Every great leap forward in your life comes after you have made a clear decision of some kind." Given the fact, we may plan and translate our dreams into reality, but full implementation depends on God. Just as you can't rehearse your way to success, you can't design your way there either. Just a simple divine intervention can open a door for you to access the life-changing success. Remember that there is only one success – to embrace the divine purpose for your life.

****

Success in business requires training and discipline and hard work. If you're not frightened by lacking these qualities you are most likely on a one-way street that is heading to a dead end. Remember that opportunities are just as great today as they ever were. The acrimonious truth is that "Success happens when preparation meets opportunity."

****

Capital is the key to beginning your own business. Switch from an employee mentality to an entrepreneurial one. Start by saving. Hard working is as good as saving. Some people are funny. They spend money they don't have, to buy things they don't need, to impress people they don't even like. The best business people have such characteristics within them: such as saving, living within ones means and creativity. They are natural planners and can juggle many tasks, and do them exceptionally well. Saving is as important as earning. It does not matter how many jobs you hop to, the number of salary increments you get or how many businesses you successfully venture into. If you lack the willpower to delay gratification, you will never have money to cover your needs. "If you cannot say no to impulse purchase or save for tomorrow instead of instant gratification, no amount of money can meet your needs. Do not attempt to incur expenses above what you can afford. Endeavor to spend less than you earn."

According to Sylvia Juuko, ultimately, money should be considered as a seed whose fruits will be determined by how you treat it. With financial discipline, you will be able to make a good harvest — wealth. Remember to reward yourself after every milestone as an incentive to even set higher targets or financial goals.

****

Having saved some money start thinking about multiplying your savings. You could start with a simple question; if you had, say one thousand dollars, or even less, how long would it take you to double this amount or triple it. Remember, we are not talking about gambling or engaging in get-rich-quick schemes.

Whenever you are considering investing, it is important to have this at the back of your mind. Invest wisely. There are numerous ways of multiplying this money. For starters, depending on your needs and financial status, you may consider saving it if the interest is attractive. You may consider engaging in trade or buying estates. Alternatively, you could invest it by becoming a shareholder in a limited company. Being a shareholder in a company usually entitles you to two things: a share of the profits, and a vote in certain company decisions. Each year, the company may decide to distribute some of its profits to its shareholders. The money is distributed proportionally according to how many shares you own. This is called a dividend.

****

There are two kinds of education in this world, there is academic education (in) which it is guaranteed that you will always work for someone for the rest of your life and there is financial education which injects entrepreneurial hedonistic traits that guarantee financial freedom, and most surely leads to the top end tier of the rainbows shades. Choose wisely.

****

Gordon B. K. Wavamunno says that: "Personally, I did not care much about employment formalities. What I wanted most was to learn the secrets of business under my father's tutelage so that sooner rather than later, I would be able to become a successful businessman in my own right." He insinuated that as a business apprentice he was prepared to do whatever his father instructed him to do in any of his business activities. All these responsibilities helped him to sharpen his business acumen and entrepreneurial spirit. After working with his father for almost a year, Gordon's dad attached him to the Merali family in Mbarara town to learn the secrets of business. He was naturally excited by this decision. It seemed to be, and indeed it was, another step in the right direction. Unlike most of his fellow Asian traders, this man treated his workers in a humane and civilized manner. He also had good relations with his customers and, for all the time he worked with him, he never lost his temper. Unlike Africans who are more inclined to spend whatever they earned, the Merali family was determined to save as much money as possible for a rainy day. This taught Gordon that saving for tomorrow is an indispensable pre-condition for business success.

****

When you run your own business, the lines between your personal and professional life blur. Your personal attributes often dictate the success of your business. When you think about yourself, you often think in terms what you are now. But when you think of your business, think of what it could be. The trick is to think of yourself much the way you consider your business -- as a growth vehicle.

****

Start on the journey to success on your own with the little you have. Engage people but never depend on others abilities. The more people you depend on the more you will be disappointed. If you wait for others to complete you, you'll never be able to have peace in your mind whenever you're alone.

****

"If you see someone greater than you in any way, acknowledge that that soul has some information you don't have - he knows something you don't know, whether you're generally more intelligent. For in truth, every new progress recorded is inseparably tied to some new information, by and large".

****

Everyone needs to be jumpstarted. Always surround yourself with people who force you to do better. You need in particular to surround yourself with people who are better than you who can challenge you to go the next level.

Treat people courteously. We were created to interact. Whosoever we meet in our lives, whether it be a stranger or somebody you know well, in one way or another, they might be your future link - boss, client, husband, wife, daughter or son.

****

We need each other. But avoid the parasite mentality because it serves temporary relief. "Self-reliance bestows benefits but it is not easy to build and sustain. When you depend on someone else you suffer some setbacks including the capacity to think for yourself. Gather courage and fight to be free from the shackles of relying on someone for your existence."

****

Endeavor to be the best person God created you to be. Have a competitive mentality but not against other people. The only person you are competing against is you. Have many friends but trust a few. Keep important information to yourself. If you don't tell your friends everything, your enemies won't know your secrets.

****

Success is not about material riches. It is striving forward and exerting self-discipline even in tough times. It the excellent person you become in the process.

****

"In order to succeed, your desire for success should be greater than your fear of failure."

****

Gain the competitive advantage by learning to swim when the tides are high or even stormy. Taking risk is part of the journey to success.

****

Success is not the key to happiness. Happiness is the key to success. If you love what you are doing, you'll succeed.

****

Gain the competitive advantage by learning to swim when the tides are high or even stormy. Taking risk is part of the journey to success.

****

Ask God what He created and gifted you to do. Avoid going into a business because of your egocentric. Professionalism matters.

****

Success is not what you see, it is what you discover. Life is traveled moment by moment. Today's moment becomes tomorrow's memory.

****

Success is the ability to move from one failure to another.

****

"Abundance is not something we acquire. It is something we tune into."

****

Notable success or achievement should be the prevailing factor in your struggles to achieve your goals.

****

"Success is not measured by what you accomplish, but by the opposition you have encountered, and the courage with which you have maintained the struggle against overwhelming odds" ~ Orison Swett Marden

****

Motivation is key to achieving your dreams. For example, the craving to be recognized by society is what drives people to work hard. If this is what motivate you to work hard, do it.

****

Take one step at the time in the right direction, and enjoy what you are doing. "When you dance, your purpose is not to get to a certain place on the floor. It's to enjoy each step along the way" ~ Sandra Gift

****

In principle, everyone has got a life to live. If you try to copy and paste, you are bound to fail. We do have different talents within us that are different from others. Work on developing what is inside you, and watch your steps as you prosper!

****

"If growth is to be meaningful and sustainable, then all the people should buy into it" ~ Her Royal Highness, Sylvia Nagginda

****

Marketing is storytelling. Whoever tells the best story gets the sale.

****

Building an innovative culture requires that you strike a balance; learning from your competitors' mistakes while pushing ahead with ideas of your own...

****

Success is our own shadow. Don't try to catch it, walk the right way, and it will automatically follow you. Remember shadow follows you only when you walk towards brightness.

****

Always pray to have eyes that see the best in people, a heart that forgives the worst, a mind that forgets the bad, and a soul that never loses faith in God.

****

The highest bravery is to remain yourself in the face of adversity. Choosing right over wrong, ethics over convenience & truth over popularity. These are the choices that measure our lives. "Travel the path of integrity without looking back, for there will never be a wrong time for the right thing" ~ Denis A Otika

****

Some body said that a successful parent is determined by watching the grandchildren and great-grandchildren. "What makes greatness is starting something that lives after you" ~ Ralph W. Sockman

****

The future belongs to those who see possibilities before they become obvious ~ John Scully

****

If you can't figure out your purpose, figure out your passion. For your passion will lead you into your purpose ~ T. D. Jakes

****

In business the customer is your boss. Even when it comes to your creditors treat them with the most utmost respect, for the trust they have in you.

****

The direction is more important than speed. Many are going nowhere fast!

****

An escalator does not get you to Success you have to take each step.

****

Attitude change is great for positive endeavors.

****

"Creativity is thinking up new things. Innovation is doing new things" ~ Theodore Levitt

****

"Success is often the result of taking a misstep in the right direction." If your mistake propels you toward a better future, then it's actually a blessing in disguise.

****

It is imperative in the design process to have a full and complete understanding of how failure is being obviated in order to achieve success. Without fully appreciating how close to failing a new design is, its own designer may not fully understand how and why a design works. A new design may prove to be successful because it has a sufficiently large factor of safety (which, of course, has often rightly been called a "factor of ignorance"), but a design's true factor of safety can never be known if the ultimate failure mode is unknown. Thus, the design that succeeds (i.e., does not fail) can actually provide less reliable information about how or how not to extrapolate from that design than one that fails. It is this observation that has long motivated reflective designers to study failures even more assiduously than successes.

****

"A winning attitude does not accept mediocrity in practice and then demand excellence on match day. Excellence is a habit. You do your very best today, not tomorrow" ~ Julius Lukwago

****

"When you have a passion in your heart, finances and resources follow vision. Where God guides, He provides" ~ Ricardo Miller

****

Brandon Sanderson in his book "the Alloy of Law" says the mark of a great man is one who knows when to set aside the important things in order to accomplish the vital ones.

****

"It's better to be significant than merely famous. Fame is about being well known but Significance is about positively touching lives" ~ Samuel Bakutana

****

"Between you and your next level of success is a person, between you and your next failure is a person"

****

"I guess it's true what they say: you can't keep a good man down." ~ Prime Minister Netanyahu.

****

My quote of the day: "Don't Facebook your problems; face them. No one is interested in reading about your problems."

****

The happiest people don't have the best of everything, they make the best of everything. The moment you come to realize that your happiness is in your hands, you start appreciating yourself as a happy and successful being. Embrace what makes you unique, even when it makes others uncomfortable. "I didn't have to become perfect because I have learned through my life journey that perfection is the enemy of greatness" ~ Jenelie Monae

****

God lets you be successful because he trusts you that you will do the right thing with it. Now, does he get disappointed often? All the time, because people get there and they forget how they got it ~ Steve Harvey

****

Generosity is a virtue. Our giving is a reflexive response to the grace of God in our lives. It doesn't come out of our altruism or philanthropy—it comes out of the transforming work of Christ in us. This grace is the action; our giving is the reaction. We give because He first gave to us. We love because He first loved us. The greatest passage on giving of all Scriptures ends not with "Congratulations for your generosity," but "Thanks be to God for his indescribable gift!" (2 Corinthians 9:15). The word "gift" is charisma: The root word (charis) means "grace" a gift of grace, a free gift. Freely we received, freely we give.

****

Proverbs 25:28 - "He that hath no rule over his own spirit is like a city that is broken down, and without walls". It is easier to conquer a city than to conquer your spirit. It is easier to tame and control others than yourself. "He who controls others may be powerful, but he who has mastered himself is mightier still." To handle yourself (self-control) involves patience. Better to be patient than powerful. Two things define you: The patience when you have nothing and the attitude when you have everything.

Effective Administration

You cannot get to your promotion without first going through your process. There are no elevators on the way to destiny, there are only steps, which will prepare you for your destination. Favor may lead you into a pit, but never mind because that pit may as well be a pathway to your palace. Look at Joseph - Genesis 41.

Numerous studies show that job stress is far and away the major source of stress for American adults and that it has escalated progressively over the past few decades. Workplace stress and anxiety affects life at work — and at home. Job stress has professional and personal consequences. Some of the factors contributing to job stress are pressure to perform in order to impress your bosses, and, of course, the anxiety over promotion. Don't let promotion anxiety derail your career. Look at God for promotion as opposed to man. Unfortunately, some people manipulate their way up - even stepping on somebody's toes to get promoted to the next level. "Be nice to people on your way up because you'll meet them on your way down."

Good administration involves good communication. To effectively communicate, we must realize that we are all different in the way we perceive the world and use this understanding as a guide to our communication with others. Most leaders do more talking than listening. Yet listening is the key to understanding. Others listen without the intent to understand; they listen with the intent to reply. They impatiently jump in on your sentences before even you finish them. "Listening is like programming a computer," author and investor James Lutcher writes. "You take stuff in, you process it, you spit life back. Learning is different. It shatters your life." Seek first to understand then make sure that you are understood.

Humility is one thing that is lacking in the workplace, both at the supervisory and leadership levels. Annie Mugisha says that instead of humility, there are a lot of egos, which in today's world connote an exaggerated sense of self-importance and an inflated feeling of pride and superiority to others. These are dysfunctional egos which can have unpleasant consequences for the organization.

Ego clashes can harm organizations, whether big or small. One or more people could deliberately be failing to consult colleagues when they should, or include them in group activities because they are driven by ego. Sometimes they may even clash during tasks and in meetings or even deteriorate into open hostility. All these have a negative effect on an organization because they affect the ability of the employees to work.

According to Steven Buckley, a human resource coach, there is a much real economic advantage to being humble. He says people who work with humble leaders are more likely to be engaged and are much less likely to quit. He explains that humility is not about self, but about what is best for others and the organization. Buckley says it values wisdom not just smartness and that leaders should be willing to say "I am sorry, I am wrong" when they are. Buckley says every choice we make has implications for the organization — negative or positive. He advises that one needs to forget the self and work in the interest of the organization. This will help get the organization out of challenging times to a level where they want it to be and keep it there.

Leadership is the ability to convince others to do things they are reluctant to do. It is not forcing them to do it but persuading them to do what is right. They are most likely to do what is right if you treat them right. Be prepared to lose your employees if you don't treat them right. A bad boss or immediate supervisor is the number-one reason people quit their jobs, according to a Gallup poll of more than 1 million workers. Your behavior directly impacts your subordinates. Not only do you have the power to brighten — or ruin — their day, you also have a whole lot to do with their overall levels of job satisfaction.

Your work is going to fill a large part of your life, and the only way to be truly satisfied is to do what you believe is great work. And the only way to do great work is to love what you do. Some people feel stuck doing their job because of various circumstances. Sadly, those who are unmotivated in their business end up slacking off and not delivering their best performance on their projects. Do what you love to do and give it your very best. Whether it's business or sports, or any field.

Choose a career you love, give it the best there is in you, seize your opportunities, and be a member of the team work. Utilize your potential resources effectively. A man has a large brain, good mind, strong faculties and brilliant talents, but yet he is not a great man unless he is inspired to use all these things in a great way. "Great work is done by people who are not afraid to be great." – Fernando Flores

You are going to be known for the solutions you provide. Yes, there are going to be obstacles but don't make excuses for why you can't get it done. Focus on all the reasons why you must make it happen. Yes, you can! The ones who say you can't and you won't are always the ones who are most scared that you will.

****

Human Resources and Human Capital, both of them involve dealing with people within an organization. The purpose is to improve the quality of life inside and outside the organization. People need jobs, and jobs need people. Jobs are what allow people to feel useful and build their self-esteem. Jobs make people productive members of the community. Jobs make people feel they are worthy citizens. Then we need people (customers) to buy our products. No business in the world happens without someone buying something.

****

Different people have different views regarding micromanaging. Management is doing things right; leadership is doing the right things. No matter how organized, proactive, conscientious or effective you are as a worker, there's a chance you'll run into a supervisor who hovers like a hungry hyena that will grab anything that ventures to pass by. The culprits are there for negativity waiting for you to fail before swooping in to wipe out what's left of your self-esteem. The opponents of micromanaging say that "Don't Micromanage: No one wants to work for someone who is constantly looking over their shoulder. Delegate work and empower people to take the lead on projects, to help them learn and grow. It's a great feeling to know that your manager trusts you."

****

In order to become an accomplished leader – among other attributes – you must possess influencing skills. Understand your motives and reassess your aims. The more you climb up the organizational ladder, the more your ability to influence others becomes and hence the distribution of labor unburdens you from executing all assignments by yourself.

****

Theodore Roosevelt said: "People don't care how much you know until they know how much you care" And this is as true as ever in organizational life. When employees perceive that you are genuinely interested in them, in their work, and in their ideas – they are much more likely to tell you what they like and what they would like to improve – and also – they are much more likely to listen to you.

****

Get to Know Your Team: Your employees are your subordinates, but they're people first. Strengthen your relationship by taking the time to get to know them on a personal level. This is a great way to improve job satisfaction levels and learn more about their strengths and weaknesses, so you can assign them to projects that fit their interests and career goals.

****

Building rapport with others is a social skill – it is your ability to find common ground and create affinity with others. Show your employees that you trust them. Complement them even in their little achievements. Show respect to the people you are over. Remember that you earn respect by giving respect. The major advantage is giving your employees a greater level of security and increase their commitment to stay.

****

Be good in anticipation of others to be good. Good people bring out the good in other people. Make it a habit to intentionally use your everyday life to bring about positive change in the lives of others.

****

"Good management consists in showing average people how to do the work of superior people"

****

Know your priorities and have them right. Put first things first.

****

Seek to do the right thing the first time. The greatest failure is succeeding in the wrong assignment!

****

Make it a habit to acknowledge your mistakes. When you acknowledge your flaws, no one can use them against you.

****

Transparency and effective service delivery remain the main theme of effective leadership.

****

Be quick to apologize, for the situation. Even if the other party is angry and abusive, do not retaliate.

****

Holding a title is not enough. You must be in position to come up with innovations tailored towards solving the problems that affect the masses or your employees. As a young boy, I always desired to be a preacher. I was always passionate about my calling. I trusted God to deliver positive results but and I always desired to do my part in an extraordinary manner. So I decided to be different and aim for the stars.

****

Men make history and not the other way around. In periods where there is no leadership, society stands still. Progress occurs when courageous, skillful leaders seize the opportunity to change things for the better ~ Harry S Truman

****

Rise above trivial talk: Don't waste your valuable time & energy responding to every petty criticism & gossip unless it's something big & potentially detrimental to your reputation.

****

"The central task for education is to plant a will and facility for learning; it should produce not learned, but learning people. The truly human society is a learning society, where grandparents, parents, and children are students together." – Eric Hoffer

****

Confront your fear and turn the mental blocks into building blocks. Willpower (that inner strength that enables you to make decisions and carry them out) is always blocked by shame (that painful feeling that is a mix of regret, self-hate and dishonor). What are you ashamed of? Stomach your shame and gain balance.

****

Leaders lead by innovation. There are times to cultivate and create; that is when you nurture your world and give birth to new ideas and ventures.

****

A leader is one who influences a specific group of people to move in a God-given direction - J. Robert Clinton

****

The most enduring skill you can bring to the workplace is the ability to learn how to learn.

****

"An effective leader develops the ability to correctly identify the pertinent detail or details - incidentals in a market, industry or sport that might create an incremental advantage" - John Wooden, Basketball Coach

****

If you are only content to follow, fine; many people are more than happy to lead you!

****

"One day you will understand that it is harder to be kind than to be clever."

****

"Making the decision to improve upon yourself, and actually following through can be one of the most rewarding experiences in a lifetime. We can all stand to become better people."

****

Study the people you lead. People's thinking is 100 percent emotional. What does this mean? This means that people think emotionally and justify logically. The subconscious mind, and our emotions actually function at several thousand times the speed of logic. For example, you may meet a person and instantly like them. You may find later that there are a lot of reasons for you to instantly like that person. Your emotions acted like a switchblade, instantaneously, but your logic followed after and you figured out the reasons.

****

People come to work mainly for self-interests. As a leader, the question you have to ask is, "What are the motivations that you need to appeal to so that they will put your interests above their interests?" The obvious answer is to boost their morale by increasing their income. People will continue to quit until you address this issue.

****

Where money is involved, time management is of great essence. Typically, some employees are used to wasting time, deploying minimum input, but assured of their pay cheque. Good management ensures that every minute counts and should be utilized effectively.

****

"Quality, Reliability, and Distinction" have been highlighted as the three pillars of Super Brands. A good leader has the ability to figure out how to maintain efficiency and make it a trademark.

****

The quality of a person's life is in direct proportion to their commitment to excellence, regardless of their chosen field of endeavor ~ Vince Lombardi

****

If you have the right knowledge you can substitute it for all the other facts of production ~ Alvin Tofler

****

Offer the feedback. People respect the opinion of their boss, so they really value your feedback. Think ahead of the people whom you lead but respect their opinions even if you are not going to implement them. Pay team members a compliment when they come up with the good ideas and when they're doing great work, and don't be afraid to offer a little constructive criticism when needed.

****

Good administrators are not bosses but they are leaders. A boss drives employees but a leader coaches them. A boss depends on authority but a leader depends on goodwill. A boss inspires fears but a leader generates enthusiasm. A boss says "I" but a leader says "We." A boss places the blames to breakdown but a leader fixes the breakdown. A boss knows how it is done but a leader shows how it is done. A boss uses people but a leader develops people. A boss takes credit but a leader gives credit. A boss commands but a leader asks. A boss says that "Go" but a leader says "Let us go".

****

Teamwork is necessary: No general is going to win a war unless he has colonels and majors who, in the thick of a fight that is going poorly, can muster the troops, galvanize them into action and help them deft the odd ~ Alex Ferguson

****

Certainly, your employees are going to make mistakes but your anticipation should not be to correct errors but to avoid them. The reality is that if you don't put an end to mistakes, they will put an end to you!

****

You are a leader not just to look for mistakes but to look for the good things done to compliment. Be a cheerleader, an encourager, and a motivator. Aspire to inspire before you expire...

****

Have a positive attitude: As the boss, you set the stage for the mood of your office. If you're generally enthusiastic and upbeat, your team will follow suit. Remember, bad attitudes are contagious, so don't let your own negative energy infiltrate your office.

****

A good administrator adjusts regarding how he handles different people. You never really understand a person until you consider things from his point of view. As we grow as unique persons, we learn to respect the uniqueness of others. It is not our differences that divide us. It is our inability to recognize, accept, and celebrate those differences. The essence of compassion is accepting others as unique individuals, without believing that they are less good for not being carbon copies of ourselves.

****

"Behold, how good and how pleasant it is for brethren to dwell together in unity!" Psalm 133:1. The word "synergy" pictures a group of people working together for a great cause, each functioning at their highest level and enjoying it. Teamwork is important because it reflects the idea that a team is 'owned' by its members. When every member of a team takes ownership, 'good things happen.'

In celebrating victory, a wise leader always takes the accolades and passes them on to others." Paul regularly paid tribute to those who worked with him, acknowledging their contribution: "Greet Priscilla and Aquila my fellow-workers in Christ Jesus, who risked their own necks for my life, to whom not only I give thanks, but also all the Churches of the Gentiles" (Romans 16:3-4 NKJV).

There's no doubt that God could get the job done without you, but you can't get the job done without the help of others. Musician George Adams said, "We are made up of thousands of others. Everyone who has ever done a kind deed for us, or spoken one word of encouragement to us, has entered into the makeup of our character and of our thoughts, as well as our success."

****

Never drop from your menu the moral and mental elements. You are only as strong as God has worked humility in your spirit, taking oversight of the mind to esteem others better than yourself.

****

Acknowledge the fact that people will love the idea of you, but lack the maturity to handle the reality of you. Pretend to be something else in order to win many. (1 Corinthians 9:19-21).

****

Stress ruins productivity. As you strive to make something of yourself, don't develop a habit of ignoring your personal life. Eat well. Exercise. Get time to relax. Learn when to take a step back from everything and appreciate what you've accomplished and what you already have. And if you are obsessed with your work, understand that you will actually be making yourself more productive by allowing yourself to enjoy life.

****

A good teacher is the one who teaches by example. While talk may not be as cheap as some people want to make it seem, well, without actions accompanying it, talk accomplishes little. Know the way, show the way, and lead the way. Be an example.

****

Keep your employees well informed. Keep Employees In the Know: It's not fun to be left in the dark. When you have important company information, you need to share it with your employees. Waiting too long to divulge key details or allowing people to hear it from another source makes it seem like you don't value them.

****

We don't become leaders to get a better life, but to help others become better and live a better life.

****

You won't know who you are until you know whose you are.

****

Mountain tops inspire leaders but valleys mature them.

****

Yes, the head should not be left behind even in leadership. While the heart is the most important component of transformational leadership, the head is a critical part that plays a cardinal role to in issues like planning, reasoning, probing, etc.! Use it please.

****

Everything changes when you love your career. This may sound dramatic but it is true. Career fulfillment can change your reality and your life. If you want it, create it. Some people need a successful career to feel whole while others can manage with less satisfaction this being a function of perceived performance and expectations.

****

Many supposedly good administrators are infatuated with money, wealth, power and sex at the expense of integrity. People are going to use your lustful desires to manipulate you. Never make a mistake of dating any of your employees. If you are doing so, you have to let go for the sake of efficiency. Then pure cosmic energy will flow without limitations. Pure cosmic energy is the complete control and awareness of your powers but is always blocked by relationship attachments.

****

Exchanging sex in return for favors has become a common phenomenon. According to NBC news, a Professor of the University of Delaware offered his female student an 'A' in Exchange for Sex. There are numerous stories worldwide involving university undergraduates manipulating their way to graduate. No wonder today's degrees are not worth the paper they are written on. "There are those whose primary ability is to spin wheels of manipulation. It is their second skin and without these spinning wheels, they simply do not know how to function." When the education system is marred with manipulations then the fabric of our society is doomed. C.S.

Lewis insinuated that education without values, as useful as it is, seems rather to make man a more clever devil.

****

It is within human instincts to crave for power, titles and promotion to high places. Unfortunately, earthly promotions do not last. Promotions change most probably compared to the attires we put on - Nobody wears the same clothes on consecutive days. The reason earthly promotions do not last is because earthly promotions depend on human merits and human favor. Unlike the earthly favor, the divine favor is forever. The word favor also means grace. Grace is the unmerited favor of God. Grace is God's riches at Christ's expense. It was first used in reference to Noah when God destroyed the world with floods: "But Noah found favor (grace) in the eyes of the LORD" (Genesis 6:8). Grace is a gift from God but we can grow in grace (2 Peter 3:18). Humility (brokenness) is the ladder towards spiritual maturity. Allow Jesus Christ to be your spring board to promotion and prosperity. There is no short cut to the divine favor.

Numerous studies show that job stress is far and away the major source of stress for American adults and that it has escalated progressively over the past few decades. Workplace stress and anxiety affects life at work — and at home. Job stress has professional and personal consequences. Some of the factors contributing to job stress are pressure to perform in order to impress your bosses, and, of course, the anxiety over promotion. Don't let promotion anxiety derail your career. Look at God for promotion as opposed to man. Unfortunately, some people manipulate their way up - even to the extent of stepping on somebody's toes in order to get promoted to the next level. "Be nice to people on your way up because you'll meet them on your way down."

****

February: February 2nd is my birthday. To all my friends. Thanks for making my birthday a memorable one. Thanks for all the lovely wishes and your thoughtfulness and blessings. Thank you for giving me such unmatched treasure of love. For me, you will always remain prime! You made me feel happy and glee. I will surely always remember this time. My day wouldn't be this special without you guys. With certainty, I can say that there is beauty in every small detail of life and we can find it only when we take time to enjoy every moment of it without worrying or fussing about the hostilities of nature. You are the most fabulous buddies in my life. God bless you all.

****

February Month for Spiritual Growth

Almighty God was referred to by a number of names and titles in the Old Testament. Jews traditionally say the divine name of God, was too sacred to be uttered, and the ineffable name stopped being uttered aloud. The letters YHWH represented the secret name of God. In Hebrew, it contained consonants but no vowels. The consensus added the vowels and God's name was rendered as Yahuweh or Yahweh. The word Hallelujah means 'Praise Yah" and shows that YH was pronounced as yah. Modern Western culture pronounced the name as Jehovah. Jehovah is a Latinization of the Hebrew. This cannot be the original pronunciation because the first letter was Y as the letter J did not exist in the Hebrew language. In the New Testament, the name was rarely enunciated. In our Bibles, the word LORD (all letters capitalized) means YHWH. Then another word "Lord" Adonai means Master.

****

Hebrews 2:11-13: "Both the one who makes men holy and those who are made holy are of the same family. So Jesus is not ashamed to call them brothers. He says, "I will declare your name to my brothers; in the presence of the congregation I will sing your praises." And again, "I will put my trust in him." And again he says, "Here am I, and the children God has given me" Father is a relationship name. Jesus made it possible for His Father to be our Father. In the Lord's Prayer, He taught us to pray to our Father who is in heaven (Matthew 5:9). After the resurrection, Jesus said, "I ascend to my Father and your Father" (John 20:17). Jesus is never ashamed to call us His brothers.

You know that you are truly His brothers or sister when you obey His Word: "For whoever does the will of my Father in heaven is my brother and sister and mother" (Matthew 12:50).

****

Salvation divided into three stages 1) Justification by faith or regeneration - This is a one-time event involving God's action on the human soul 2) Sanctification by truth - Process of life involving obedience to the Word as convicted by the Holy Spirit. 3) Glorification - God's final restoration upon the resurrection of the bodies. We were saved; we are being saved; we shall be saved.

****

Jesus promised to indwell our bodies (temples) and to manifest Himself to us. Indwelling takes place when we are born again (regeneration). His Spirit comes in to sit on the throne of our hearts to sanctify us. We are supposed to constantly seek the manifestation of the Holy Spirit. He comes in to work in us as a helper and to work for us and through us (manifestation). He wants a full-time job as opposed to a part-time job. Quenching the Holy Spirit is denying Him to do what He came to do.

****

Have you ever wondered why the words unlawful, illegitimate, illegal, insurgence, insurrection and etc. are applauded and embraced with two hands in our culture today? It is because the world is obsessed with rebellion, disobedience and disrespect to the authorities. We have a situation where there is no absolute right. This is the main reason why there is even no fear of the Supreme God. Antinomy means "anti-nomas," or anti-law. Antinomianism in modern times is commonly seen as the theological opposite to Legalism or Works righteousness, the notion that obedience to religious law earns salvation. True, justification is by faith alone in the finished works of Jesus Christ. However, after justification, our Good works of obedience are necessary for our sanctification. This is the process when the Holy Spirit cleanses the minds of a regenerated person of unrighteousness through the Word. The evidence is loyalty to the statutes of God. This process goes on until glorification. No man is autonomous or self-directed.

"Keep my commands and you will live; guard my teachings as the apple of your eye." (Proverbs 7:2). God's sovereignty demands absolute obedience. However, rules without relationship equals to rebellion. God chose to be a parent to us as He is the Father to Jesus Christ. The advantage of parenthood is that a parent can never resign from being a parent. Disobedience dents our communication with God but does not temper with the relationship. The best love of all is that of our heavenly Father! What a blessing it is that He loves us! He fills the hole in our heart with a love that can't be matched!

****

"Be ye holy; for I am holy" (Leviticus 11:44; 1 Peter 1:16). God declared His character in both the Old and the New Testaments (covenants). He gave the Ten Commandments (Moral Law) to reveal His character. Finally, He gave His Son Jesus Christ to make His character accessible to man. God does not dare us to do what He Himself does not dare to do. Therefore, when God says that "Be holy; for I am holy" He is not making a suggestion; He is instructing us to be holy, with severe consequences for those who dare not be.

****

The most influential man on the universe is no longer in the world but He is well and alive in believers by His Spirit. Jesus establishes His character in us through His Word. Questioning and doubting His Word means questioning God's character and integrity. Unbelief is disbelieving what God said and promised to do and believing all kinds of lies. Unbelief was the greatest challenge to the ministry of Christ when He walked on the universe and it still is today. Unbelief is compared to the sin of witchcraft: "For rebellion is like the sin of divination, and arrogance like the evil of idolatry" (1 Samuel 15:23).

****

Spiritual maturity is measured by your faith and inner peace. It is called the discipline of the Christian living. Our character is renewed daily from inside (2 Corinthians 4:16). To know the mechanics does not mean that we are practicing the Lord's disciplines. The spiritual disciplines are an inward and spiritual reality of the transformed heart. The fruit of the Spirit is a physical manifestation of a Christian's transformed life (Galatians 5:22-23). A fruit is evidence of maturity. We learn from the scripture that these are not individual "fruits" from which we pick and choose. Rather, the fruit of the Spirit is one nine-fold "fruit" that characterizes all who truly walk in the Holy Spirit. I mean that the fruit of the Spirit is a collective noun meaning one fruit consisting of nine virtues. Collectively, these are the virtues (singular - fruit) that all Christians should be producing in their new lives in Christ.

****

James 2:14-26 – "Faith without works is dead." The word "dead" is the word "nekros" the same word that God uses to describe the pre-salvation condition of a Christian. The word carries with it the meaning of "useless, lifeless, and void. Yes, God saves us when we cannot save ourselves, and God helps the helpless. However, our faith must be proven by our works. This time, decide to pray with your heart, hands and legs. Don't just ask for blessings; Give God something to bless. Swing into action when believing God to bless the works of your hands.

****

Hebrews 11:6 – "But without faith it is impossible to please God; for he that comes to God must believe that he is, and that he is a rewarder of them that diligently seek him." Faith is embracing the existence of God, and believing that He will keep His promises. Faith sees with the spiritual eyes and receives with the sincere heart. Faith begins with relationship and grows with the truth (Word). The more you know what God is like, the more conformed to His greatness will be your faith. You will be more and more assured of things hoped for and more and more convinced of things unseen. And God's existence and fullness will be wonderfully displayed in your life.

****

Psalm 119:105 - "Thy word is a lamp unto my feet, and a light unto my path." One third of the Bible is prophetic involving promises to be fulfilled in future. Yet the Bible is not necessarily the spot light for us to make one giant leap into the future. It is the lamp to light your path so that you can make a series of small steps forward in the right direction. Each step reveals a new horizon challenging you to take another step without a possibility of stumbling.

****

Proverbs 16:6-7 – "When a man's ways please the Lord, he makes even his enemies to be at peace with him" The inner peace is never enforced, it is imparted in humbleness, and it conquers by love. "True humility is not thinking less of yourself; it is thinking of yourself less." John the Baptist is the most humble person. He said concerning Jesus that "He must increase, but I must decrease" (John 3:30). The heart is restless until it finds its rest in Christ. Reconciling with God means reconciling with your neighbor.

****

It takes a round turn to turn around. A partial turn is tantamount to reversing and creeping around in the same direction, leaving you pedaling in obviation. Repentance involves the change of direction. It is completely turning around 360 degrees. It doesn't matter how fast or slow you are going off the cliff the end result is disaster. The narrow way is the only exit from the broad way of destruction.

****

Genesis 22:2 – "Then God said, "Take your son, your only son, whom you love--Isaac--and go to the region of Moriah. Sacrifice him there as a burnt offering on a mountain I will show you." Obedience involves giving up something that you love most. The reason is because your will is closely attached to the things we love. Something you love is interfering with God's love for you. Surrender it to God then watch and see how life suddenly starts working for you rather than against you. The circumstances and the world change when we change.

****

Unbelief is a master carpenter at cross-making; neither are you permitted to choose your own cross, although self-will wants to be lord and master. But your cross is prepared and appointed for you by divine love, and you must cheerfully accept it; you are to take up the cross as your chosen badge and burden, and not to stand complaining. Take up your cross, and by the power of the Spirit of God you will soon be so in love with It. "Jesus bids you submit your shoulder to His easy yoke. Do not kick at it in petulance, or trample on it in pride, or fall under it in despair, or run away from it in fear, but take it up like a true follower of Jesus." ~ Alistair Begg

****

Somebody asked "What is lust?" The Bible says that, "For all that is in the world, the lust of the flesh, and the lust of the eyes, and the pride of life, is not of the Father, but is of the world. And the world passeth away, and the lust thereof: but he that doeth the will of God abideth for ever" (1 John 2:17). God created us with perfect desires but they were corrupted by sin. Lust is uncontrolled desires that cannot be fulfilled by material things. The etymology of the word in Greek is "to be hot after something." In this context, lust is any sinful desire that is contrary to the will of God. The third phrase, "the pride of life," describes the arrogant spirit of self-sufficiency or human ego that will not seek godliness. Everything from sensualism and self-indulgence to self-conceit; the ungodly gratification of fleshly appetites, of mental self-satisfaction, of egotistic arrogance; this is the pride of life.

****

Who doesn't love a makeover? God gave to me a Makeover. It wasn't like Extreme Makeover where I got a nose job or anything. It is a character Makeover. Now, I do not have go to the mirror to see how I look. I go to the Scriptures.

****

Sometimes, you have to shut up, swallow your pride and accept you are wrong. It's not giving up, it's growing up.

****

The Israelites went out into the morning mists and the ground was covered with the fine, flake-like thing like the frost (manna) from heaven (Exodus 16:1-36; Numbers 11:1-9). It came each morning, except on the Sabbath day. When the Israelites saw it for the first time, they asked each other, "What is it?" (Heb. man hu [aWh'm]). This led to the name "manna" meaning "what is it?" Although they had no concept of what it was, they had no choice but to diet on God's choice for them in order to sustain their lives. The purpose of manna was to sustain life but also to test their faith and to humble them. Eventually, the rebellious Israelites grew tired of the manna and regretted the day they were delivered from their bondage (Number 11:6).

Likewise, we have no choice but to partake of the gospel in its simplicity as it is presented to us because Jesus is the source of life. Only the rebellious people reject the gospel hence rejecting the divine plan of salvation and deliverance. Manna was symbolic of Jesus: "For the bread of God is that which comes down from heaven, and gives life to the world". They said to him, "Lord, give us this bread always." Jesus said to them, "I am the bread of life" (John 6:30-34). Jesus made the claim which only God can make: I am the bread of life. The bread which Jesus offers is none else than the very life of God. This is the true bread which can truly satisfy the spiritual hunger in our hearts.

****

Ephesians 2:8-9 - "By grace you have been saved through faith; and that not of yourselves, it is the gift of God; not by works, so that no one may boast". We need to hear the gospel and receive Jesus Christ for our new beginning in Christ (transformation). Also, we need to hear the gospel over and over again in order to grow in the awareness of His love. The Bible says that every person is given a measure of the saving faith (Romans 12:3). Paul specifically says that God gives varying measures of faith to his people. We ought "to think so as to have sound judgment, as God has allotted to each a measure of faith". We (believers) need to exercise the same faith to grow daily into loving and trusting God (Galatians 2:20). It is this ordinary faith with which we receive and use our varying gifts. Each believer is given a gift but you cannot know what God wants from you until you know what He put inside you! Definitely, we cannot know the will of God by Carnal wisdom. We must be Spirit filled and Spirit driven in order to know the will of God. Jesus said that "My Words are spirit and they are life" (John 6:63). Also, "Anyone who loves me will obey my teaching. My Father will love them, and we will come to them and make our home with them" (John 14:23).

****

1 Peter 1:16 – "You must be holy because I am holy." We are called to be holy because our Master is holy. We do not belong to ourselves. We were bought by the precious blood of Jesus. We belong to Him. We are supposed to be like Him. The one who sanctifies (the sanctifier) and the sanctified are the same; they are holy. Justification is the

transformation of the heart. Sanctification begins with the change of minds and grows into acquiring the minds of Christ.

****

1 John 5:13 - "These things have I written unto you that believe on the name of the Son of God; that you may know that you have eternal life, and that you may believe on the name of the Son of God." We are called to believe in Jesus Christ in order to be saved. Also, we are called to know beyond doubt that we are saved (have assurance of our salvation). We are saved by putting our faith in the finished works of Jesus Christ (John 3:16). We are assured of our salvation by manifesting the life of Christ (our good works). The Bible warns that: "Whoever says, "I know him," but does not do what he commands is a liar, and the truth is not in that person" (1 John 2:4).

****

Knowing increases by repetition or recurrence. That is why when you fail a subject or a class you are asked to repeat it. They say that when people are married for a long time they tend to look alike. The same applies to our spiritual maturity. The more time we spend in the presence of God, the more we look like Him. We know God by intimately knowing Jesus Christ. The more we know Christ the more we know God, and the more we know ourselves. Such knowledge increases as our faith grows. Faith supersedes feelings and seeks the guidance of the Holy Spirit.

****

James 1:23 – "For if anyone is a hearer of the word and not a doer, he is like a man who looks at his natural face in a mirror; for once he has looked at himself and gone away, he has immediately forgotten what kind of person he was". The Word of God is a mirror where we go to check ourselves to see the uncleanness. It shows our uncleanness not to condemn us but so that we might clean up. Jesus alone can clean up your mess but you must let Him do it for you.

****

The Bible is the infinite mind of God revealed to mankind. It is the road map during our spiritual journey. When you ignore it you tear apart the only map at your fingertips and you are left to wonder in circles without direction to your intended divine destiny. When you read the Bible without the help of the Holy Spirit you read it in darkness without any possibility of a revelation and illumination. Then the Bible becomes like any other books on the shelve.

****

Matthew 6:10 - "Your will be done, on earth as it is in heaven." God's will is already perfectly done in heaven but He is waiting for it to be done on earth. God has already revealed His will to us in His Word. Our problem is not what we do not know but implementing what we already know. It is imperative to have complete compliance in the revealed truth (full gospel) in order to obviate incompetence.

****

Luke 18:16 - "Truly I say to you, whoever does not receive the kingdom of God like a child will not enter it at all." Why little children? The Christian life is that of dependence compared to little children. Jesus taught us practically the life of dependence: "Very truly I tell you, the Son can do nothing by himself; he can do only what he sees his Father doing, because whatever the Father does the Son also does (John 5:19). Therefore, the discipline of the Christian life is praying (1 Thessalonians 5:17) and seeking the guidance of the Holy Spirit in our consciences (Romans 9:1) and through the Scriptures (John 14:26)

****

A commander-in-chief is a person or body that exercises supreme operational command and control of a nation's military forces or significant elements of those forces. We are in a spiritual warfare. Our commander in Chief (Jesus) will never give us marching orders leading us into disaster. In Christ, God has given us all answers to our current problems. Our arch-enemy (Satan) was defeated but he still has the power to vex us. The raging battle is primarily within us; it is a battle between our minds and the mind of Christ. The Bible says that "The mind governed by the flesh is hostile to God (Romans 8:7). It is time to point the arrow in the right direction by reading and heeding the Word. Renewing your mind is saying what God says (confession); thinking as God thinks (acquiring the mind of Christ) and doing as God says (heeding).

****

1 Peter 5:8 - "Be sober, be vigilant; because your adversary the devil walks about like a roaring lion, seeking whom he may devour." Every Christian has an enemy. Although unseen by the natural eye, this adversary is not imaginary nor a mythological character. Satan, the Devil, is a real person... a spirit being, with intelligence, tangible characteristics, and whose incessant goal and ambition is to "steal, kill, and destroy" (John 10:10). The good news is that, although the Devil is described "like" a "roaring lion," in reality he has no actual authority over believers. He is not really a lion but roars "like" a lion would, to bluff his victims into fear and intimidation. Satan is a liar and a deceiver and uses deception as his weapon to gain advantage over those who are ignorant of the limitations of his power.

****

Faith is deeper than desire. Faith is diligently seeking God in love.

****

Faith is seeing the light with your heart even when all your eyes see darkness.

****

Show God your faith, and He will show you His faithfulness.

****

To know God is to love Him. To love Him is to trust Him.

****

Keeping the commandments of God is our obligation but it is not a security for our salvation; it is the assurance of our salvation.

****

Matthew 5:17 - "Do not think that I have come to abolish the Law or the Prophets; I have not come to abolish them but to fulfill them". Jesus fulfilled the Moral Law (Ten Commandments) in three main ways. First is His sinless life. He was born under the Law (Galatians 4:4), and He observed it without breaking it (2 Corinthians 5:21; 1 Peter 1:18-19). The second way is that He rightly interpreted the laws for us. He spoke with the authority of the Law giver: "You have heard that it was said to those of... old------But I say to you". For example, He explained to us the right way of observing the Sabbath. He established the Moral Law rather than diminishing it. The third way is that He paid the penalty of the broken laws (wages of sin is death) on our behalf. Therefore, the Law has no demand on a believer. We can now observe the Ten Commandments without fear of the consequences when we unintentionally break them. "Therefore, there is now no condemnation for those who are in Christ Jesus" (Romans 8:1).

****

Matthew 6:33 - "But seek ye first the kingdom of God, and his righteousness; and all these things shall be added unto you". To be changed and transformed is man's utmost desire. The rest of the things are embodied in this one desire! The kingdom of God is God's way of doing things. The kingdom of God is the domain where His will is paramount. The best way to interpret a scripture is by using other scriptures. Let us examine other parallel scriptures about the kingdom of God. In the Lord's Prayer Jesus instructed us to pray that "Our Father in heaven, hallowed be Your name. Your kingdom come. Your will be done on earth as it is in heaven." (Matt. 6:9-10). Elsewhere, Jesus said that, "Behold, the kingdom of God is within you" (Luke 17:21). The kingdom of God is in future when the King returns to earth, and it is in present beginning in the hearts where the sovereignty of God is acknowledged, backed by the authority and sponsorship of the God of Heaven. It begins in the heart then it subdues the total man including the will and the emotions. The kingdom of God must have impact on you and your environment or surroundings. Grace is the divine influence upon the human soul.

****

Matthew 7:13-14 - "Enter through the narrow gate. For wide is the gate and broad is the road that leads to destruction, and many enter through it. But small is the gate and narrow the road that leads to life, and only a few find it." Salvation is extended to all but just a handful of people are saved. The Bible states concerning God's past judgments that there were only eight survivors of Noah's flood (I Peter 3:20). The days of Noah were days of apostasy as today. Likewise, God destroyed Sodom and Gomorrah with brimstone and fire from heaven and overthrew those cities and all the inhabitants of the cities because He did not find ten righteous people in the cities. There had been six righteous people in Sodom: Lot, his wife, his two daughters and their fiancés - four short of the ten required for sparing the city. Three of these lost their lives due to disobedience leaving only three survivors of the catastrophe: Lot and his two daughters. We are living in the end times when God is sifting our faith. Only those who are genuine, whose faith is proven by good works, will stand the test of time. The question is, "Are you numbered among the remnants that are saved?"

****

Renewal of the Mind, Sanctification of thoughts & bringing the body under subjection are today's chapters: Romans 12 verse 1-3. Ephesians 4 verse 22-24 James 1 verse 13-15. 2nd Corinthians 3 verse

18. Job 10 verse 11. 1ˢᵗ Corinthians 9 verse 24-27. Colossians 3 verse 5. Romans 6 verse 13-15. Read for yourself, meditate and implement.

****

Lights have a very cheering influence, and so do Christians. A Christian ought to be a comforter, with kind words on his lips and sympathy in his heart; he should carry sunshine wherever he goes and diffuse happiness around him. He should portray the goodness of God and the God of the goodness. Jesus declared the kingdom of God so that we might demonstrate it.

****

"Until Christ's return, there is only a pilgrim church here on earth, not a perfected one" ~ Sinclair Ferguson

****

The reason the world is not seeing Jesus is because some confessing believers are not filled with Jesus. Inspiration is the movement of the Holy Spirit in man's mental faculty. The Holy Spirit teaches us the Word of God. The Word says what it does, and does what it says!

****

Christianity is faith oriented. Faith is not limited by space and time. Look at the following quotations of Jesus: "Verily, verily, I say unto you, If a man keep my saying, he shall never see death. Then said the Jews unto him, Now we know that thou hast a devil. Abraham is dead, and the prophets; and thou sayest, If a man keep my saying, he shall never taste of death. Art thou greater than our father Abraham, which is dead? and the prophets are dead: whom makest thou thyself? (John 8:52-58). The object of his exultation is conceived as the goal to whose attainment the joyous movement of the heart is directed. He rejoiced in the anticipation of seeing my day, i.e. of witnessing the day of my provision as the perfect sacrifice for the redemption of mankind. By faith Abraham saw it; his faith was invested in the future, one thousand years ahead when Jesus was crucified at Calvary. Today, we invest our faith in the past, two thousand years ago, when Jesus died on the cross at Calvary. Elsewhere Jesus said that Abraham though physically dead, he is still spiritually living: "I am the God of Abraham, and the God of Isaac, and the God of Jacob? God is not the God of the dead, but of the living" (Matthew 22:32). For all those who invest their faith in Him live for Him, in Him, and unto Him. As Paul said, "For in him we live, and move, and have our being; as certain also of your own poets have said, For we are also his offspring" (Acts 17:28).

****

Uncle J. Z. responded to the above posting in this way: *"These people are actually dead, but they died with the FAITH of Jesus [Revelation 14:12, 13] and so they were SURE of resurrecting in the FIRST Resurrection. Revelation 20:4-7. John 5:24-29. Jesus Himself said He had to go and prepare a place for His people then come back for them. John 14:1-4. Abraham has not yet received what he wanted. Hebrews 11:13-19. The Apostles said the saints are still dead. Acts 2:29. 1 Thess. 4:13-18. Revelation 3:21; 4:1-11. They could not be alive UNTIL the Judgment is over when Christ then receives his Kingdom. Luke 19:12-27. Hebrews 9:27. The Judgment of the dead began in 1844 Oct. 22. Daniel 8:13, 14. When the seals were opened. Rev."*

I replied: Thanks, Uncle. John 5:24-29. Jesus Himself said He had to go and prepare a place for His people then come back for them. John 14:1-4. The audience of Jesus whom He was addressing were the Jews of His time in the Bible Land (Palestine). Jesus indeed came for them and for all believers on Pentecost. Pentecost is Jesus coming to indwell His body (the Church). Regeneration is the rebirth of the spirit. The Second Coming is for the resurrection of the bodies. We are the spiritual body of Christ (Ephesians 1:22-23). The name of Jesus Emmanuel means God with us (Matthew 1:23). For we were all baptized by one Spirit so as to form one body--whether Jews or Gentiles, slave or free--and we were all given one Spirit to partake of

(1 Corinthians 12:13). Through His Spirit, we have fellowship with the Father and the Son. This is the Church that is spiritual that is not built with bricks and stones (1 Peter 2:5). Yes, we shall in future occupy a new city (Jerusalem) coming down on the earth after we acquire the glorified bodies when Jesus comes for His bride. But as per now the body of Christ consists of the living saints on the earth and those departed souls in heaven.

****

True, Jesus will return in His person to take His bride (Church). The Holy Spirit is the third person of the Godhead. The Christian doctrines of the Trinity (from Latin trinitas "triad", from trinus "threefold") defines God as three consubstantial persons, expressions, or hypostases: the Father, the Son (Jesus Christ), and the Holy Spirit; "one God in three persons". The three persons are distinct, yet are one "substance, essence or nature" In this context, a "nature" is what one is while a "person" is who one is. Three distinct persons yet one God in a non-separate manner. The Spirit proceeds from both the Father and the Son. The Holy Spirit is referred to in Scripture as both the Spirit of the Father (Mt 10:20, Rom 8:10-11, 2 Cor. 1:21-22, Eph. 3:14-16) and as the Spirit of the Son (Rom 8:9, Gal 4:6, Phil 1:19, 1 Pt 1:11). The Holy Spirit is the presence of Christ in the believers. Jesus promised that He will be with us up to the uttermost ends of the earth (Acts 1:8).

****

Faith is calling things that have not manifested as though they are. God called Abraham the father of many nations when he wasn't the father of any. God taught us that faith is believing that the promises of God are as good as the tangible real substances. He says concerning you that you are the head, not the tail; you are a designer's original made in His very image; no weapon directed against you shall prosper! High five someone right now and tell them that your life is changing for the better because your destiny is predetermined by God.

****

Faith is hearing from God. Faith is not naming it and claiming it but it is claiming what God has named.

****

Both faith and fear sail into the harbor of your mind, but only faith should be allowed to anchor.

****

Faith is the giant killer. Faith puts God between me and my problems.

****

Faith defies logic. The reason is because the art of thinking and reasoning is within the limitations and capacities of the natural man. Logic, when overemphasized, loses its beneficial effect. For example, logic can define evil but cannot dispel it. Faith gives us wings to sail into the spiritual realm. No wonder God said that without faith it is impossible to please Him (Hebrews 11:6). Faith has an object which is Christ. It is not how big your faith is but how big your God is. Jesus recommended the faith as small as a mustard seed which has the capacity to blossom (Matthew 17:20). It's not the size of your faith that counts, but the God behind your faith!

****

Hebrews 12:26b-27 - "Yet once more I will shake not only the earth but also the heaven." This phrase, "Yet once more," indicates the removal of what is shaken, as of what has been made, in order that what cannot be shaken may remain. God is in the process of shaking up things. God and His kingdom alone cannot be shaken. Faith is trusting in the God that cannot be moved. Remember when you're worrying, you're not trusting, and when you're trusting, you're not worrying.

****

Genesis 1:28 - And God blessed them, and God said to them, Be fruitful, and multiply, and replenish the earth, and subdue it. Before the Bible was translated, *repleo*, the word that gave us 'replenish', normally meant just 'fill'. God created Adam in His image with the prior intention of filling the world with people made in His image. Adam failed when he corrupted the image of God with sin. He replenished (filled) the world with corrupted souls. Jesus, the Son of God, came to the earth so that through Him God might have other sons, made in His image, filling the world with His glory.

****

Mark 10:18 - And Jesus said unto him, Why callest thou me good? No one is good--except God alone." God alone is good and He alone can determine what is good. Wickedness arrays itself in fine clothes and imitates the language of holiness. The Gospel defines the holy life of Jesus, and at the same time reveals to us our sins. The Gospel is opposed to wickedness in every shape. "Jesus hated wickedness so much that He bled to wound it to the heart; He died so that wickedness might die; He was buried so that He might bury wickedness in His tomb, and He rose so that He might forever trample it beneath His feet". The cross and resurrection are the core strength and center of the gospel; the only hope for humanity. Jesus did everything so that He might present you spotless before God. The only righteousness God will accept is based upon the perfect and finished works of Jesus Christ at the cross. Jesus said "It is finished". It means paid in full once for all. Death is no long the end but the beginning.

****

God created everything by His Word but dipped His hands in clay to make man and breathed into him His Spirit to make him a living soul. We are special in the eyes of the Father because we are the embodiment of His grace. Glorious is the champion of right, and destroyer of wrong, for this cause God has anointed you with the oil of gladness to impart others. The joy of the Lord is contagious. Pass it on!

****

The necessity to be born again implies that there is nothing in the old nature (flesh or Adamic) that is redeemable. "There is no power in self." We cannot grit our teeth and clench our fist and say, "I am going to redeem myself!" We are dead in our sins. A dead man cannot do anything for himself. We are like Paul, as he cried out in Romans 7, "For I do not do what I want, but I do the very thing I hate," (Romans 7:15 RSV). "Wretched man that I am! Who will deliver me from this body of death?" (Romans 7:24 RSV). Once again the answer comes -- we are delivered by the activity of God at work within us: "Thanks be to God through Jesus Christ our Lord!" (Romans 7:25a RSV).

****

Worrying is the major cause of depression. Depression is when the body cannot take in (handle) any more burdens of the minds. The word worry comes from two words meaning divided minds. Jesus calls us to rest in Him.

****

We offended God beyond reasonable but God decided to forgive us and to love us unconditionally. He instructs us to extend the same grace to others. "To be a Christian means to forgive the inexcusable because God has forgiven the inexcusable in you."

****

"Christians disagree about almost everything. And when we disagree, we usually start a new church." - Pr. Ray Pritchard

****

When Martha grumbled because Mary wasn't helping her, Jesus said, "Mary has chosen what is better, and it will not be taken away from her (Luke 10:39-42). Jesus' words remind us that our relationship with Him is more significant than other things we do for Him. Do the right things but never allow them to temporary capture your attention from Jesus. "It has been said that good things are the enemies of great things. As for the followers of Jesus, the greatest thing in this life is to know Him, to walk with Him and to make Him known.

****

Being a Christian is not just worshipping God for an hour on Saturday or Sunday. A true follower of Jesus Christ is committed to a life of obedience to Him for the rest of his or her life. And it is a full life and an exciting adventure (John 10:10)! Obedience is a lifestyle. Strictly do what God instructed you to do. Consider the ministry of Jesus. There was nothing professional about it. The righteousness He earned for you was not limited to forty-hour work weeks. It encompassed of a shred of His life. He went to the cross and bore all our cheesy professionalism on His shoulders. Obedience relates to every aspect of our lives: observing God's commandments; relationships with family and friends, our jobs, career plans and future ambitions — everything must be surrendered to God's plans.

****

Luke 19:10 - "For the Son of Man came to seek and to save the lost." This is the mission statement of Jesus. Preaching the gospel by mouth and deeds is the evidence of intimacy and fellowship with Christ. This is called impartation by association with Christ, and walking within His anointing.

****

1 John 1:8-9 - "If we say that we have no sin, we are deceiving ourselves and the truth is not in us. If we confess our sins, He is

faithful and righteous to forgive us our sins and to cleanse us from all unrighteousness." It looks as if John is contradicting himself because he says that, "If we confess that we have no sin we are lairs", then he goes on to say that, "Sin not." John is basically appealing to us to live by our new nature that is guided by the Spirit of God that sins not. But still our old nature can surface causing us to sin, without prior intention to sin. In such case, the grace of God fills in to cover our failures and the blood of Jesus cleanses us when we repent. It is from this prospective Paul wrote: "So I say, walk by the Spirit, and you will not gratify the desires of the flesh" (Galatians 5:16). The anointing is the yoke destroying mechanism that Satan does not want you to have. No wonder religiosity ignores the anointing!

****

The more you focus on something the more you program your minds on it. It doesn't matter whether your opinion is positive or negative towards it. No wonder we are a society of paranoid people. Too paranoid to show love and even more paranoid to receive it. The good news is that Jesus gave us His sinless life to be ours and to manifest. Paul said that "And I no longer live but in me Christ lives" (Galatians 2:20). His life can neither be imitated nor duplicated. It is lived by our fellowship with the Holy Spirit (Romans 8:9-11). Therefore, the degree to which Jesus Christ dwell in us depends on the degree to which we follow the guidance of the Holy Spirit through the Scriptures.

****

Oils and precious ointments were emptied upon priests and kings as mere symbols or acknowledgments that God's Spirit had chosen to rest upon them. Normally they had only one anointing, and it came at the beginning of their career. God was the originator, and such men were therefore called "the anointed of the Lord" or "the anointed of God." The anointing came with their appointing—anointing and appointing go together. The anointing was given solely to equip and condition ordinary people to serve the Lord. It was not available apart from service. Today the anointing is for all believers, for all are called to serve. We are "a royal priesthood" (1 Pet. 2:9).

Jesus was God's alabaster box of perfumed ointment, broken for us on the cross and now filling the world with His fragrance. The Holy Spirit that descended on Jesus at baptism is now available on His body (the Church). The purpose of the anointing is to break the yoke. The anointing is the Holy Spirit at work in and among us. In order to be anointed, you must be available to serve others. Any strong man does not feel his strength while sitting down; he feels it only when he exerts himself. David did not feel anointed in any particular sense, but when he faced Goliath he knew he was. Samson became strong only when he went into action for God, for it was then that the Spirit of God came upon him (Judges 14:6).

Note carefully, though, that anointing is not a kind of emotional pleasure. It is the divine influence on humanity that comes to perfect our works when we serve. The anointing is not for selfish personal benefits. Reinhard Bonnkie said that "I know of no profanity worse than healing the sick in Jesus' name to get rich, make a name for oneself or obtain the gratification of wielding power."

****

"You never know how big a threat you are to the enemy until you start doing something for God".

****

Acts 17:11: "The people of Berea were more open-minded and they listened eagerly to Paul's message. They searched the Scriptures daily to see if Paul's teaching was true." We are called to be meat inspectors. Satan targets the Word of God because it is the most important thing to us. Counterfeits are made after big currencies. The most common counterfeits involve fifty dollar bills and above but none for a one dollar bill because it is valueless. Never be turned off because of the existence of counterfeits because they are modeled after the real things. The best way to recognize a counterfeit is to know the real thing! Spiritually, most of us will not fall for an obvious lie, but we can be fooled by a slight twist of the truth.

****

Paul called himself a bond slave of Jesus Christ (Rom.1:1). That is what all the early apostles were. Jesus is looking today for bond slaves - not servants. There is a difference between a servant and a slave. A servant works for pay. A slave gets no salary. God has no servants under the new covenant, only bond slaves. To be a bond slave means willingly devoted to absolute obedience and loyalty to Jesus Christ. It means spiritually made free by the Lord from sin. The gospel cannot be bought or sold otherwise it ceases to be of grace. "The passion of Christianity is that I deliberately sign away my own rights and become a bond-slave of Jesus Christ. Until I do that, I do not begin to be a saint."

Romans 6:22 speaks of the past present and future of a true bond slave of God. (1) In the past - freed from the guilt and conscious sin. (2) In the present - the fruit of progressive sanctification. A life of victory over sin. It does not mean sinless; it means constantly bending towards the righteousness of God. It means aiming to manifest the righteousness of Christ. Yes, at times we are going fail; it is called to miss the mark. But our target is to obey the commandments of God. (3) In the future – glorification of the total man into the fullness of the divine stature.

****

Life is about making choices - good and bad choices as well. In the end, we cannot escape the consequences of our choices. "In every life, there comes a day of reckoning - a time when unsettled scores demand retribution, and our own lies and transgressions are finally laid bare." Therefore, if you have the guts to do something, then you better save enough guts to face the consequences. The law of harvest is to reap more than you sow!

****

"In an extroverted society, the difference between an introvert and an extrovert is that an introvert is often unconsciously deemed guilty until proven innocent." God declares innocent the condemned sinner by the substitutional death of Christ. Grace is therefore not the absent of justice.

****

John 3:16 – "For God so loved the world that he gave his one and only Son, that whoever believes in him shall not perish but have eternal life." The thirsty of God's love could only be quenched by giving His only Son to die on your behalf. Think about it!

****

Luke 9:23 – "Take up his cross daily and follow me." (Luke 9:23) Following Christ is about self-denial. It is a calling to make it the daily habit of denying your old nature an opportunity to take its course, and manifesting the new nature born in you. The new nature involves the will and purpose of God as projected in the Scriptures. "Die to self" means "Trusting Jesus instead of the flesh." It means to live each and every day out of the glorious relationship you have with the Lord instead of religious obligation. The message of self-denial is contrary to the Pharisaical self-righteousness legalistic practice of asceticism dressed up in religious jargon. Carrying your cross is a willful act of self-judgment done out of conviction as opposed to being coerced or judged by others. Paul said that I have been crucified with Christ and I no longer live, but Christ lives in me… (Gal 2:20). Take your flesh to Christ's cross, where your sins were crucified. The only weapon to fight sin with is the spear that pierced the side of Jesus. You must kill your anger, temper, lust, pride and etc., in the same way. Let them die!

****

Love for God is born into us after we are born again. But after it is divinely born, it must be divinely nourished. It is not like a perennial plant, which will flourish naturally in human soil--it must be watered from above by His Word. Love for Jesus is a flower of a delicate nature, and if it received no nourishment, as a result of hardened hearts (rock of our hearts), it would soon wither.

****

1 Corinthians 13:13 - "And now these three remain: faith, hope and love. But the greatest of these is love." When we go to heaven, we will never need faith because we will see Jesus with our eyes. When we go to heaven, we will never need hope because we shall already have our blessed hope. But we shall take love with us to heaven because the love of God is eternal. Perfect love comes from God to us.

****

Question: "How can I have the mind of Christ?" Answer: It is to think as Christ would have thought — clearly, positively and concretely. In 1 Corinthians 2:16, Paul quotes Isaiah 40:13 and then makes a statement concerning all of the faithful believers: "We have the mind of Christ." Having the mind of Christ means sharing the plan, purpose, and perspective of Christ, and it is something that all believers possess. It is having a clean conscience that pursues the righteousness of God.

In order to have the mind of Christ, one must experience the new birth after investing their faith in Jesus Christ to be saved (John 1:12; 1 John 5:12). A believer's life is influenced by God. The divine influence (grace) is the guidance of the indwelling Spirit of God (Ephesians 4:30). The Holy Spirit indwells and enlightens a believer, infusing him with wisdom—the mind of Christ. Yielding to the Holy Spirit is the process of conversion by renewing the minds (Romans 12:1-2). Jesus promised that "But when he, the Spirit of truth, is come, he will guide you into all truth" (John 16:13). The Holy Spirit teaches us to obey the Word of God. The Word of God is the mind of God written down by man for man through inspiration. We get into the Bible so that the Bible gets into us.

****

1 Corinthians 12:13 - "For by one Spirit are we all baptized into one body, whether we be Jews or Gentiles, whether we be bond or free; and have been all made to drink into one Spirit." The Church is made up of believers who were redeemed and baptized with the Holy Spirit. Baptism of the Holy Spirit is what God does to your soul at regeneration. It is not because you deserve it but because of how gracious your God is. After the baptism of the Holy Spirit, we are required to maintain the status by being filled with the Holy Spirit. To be filled with the Holy Spirit is our responsibility (Ephesians 5:18).

****

The Ark of the old covenant represented the Holy Temple of God in heaven. The mobile tent was later replaced by the temple. The temple is the dwelling place of God - symbolic of Jesus Christ the true temple. All believers make up the temple of God because the Holy Spirit indwells their hearts. Every believer has a throne where Christ rules by His indwelling Spirit. Every redeemed soul is supposed to be filled to the brink, and rivers of living waters and love flowing from them for others to partake of. Like the stars shine in the heavens, we are the light lightening the whole earth. Wherever there is a believer there is a fiery glow of the Holy Spirit, mapped in every corner of the universe. The Holy Spirit is the best gift we can receive from God. Indeed, God always gives His best to those who leave the choice to Him!

****

Get you up to a high mountain (Isaiah 40:9). Each believer should be thirsting for God, for the living God, and longing to climb the hill of the Lord and see Him face to face. Sadly, many saints are content to live like men in coal mines, who do not see the sun; they eat dust like the serpent when they might taste the food of angels; they are content to wear the miner's garb when they might put on king's robes; tears disfigure their faces when they might anoint them with celestial oil. What fully enchants you to remain in a pit when you may sit on a throne? "Do not live in the lowlands of bondage now that mountain liberty is conferred upon you. Do not be satisfied any longer with your tiny attainments, but press forward to things more sublime and heavenly. Aspire to a higher, a nobler, a fuller life" ~ Alistair Begg

****

Amos 3:3 - "Can two walk together, except they be agreed?" (KJV). We cannot walk with God unless we agree with Him. God does not have to agree with us, we must agree with Him.

****

Galatians 6 - "Do not be deceived: God cannot be mocked. A man reaps what he sows." God is not too good to punish sin; He is too good to let sin go unpunished!

****

Remember this, Christian, and let it comfort you. However difficult and painful your road, it is marked by the footsteps of your Savior; and even when you reach the dark valley of the shadow of death and the deep waters of the swelling Jordan, you will find His footprints there. Wherever we go, in every place, He has been our forerunner; each burden we have to carry has once been laid on the shoulders of Immanuel. His way was much rougher and darker than mine. Did Christ, my Lord, suffer, and shall I repine? Take courage! Royal feet have left a blood-red track upon the road and consecrated the thorny path forever.

****

John 11:49-51- Caiaphas, who was the high priest that year, spoke up, "You know nothing at all! ---- do you take into account that it is expedient for you that one man die for the people, and that the whole nation not perish." Now he did not say this on his own initiative, but being high priest that year, he prophesied that Jesus was going to die for the nation, and not for the nation only, but in order that He might also gather together into one the children of God who are scattered abroad...." God can use various people to speak to us the words of knowledge and wisdom from God even when they are not aware that they are delivering a message from God. He used the mouth of a donkey to speak to Balaam (Numbers 22:28).

****

Jesus commanded Nicodemus that, "Do not be amazed that I said to you, 'You must be born again. The wind blows wherever it pleases. You hear its sound, but you cannot tell where it comes from or where it is going. So it is with everyone born of the Spirit" (John 3:7-8). As the wind, He brings the breath of life to men; blowing where He wills, He performs the quickening operations by which the spiritual creation is animated and sustained.

****

The Kingdom of God is the only remaining place where we can find doubtless love and security. Don't seek fulfillment, perfect love and security 'out there' through other sources other than from your cleansed conscience. Enjoy the privileges of the world but not at the expense of your soul. True joy comes from the Lord. See beyond the current system of the world by cultivating for peace that surpasses your wisdom from within. Our Lord and Master taught that the "Kingdom of God is within you."

****

John 5:39 – "You search the Scriptures, for in them you think you have eternal life; and these are they which testify of Me." Elsewhere,

Jesus said to His disciples that, "These are My words which I spoke to you while I was still with you, that all things which are written about Me in the Law of Moses and the Prophets and the Psalms must be fulfilled." (Luke 24:45). The Bible is a story about the creation, fall and salvation of man. Jesus is in the background of every moral biblical story and character. The story of salvation narrates the sovereign work of God in history. Virtually every story, poem and proverb in the Bible contribute to the ongoing plot conflict between good and evil. The biblical characters, as portrayed in the scriptures, are the historical truth but not patent truth. They either chose to be for God or against God. We are called not to embrace everything they did but to learn from them. The life and words of Jesus are the patent truth which we are supposed to follow. Jesus said that ultimate goodness is in God alone: "No one is good except God alone" (Mark 10:18). For this reason, Jesus came to reveal the goodness of God to us and by His grace He made it possible to be ours. Celebrating Jesus is the only way of silencing the devil!

****

Psalm 119:130 - "The unfolding of your words gives light; it gives understanding to the simple" The Holy Spirit uses the scriptures to inform us and illuminates our minds, convicting us towards the moral truth we need to know to make adequate sense of what we encounter in our daily activities. The Bible is the living powerful force for us to overcome adversity and to protect our minds from the intrusion of worldliness (Hebrews 4:12). You can count on the Bible because it is God's Word that endures forever (Isaiah 40:8; Mark 13:31).

****

You can't be influenced by what you don't know. The prescribed pills on your table will not heal you unless you swallow them, in the same manner you need to read the Bible and digest the truth in order to acquire the mind and character of God.

****

In order to appreciate Gods work through his Word, believers need to study the Bible. This is how we can know what God is saying to us. God is real and his word is alive. But we must rightly divide the Word. Proper biblical interpretation involves proper word study; proper understanding of the history, culture and language of the writer and the people he wrote to. Then the application of the truth within Gods Word to our lives. This is what the Church needs today to be effective in contending for the faith. We need value time to read the Bible with the help of the greatest teacher (the Holy Spirit). That is when we can say that it works; His Word works!

****

Romans 11:29 - "The gifts and callings of God are without repentance." Actually, this scripture refers to God and not man. It is God Who has never repented (changed His mind) about the promises that He made to Abraham and his seed. The word repentance in this case has nothing to do with man.

****

"You will say then, "Branches were broken off that I might be grafted in" (Romans 11:19). Jesus was sent first to the Jews but because of unbelief they were broken off like branches from the tree so that the gentiles might be grafted in. "For if God did not spare the natural branches, He will not spare you, either. Behold then the kindness and severity of God; to those who fell, severity, but to you, God's kindness, if you continue in His kindness; otherwise you also will be cut off" (Romans 11:21-22) Read the above scripture regarding the goodness and severity of God and pay attention to the "If" and "Continue". The words are the key to proper interpretation of the scripture. God's tough love to forsake a soul is not intended for total destruction or leave it to ruin, but for conviction that yields to repentance so that there can be restoration.

****

When you reject truth, you become vulnerable to deception and you are unable to see things from the divine prospective. Free will without spiritual discerning is terrible danger. It is a totally unreliable instrument. The scriptures warn against it. "Trust in the Lord with all of your heart, and lean not to your own understanding. In all your ways acknowledge him, and he will direct your path," (Proverbs 3:5-6 KJV). It is absolutely impossible to understand what is happening in life unless you see life from God's point of view.

****

The greatest story ever told is the biblical story of salvation. Christianity is unique such that people, after they reach the age of accountability, must be converted in order for them to become true believers. Unlike other religions whereby the vast majority of the people are born into their respective religions and are held captives simply because their parents belonged to the same religions. Christianity is unique because every true Christian must have the testimony of the transformed life and an encounter with the living Christ.

****

The Bible says that Jesus adds to His Church: "And the Lord added to the church daily such as should be saved" (Acts 2:47). Yes, we are saved by God but after that we are called to stay holy by devotion. The Word is as important as the teacher of the Word (the Holy Spirit). Jesus said that, "But the Advocate, the Holy Spirit, whom the Father will send in my name, will teach you all things and will remind you of everything I have said to you" (John 14:26). Notice that the Holy Spirit is called "the Spirit of truth" in John 14:17. Apart from Him, men cannot know or understand truth. The Bible warns that "The person without the Spirit does not accept the things that come from the Spirit of God but considers them foolishness, and cannot understand them because they are discerned only through the

Spirit." (1 Corinthians 2:14). Jesus said, "The world cannot receive [the Spirit of truth], because it does not see Him or know Him" (v. 17). The apostle Paul said that Christ in us is the hope of glory (Colossians 1:27), and Christ promised His Spirit would reside in us (John 14:17). And He will reside in us permanently. He will never leave or forsake us (Hebrews 13:5).

****

Adam and Eva sinned by deciding to act independently of God. The religious leaders of the times of Jesus decided to act independently of Christ. The people of the world have no fellowship and communication with the Holy Spirit. They act independently of the Holy Spirit. Self-efforts to transform ourselves is the ultimate self-destruction. Faith is coming to the end of yourself, and acknowledging and trusting what God can do in you through Jesus Christ. It is called surrendering your heart to Jesus and committing your will to Him.

****

One of the Ten Commandments in the Old Testament states: 'You shall not take the name of the Lord your God in vain, for the Lord will not hold him guiltless who takes his name in vain' (Exodus 20:7). Dr. John Hagee, the founder and senior pastor of the Cornerstone Church, said that The word vain means for "no reason" or 'useless", 'In this world of crimes and deaths that surround us, a simple blasphemy does not get that much attention when it should. No wonder nowadays people are partaking of iniquity compared to drinking water. There is the fantasying of sin everywhere you look'.

****

Somebody asked that "Are our bodies evil?" The term flesh is used interchangeably when referring to our human bodies and to our old Adamic nature that is corrupted with sin. Our current bodies are corrupt in nature such that they cannot see God. Corruption came to us because of the curse of sin but sin does not reside in our bodies.

Sin resides in our hearts. Our bodies can be clean or unclean vessels depending on who seats at the throne of your heart. The Bible says that "I beseech you therefore, brethren, by the mercies of God, that ye present your bodies a living sacrifice, holy, acceptable unto God, which is your reasonable service" (Romans 12:1). Holy in this case means set apart to be used by God compared to the vessels (cups) which were used to serve in the temples; they were not holy in sense of morality but they were set apart to be used at the altar of God and could therefore not be used to serve others gods.

****

There is a moral lesson to learn from the Namugongo pilgrims. I am in particular thrilled with the elderly and the 14 years old teenager that persevered the hostile environment trekking hundreds of miles from Lira to Kampala on feet. "Character cannot be developed in ease and quiet. Only through experience of trial and suffering can the soul be strengthened, ambition inspired, and success achieved." ~ Helen Adams Keller

****

"We live in a time when faith is thin, because of our aching for what is above us and beyond us has been anaesthetized and our capacity for wonder reduced to clever tricks" ~ Abraham Herschel

****

Proverbs 20:27 -"The human spirit is the lamp of the LORD that sheds light on one's inmost being." The human spirit is the lamp that cannot light without oil. The Holy Spirit is the oil that lights up the human spirit (lamp). God put His Spirit in our spirit to illuminate our minds and to bring awareness of His presence. Jesus promised that "I will not leave you comfortless: I will come to you" (John 14:18). He sent us to light the world with His light: "Let your light shine before others, that they may see your good deeds and glorify your Father in heaven" (Matthew 5:16).

****

The total man is divided in three parts: spirit, soul and body. The tabernacle was divided in three parts, and lighted by three kinds of lights. The outer court was lighted by natural sun – representing the natural light for the natural body. The inner court (holy place) was lighted by the lamp stand – representing the Word lighting the human soul. The holy of holies lighted by the presence of God (Shekinah) – representing the indwelling Spirit of God in the human spirit.

****

We are sons of God by virtue of our fellowship with the Holy Spirit (Ephesians 3:16). The begotten Son of God (Jesus) is God coming down to us when wrapped in human flesh. A believer is the Holy Spirit (God) wrapped in human flesh going back to God the Father. Christ enables us to live in Him all that He Himself lived (sinless life) this being the only acceptable life before God, and He lives it in us. We are called only to become one with him, for He enables us as the members of His Body (Church), to share in what He lived for us in His flesh as our model. Jesus Christ came down from heaven, and yet heaven was in Him: "And no man has ascended up to heaven, but he that came down from heaven, even the Son of man which is in heaven" (John 3:13). Heaven was in Him before He went to heaven. In the same manner heaven must be in you before you go to heaven!

****

2 Corinthians 10:3-4 - "Though we walk in the flesh, we do not war according to the flesh. The weapons of our warfare are not of the flesh, but have divine power to destroy strongholds". Our enemy (the devil) is spiritual. Satan is not a mere force; he is a real entity with supernatural capabilities. We are not called to follow him but to flee from him by our godliness. We are called to fight the good fight of faith and stand against the wiles of the devil. But this warfare does

not involve carnal weapons. Faith is trusting in the spiritual and supernatural capabilities of God extended to us through Jesus Christ.

The Church is the body of Christ supposedly to be the embodiment of TRUE Christianity, and TRUE Christianity is supernatural, or it is nothing! Jesus used for the first time the word 'Church' in Matthew 16:18 (εκκλησια) meaning "the called-out" people from the world of sin. Jesus made this great pronouncement about His Church: "I will build my Church, and the gates of Hades shall not prevail against it". He intimated three things: 1) That He would build a definite entity called His Church. 2) That the Church would encounter an opposing force. 3) That the opposing power (even death) will not prevail against the Church. The fundamental and essential supernatural nature of the Church is evident in the supernatural new birth from heaven of every individual in the Church (John 3:4-8). The Church was born on Pentecost when the Holy Spirit came to dwell in us. He came to help us to do what we could not do naturally. Jesus made this profound radical statement: "Without me you can do nothing" (John 15:5). Jesus promised to be with us by His Spirit even unto the end of the world (Matthew 28:20).

****

Some unconventional wisdom here for you: "The highest purpose of God in the believer is not to make him so much a powerfully-used instrument, as to bring forth in him the fullest manifestation of Christ in every aspect of His character, and this can only be done in the winepress valley of fellowship with His sufferings."

****

It is our conviction that all the activities of the children of men, which are not guided by the Spirit and counsel of God will bear no lasting fruits; they will not be acceptable in the sight of God. This is my earnest prayer: "Search me, God, and know my heart; test me and know my anxious thoughts" (Psalms 139:23). Examine me; keep on always searching me out trying my reins and my heart (Psalm

26:1 - 2) and see if I have not misrepresented you in my actions or acted contrary to my conscience. As the Lord knows us thoroughly, and we are strangers to ourselves, we should earnestly desire and pray to be searched and proved by his Word and Spirit. According to the psychiatrists, we are emotional animals. Emotions are at the center of our thinking. Emotions are not separate from reason but they are the foundations of reason because they tell us what to value. My desire is to be proved and tested by God because I don't want my decisions to be influenced by my emotions.

****

The saving love of God is our saving faith. Christianity is not a religion but it is the relationship with God and the neighbor. Give love because God gave love. Whatever God does is the best for us to do. Generosity is one of the evidences of spiritual maturity because our God is generous. The bible recommends giving cheerfully (2 Corinthians 9:7). Psychology suggests that when you give to another person, there's a physiological response. Your brain's pleasure and reward centers light up as if you were the recipient of the good deed - not the giver. We are called to love God with all our hearts and love neighbor as we love ourselves. According to the story of the Good Samaritan (Luke 10:25-37), Jesus insinuated said that your neighbor is the one who has a need, and you are able to meet their needs.

****

Success is certain when the Lord has promised it. Never despair in case you pleaded for something for months without manifestation of tangible evidence. God will not turn a deaf ear when His people are serious about a matter that concerns His glory. Jesus asked us to forgive seventy times seven times (Matthew 18:22). Likewise, we must not dream of unbelief but to hold on to our faith even to seventy times seven (endlessly). Faith restores expectant hope in a hopeless situation and resists any possibility to be crushed by repeated disappointment. "Faith is quickened to plead more fervently with her God. She is humbled but not crushed: Her groans are deeper, and her sighings more vehement, but she never relaxes her hold or stays her hand" ~ (Alistair Begg)

****

Where there is a mountain, there must be a valley. When you up expect to come down. You can count on the fact that the God of the mountain is the God of the valley.

****

God is love, and His love is forever but His grace is not forever. Don't take God's love for granted. Self-evaluation, self-examination and swot analysis will help you to move in the right direction.

****

Trusting in the God that still performs miracles will take you to a higher level in Him; into the realm where impossibilities become possible! Activate your faith and use it effectively in order to give the people around you a reason to believe.

****

Politicians call for reforms. God calls for renewing. He is in the business of renewing of hearts by transformation. The Bible says that "Do not conform any longer to the pattern of this world, but be transformed by the renewing of your mind. Then you will be able to test and approve what God's will is-his good, pleasing and perfect will" (Romans 12:2). God uses His word to penetrate our hearts. The Word of God equips us and prepares us to face the adversity of this world. Peter said, "His divine power has given us everything we need for life and godliness through our knowledge of him who called us by his own glory and goodness. Through these, He has given us his very great and precious promises, so that through them you may participate in the divine nature and escape the corruption in the world caused by evil desires" (II Peter 1:3-4). When we receive Jesus Christ, He transforms our hearts. Then the process of renewing our minds through His Word initiates, purposely to purge ourselves of the bad. The mind is the powerhouse of the body where every thought is buried, both good and bad.

****

Praying, fasting and giving are the pillars of Christianity. God expects us to pray, to fast and to give to the needy. That is why Jesus said, "When you pray, not if you pray." But God looks at the quality of the quantity. God minds how we pray, fast and give. Jesus said that "And when you pray, do not be like the hypocrites, for they love to pray standing in the synagogues and on the street corners to be seen by others. Truly I tell you, they have received their reward in full" (Matthew 6:5). Also, "But when you give to the needy, do not let your left hand know what your right hand is doing" (Matthew 6:3). Also, "When you fast, don't make yourselves look sad. The hypocrites do that. Don't be like the hypocrites. They make their faces look strange to show people that they are fasting. I tell you the truth, those hypocrites already have their full reward" (Matthew 6:16-18). God looks at the intents of our good works. We do not pursue the spiritual disciplines to gain us notoriety and respect. They are of value when we offer them to God and go about our daily routine as if nothing were different, except our character. Our character is to be transformed to be more like our Father in Heaven. A fast to God is not about looking like we're fasting on the outside, but that we're being transformed on the inside. That transformation will show itself over time, and in the meantime, the fruit of fasting will be its own reward.

****

Psalm 37:23 – "The steps of a good man are ordered by the Lord: and he delighteth in his way." The discipline of life involves doing something that you do not necessarily want to do. Rise up against the odds and do it because it the right thing to do, and because it is pleasing to God.

****

Truth leads us to grace. The grace revives and awakens the soul moment after moment till glorification. Paul said that: "Whereunto I also labour, striving according to his working, which works in me mightily." (Colossians 1:29). The Christian life is like running a race. Except that, regarding faith, you don't have to train hard and make the giant strides in order to win. Christ, inside you, is the hope of all glory. He is running the race on your behalf. He is taking every necessary step to change you into the person God wants you to be. All you have to do is to surrender and allow Him to do what He came to do in you. Whenever you choose to do the opposite, you will suffer the consequences of your choices. "You may choose your kicks but you have no choice regarding the kickbacks."

****

Jesus said that our eyes are the windows of our heart. We see people through the spiritual lens of our hearts. For example, if we have a scratch on our glasses, it may seem like everybody around us has scratches too, but the problem actually lies with us because our vision is impaired. "You need to reconsider before you assume that everybody is bad to you, and you are the only Mr. or Mrs. Perfect!"

****

The greatest commandment is to love God with all our heart (Matthew 22:37). That means the greatest sin is doing the opposite. Jesus taught us how to love God: "If you love me, obey my commandments" (John 14:15). There are three reasons why we obey. The first one is out of fear of the consequences of breaking the given rules (Ephesians 5:5-7). There is assured retribution (physically, emotionally and spiritually) whenever we break the established moral laws. Most of the calamities in this world could be averted if only we adhered to the laws of God. The second reason why we obey is to enjoy the benefits of obedience (Mathew 19:28). Of course, the greatest benevolence is our good communication with God the creator. The third reason why we obey is because we love God. The rest of the reasons are embodied in the third one. God demands obedience based on relationship rather than out of obligation. You cannot live Christ's life but you can allow Christ to live His life through you.

****

According to Alistair Begg, life is a precious thing, and in even its humblest form it is superior to death. This is eminently true in spiritual matters. It is better to be the least in the kingdom of heaven than the greatest out of it. The lowest degree of grace is superior to the noblest development of unregenerate nature. Where the Holy Spirit implants divine life in the soul, there is a precious deposit that none of the refinements of education can equal. The thief on the cross excels Caesar on his throne; Lazarus among the dogs is better than Cicero among the senators; and the most unlettered Christian is in the sight of God superior to Plato. Life is the badge of nobility in the realm of spiritual things, and men without it are only coarser or finer specimens of the same lifeless material, needing to be made alive, for they are dead in trespasses and sins.

The same holds true of our prayers and other religious exercises: If we are quickened in them by the Holy Spirit, they are acceptable to God through Jesus Christ, though we may think them to be worthless things, while our grand performances in which our hearts were absent, like dead lions, are mere carcasses in the sight of the living God. We need living groans, living sighs, living despondencies rather than lifeless songs and dead calms. Anything is better than death. The snarlings of the dog of hell will, at least, keep us awake, but dead faith and dead profession—what greater curses can a man have? Quicken us, quicken us, O Lord!

****

God created a perfect universe with perfect people. We make a grave mistake whenever we think that our world and humanity are our problems, instead of our sin and the corrupt system of the world. The difference between this world and the future world to come is the absence of sin. Jesus came to redeem our humanity and nature by eradicating sin. He destroyed sin by liquidating the wages of sin (death). The Moral Law (prescribed moral righteousness of God) demanded death for every bit of it that was violated. Jesus saves us from the consequences of breaking God's laws. Now, the Law has no demand on a believer. Jesus Christ reconciled us to God and to God's image bearers (neighbors). He said, "Behold, I make all things new" (Revelation 21:5). It means a new man born of God/heaven on earth. Man to whom it is accounted righteous because of the grace. New people and new world belong to God. Abraham Kuyper, a well-respected Dutch theologian made the following comment: "There's not a single square inch in the whole domain of human existence over which Jesus Christ who is Lord of all does not cry out, 'Mine!'" Chuck Colson quoted Kuyper, and added that, "And so, there's not a single square inch in the whole domain of human existence over which we, as follower of Christ, do not cry out 'His!'"

****

Take your sins to Christ's cross, for the flesh can only be crucified there: We are crucified with Him. Our corrupt bodies have got a permanent place at the cross to hang there. The only weapon at our fingertips to fight sin with is the spear that pierced the side of Jesus. I must kill my angry, temper and bitterness in the same way. This is how Jesus delivered us from our burdens. This is the only way to give them a deathblow. Let them die!

****

A good name is to be chosen rather than great riches. Proverbs 22:1-5 - Reputation is fragile; once it's damaged, it's hard to restore. It is not uncommon to sacrifice a good reputation on the altar of power, prestige, or profit. This too could be our story. Scripture encourages us: "A good name is to be chosen rather than great riches." God is telling us that true value must be placed not in what we have but in who we are. Ancient Greek philosopher Socrates said, "The way to gain a good reputation is to endeavor to be what you desire to appear." As followers of Jesus, we bear His name. Because of His Love for us, we strive to walk worthy of Him, reflecting His likeness in our words and deed. Doing the opposite is taking the name of God in vain. By our example, others around us will be led to praise the God who has redeemed and transformed us - for the name of the Lord is worthy of glory, honor, and all praise.

****

Philippians 3:1-11 – "I also count all things loss for the excellence of the knowledge of Christ Jesus my Lord". It is not Christ and the world but Christ or worldliness; it is either Christ alone or no Christ. Ego is the manifestation of our corrupt nature. It is that passionate desire that objectively focuses on you. "Our desire for recognition wouldn't be such problem if it didn't tend to replace Jesus as the focus of our attention. But being absorbed with ourselves crowds Him out of the picture" ~ Dorothy Johnston

****

"Things are valued differently depending where you are. Only the Word of God, the Bible, means the same thing, all the time, but only to God's True People. Those who feed in The Gilead pasture. Micah 7:14." ~ Jonathan Zake

****

Romans 8:23 – "Not only so, but we ourselves, who have the firstfruits of the Spirit, groan inwardly as we wait eagerly for our adoption to sonship, the redemption of our bodies." Inside each of us is a rebellious nature that inclines towards lawlessness (anti-nomos). Also inside every one of us is a person that God intended us to be. The Holy Spirit is the chisel that can bring that person out. Discover your inner-self by regeneration, and from that place spread love contagiously to the left and to the right - in every direction. Freely you received, freely give!

****

We live in a disposable society. It's easier to throw things out than to fix them. To avoid this impotence, we engage in frantic, obsessive activities- we call it recycling. We recycle old paper, plastics, garbage's and etc. "All the human and animal manure which the world wastes, if returned to the land, instead of being thrown into the sea, would suffice to nourish the world." We basically recycle all things that used to be regarded as the rejects of the world; but what about your miseries? Put your problems into the hands of God because He alone can recycle evil into good. "But as for you, you thought evil against me; but God meant it unto good" (Genesis 50:20).

****

The Biblical story of the handwriting on the wall (Dan. 5:1-31). Belshazzar was the king of Babylon. His father, Nebuchadnezzar, had conquered the nation of Israel and brought all the wealth of the temple, along with most of the inhabitants of Jerusalem, back to Babylon. Daniel interpreted the dreams and visions of Nebuchadnezzar when no one else could. Daniel was summoned to explain the writing on the wall. The message from God revealed that Belshazzar had been weighed in the balances and was found wanting. Therefore, his kingdom was divided and given to the Medes and Persians. This came to pass that very night. Belshazzar was overthrown, and Darius, the Mede (Persian), took control. If we were weighed in the balances against God's righteousness as Belshazzar was, we too would come up short. God's righteousness is always more in quantity and quality than ours will ever be. Our righteousness is as filthy rags compared to God's righteousness (Isaiah. 64:6). Righteousness is a gift that comes from the Lord to those who accept what Jesus has done for them by faith (Rom. 5:17-18). Unfortunately, the word "righteousness" has become a religious cliché that has lost its meaning to many people.

Even Christians are confused about what righteousness is and how to receive it.

****

<u>End of February Romantic Month:</u>

The celebration of St. Valentine's Day has become an annual traditional ritual amongst people especially of my generation. The need for attachment during this period has forced people into unplanned relationships just to appease their boredom & quench their thirsty desire for a companion; the euphoria of which is always short-lived. If Valentine's Day is the "Holiday of Love," isn't this the perfect time to love yourself a little more fiercely? To remind yourself of how strong, and spirited, and independent you are? To celebrate yourself and your life a little? To avoid the emotional agony that accompanies the termination of impromptu unions. February 14 should be celebrated for being single and dating yourself too. Trust in God's perfect timing, knowing that every moment of waiting is worthy because He is preparing you for someone special.

****

During Valentine's Day each year, nearly $18.6 billion dollars are spent—$1.6 billion of which is spent on candy and $4.4 billion spent on jewelry! We're so driven by consumerism these days that we can come to believe that romantic love revolves around gifts. We can even begin to think that the best way to know if someone really cares about us is if they're willing to buy something we want (and even better, something really expensive!).

Unfortunately, we often apply this same principle to God—assuming that He best shows His love for us by giving us what we want when we want it. When we get the goods, we're confident of God's love. But when we don't, when things don't go our way, or if we don't receive what we want, we're tempted to wonder if God really loves us. Although I am loath to admit it, I am definitely guilty of this tendency. While gifts can be a demonstration of love, they're not the only way we can be sure of someone's affections, nor are they the best way.

The best way to know that someone loves you is if they're willing to suffer for you. And that's precisely what we read in Romans 5:8, that God demonstrated His love for us most clearly not by giving us a diamond ring or a shiny new toy, but by sending His only beloved Son to die for us—something more precious by far. This is a calling that Jesus took up willingly for the sake of the sheep that He loves. For us. Jesus said, "No one can take my life from me. I sacrifice it voluntarily" (John 10:18). The next time we begin to wonder if God really loves us, may we look to the cross. God loves us enough to suffer for us. There's no greater nor better symbol of true love.

****

Exodus 20:3-5 - "You shall have no other gods before me". God is Love but He is also a jealous God. Sincere love is jealous: "Place me like a seal over your heart, like a seal on your arm; for love is as strong as death, its jealousy unyielding as the grave. It burns like blazing fire, like a mighty flame" (Song of Solomon 8:6). Love is possessive. Love says to your spouse that, "I have put a seal on your hand so that it cannot be wrapped around any other person other than me." Jealous with intent to protect whom you love should never provoke moral indignation!

****

"If you hesitate between me and another person, don't choose me"

****

Love demands full attention. "I want to be the reason why you fall asleep with your phone in your hand!"

****

"Don't tell a woman she's pretty; tell her there's no other woman like her, and all roads will open to you" ~ Jules Renard.....

****

True love sees not with the eyes, but with the mind. One of the scams of technology is the lost romance which we used to enjoy before the digital era. I reminisce with nostalgia my youthful age when I used to write pages of love letters made out of insight, understanding, love and compassion. Unlike today in the digital era whereby love letters are texted in a couple sentences. According to experts, technology makes it easier to bring up thorny topics while avoiding confrontation. And in our busy world, typed-out messages are fast becoming a substitute for the meaningful conversations that keep people connected. Don't forget that, "Romance is the glamour which turns the dust of everyday life into a golden haze." Happy Valentine Day to all of you warriors of love!

****

A man can love a million girls but only a real man can love one girl in a million ways!

****

Beauty is not just mere external looks. Your intelligent, ambitious, mentally fine qualities walk past a mirror, stop. Look at that beautiful soul staring back at you & tell her, "You are beautiful."

****

The body will heal with rest.

The mind will heal with peace.

The heart will heal with love.

The soul will heal with joy.

The home will heal with laughter.

The world will heal with kindness.

****

Be the girl his ex-girlfriend will hate, his mother will love, his sisters will admire, his brothers will welcome and the one he will always cherish..

****

Proverbs 5:3-6 - The lips of a seductive woman are oh so sweet, her soft words are oh so smooth. But it won't be long before she's gravel in your mouth, a pain in your gut, a wound in your heart. She's dancing down the primrose path to death, she's headed straight for Hell and taking you with her. She hasn't a clue about real life, about who she is or where she's going.

March Month of the Resurrection of our Lord and Savior

Today is Ash Wednesday, the beginning of the season of Lent. The concept originated by the Roman Catholics somewhere in the 6th century. Though the exact origin of the day is not clear, the custom of marking the head with ashes on this Day is said to have originated during the papacy of Gregory the Great (590-604). In the Old Testament ashes were found to have been used for two purposes: as a sign of humility and mortality; and as a sign of sorrow and repent. Putting a 'cross' mark on the forehead was in imitation of a ritual practiced by the Roman Catholic and Protestant churches of putting a mark, when using water, on the forehead of a Christian at baptism. This was symbolic of being delivered from the slavery of sin and the devil, and made a slave of righteousness and Christ (Rom. 6:3-18). Whether or not your own church participates in this ritual of the smudge ash, there is a moral lesson in fasting. I mean self-denial; taking into account that we are living in a culture that is obsessed with "self" and committed to the pursuit of self-fulfillment and feeling good about oneself. Also, the ash diminishes our contemporary illusions of autonomy and self-determination. It is a reminder that I am not my own. And I will die one day - Remembering that "thou art dust and to dust thou shalt return." What happened on that Resurrection Day, which we'll commemorate 40 days from now, is the most important event in the history of the world. Jesus defeated death on our behalf.

****

Palm Sunday is celebrated a week to the Passover (Pasika) holiday. On this day according to the Bible, Christians took palm branches and lined the streets to welcome the son of God, shouting, "Hosanna!" "Blessed is he who comes in the name of the Lord!" as He rode on a donkey to Jerusalem (John 12:12-13). Jesus had been in Jerusalem before but, this time it is a unique entry in Jerusalem. It is His last entry of triumph. This season of the year the city had heightened excitement because of the many pilgrims who had come to the city for Passover. Also, the excitement caused by the resurrection of Lazarus. His entrance, therefore, captured the curiosity of many people.

Several weeks earlier, some Pharisees came to lure Him back to Judea. Jesus said that He would not return until such time as the citizens of Jerusalem would say, "Blessed is He who comes in the name of the Lord" (Luke 13:31-35). Perhaps He intended this to further establish His credentials as the promised Messiah. When Jesus came to Jerusalem for the last time, He arrived to the adulation of many and the cheering approval of the crowd. They followed shouting, "Hosanna to the Son of David!" "Blessed is he who comes in the name of the Lord" (Matthew 21:9). His coming in this manner had been revealed clearly in the Old Testament: the method, the timing, and the meaning. Zechariah 9:9 had told of the King's coming on the colt of a donkey so that Israel would recognize Him. From Daniel 9:25-26 the exact time of the Messiah's arrival can be calculated. Psalms 118:21-29 had announced the meaning of Christ's arrival, which the crowd realized in their shouts.

****

Palm Sunday or Triumphal Entry, as it is called, served a deeper purpose than simply a parade in the honor of Jesus. Traditionally, the Jews used the palm branches on the Feast of Tabernacle [Booths] (Lev. 23:29-43). The Triumph Entry happened when the Jewish people were in preparation to celebrate the Passover Feast. This time, Jesus entered Jerusalem to save. They waved the palm branches, shouting "Hosanna", meaning "save, rescue, savior". The significance of the palm branches (normally waved at the Feast of the Tabernacle) is that God tabernacled (dwelt) among us. The religious leaders trying to steal the show asked Jesus to tell His disciples to be silent. Jesus replied that if they keep silent these stones would cry out (Luke 19:40). The stones which Jesus was talking about are the bricks making up the temple building at Jerusalem. Jesus is the true temple (John 2:19), and we are the living stones making up His temple [body] (1 Peter 2:5). The term "living stones" is used as a metaphor to illustrate the secure and intimate relationship believers have with Jesus. We are a temple being built by God Himself for His praising. We cannot be silenced because Jesus put a new song of salvation in our hearts; a song which those who are silent (the world) cannot sing. Give Him a big praise today!

****

Matthew 27:2 – "And they bound him and led him away and delivered him over to Pilate the governor." Humility is power under control with restraining. In Jesus, we see humility at its best. The One that created the universe decided to become a speck of dust (human). He allowed His hands to be bound by an insignificant creation (soldier). These are the same hands that created the universe (the heavens and the earth, sun, moon and stars) but could not resist humiliation by the speck of dust. He did it for me and you. Self-sacrifice is the essence of love. The humility of Jesus is indeed love at its perfection.

****

The book Leviticus says the lamb of sacrifice had to be perfect without a broken bone. John 19:31-37 – "The Jewish leaders didn't want the victims hanging there the next day, which was the Sabbath (and a very special Sabbath at that, because it was the Passover), so they asked Pilate to hasten their deaths by ordering that their legs be broken. Then their bodies could be taken down. So the soldiers came and broke the legs of the two men crucified with Jesus. But when they came to Jesus, they saw that He was dead already, so they didn't break His legs. One of the soldiers, however, pierced His side with a spear, and blood and water flowed out. This report is from an eyewitness giving an accurate account; it is presented so that you also can believe. These things happened in fulfillment of the Scriptures that say, 'Not one of His bones will be broken (Psalms 34:20),' and 'They will look on Him whom they pierced' (Zechariah 12:10).

****

Somebody asked that "If Jesus was strangled could He have saved us?" The answer is No. The Bible forbids even eating strangled animals (Acts 15:29). Jesus had to die on the cross in order to fulfill prophecy (Psalm 22:16–17). The cross is the greatest altar on the face of the earth where God sacrificed His Son. There must be the spilling of the blood in order for a sacrifice to be valid and acceptable to God. The Bible says that all sins are by the law purged with blood, and without shedding of blood there is no remission (Hebrews 9:22). Life is in the blood. The wages of sin is death. It means that the curse of sin (death) is in the blood. The curse of death was against Adam as opposed to Eva because all of us have the blood of Adam. The same contaminated blood is transmitted to all human races. Because sin is a disease of the blood, it can be cured by the application of sinless blood, for it is the blood that maketh an atonement for the soul. In Egypt, God passed over the firstborn of Israel: "When I see the blood I will pass over you" (Exodus 12:13). God did not see the sins of the people but instead, the blood of innocent animals painted on door posts. He was satisfied because of the substitute death of the animals in the homes of the Israelites. In the old covenant God instructed Moses to temporarily atone (cover) for the sins of the people with the blood of the innocent animals: "For the life of the flesh is in the blood: and I have given it to you upon the altar to make an atonement for your souls: for it is the blood that makes an atonement for the soul (Leviticus 17:11).

Jesus shed His blood in seven areas: In the Garden of Gethsemane His sweat turned to blood; He took 39 stripes on His back that you might be healed; the Crown of Thorns placed on Jesus' head to wound him and mock Him; they drove nails into His hands; the Roman soldiers drove spikes into his feet; the soldier shoved a spear into His side and blood and was poured out; He was bruised. In summary, the death of Jesus is the substitute death necessary to pay the wages of our sins, and His blood is necessary to atone for our sins and to clean our conscience of guilt. It is only the perfect blood of God that can redeem the imperfect sinners.

****

Somebody asked this question: "Are the people who killed Jesus innocent since they were fulfilling prophecy because Jesus came to die for our sins?" I want to say that it is true that Jesus came with prior knowledge and plan to die for our sins. Jesus said, "Everything written about me in the Law of Moses and the Prophets and the Psalms must be fulfilled" (Luke 24:44). Prophetic messages certainly alert us of the good things from God and the evil plans of the devil that will come to pass but the warnings (prophecies) do not cause the evil plans to prevail or to come to pass because God is not the author of evil. People have free-will to act the way they do.

Peter lamented that, "This Jesus, delivered over by the predetermined plan and foreknowledge of God, you nailed to a cross by the hands of wicked (godless men) and put Him to death" (Acts 2:23). The point is that these people did what they did out of their free-will without any coercion. Nobody forced them. They ignored the Scriptures projecting that Jesus was the promised Messiah, and they danced at the music of the devil for their own destruction. Jesus told the religious leaders that they had no excuse for not knowing who He is because the Scriptures point to Him: "You search the Scriptures because you think that in them you have eternal life; and it is they that bear witness about me, yet you refuse to come to me that you may have life" (John. 5:39, 40). Elsewhere Jesus told them that, "If you don't believe my words, believe my works" (John 10:37-38). Jesus asserted that, even if the Jews couldn't accept His claims of deity, the miracles He had done are without doubt from God. Therefore they are without excuse! Given the fact, the blood of Jesus which they spilled rebelliously had the power to save them too.

****

Jesus was truly God and truly man. He was not one of the two natures, and He was not a mixture of the two natures. The Gospel records provide many examples of how completely Jesus had human nature. It is recorded that he was weary, and had to sit down to drink from a well (John 4:6). "Jesus wept" at the death of Lazarus (John 11:35). Most supremely, the record of his final sufferings and death should be proof enough of his humanity: "Now is my soul troubled", he admitted as he prayed for God to save him from having to go through with his death on the cross (John 12:27). He "prayed, saying, O my Father, if it be possible, let this cup (of suffering and death) pass from me; nevertheless not as I will, but as thou wilt" (Matt. 26:39). This indicates that in His humanity Christ's 'will', or desires, was different from that of God. Jesus died as a man. Of course, God cannot die.

****

Luke 22:42 - "Father, if you be willing, remove this cup from me: nevertheless not my will, but yours, be done." Because of the corruption of sin, we are all children of wrath unless saved by God. When Jesus decided to partake of the cup of God's wrath, He saved us from God's wrath against sin. This is exactly what we are saved from. We are sinners under the grace. We were justified by the perfect life of Christ and His death on our behalf. Thank God for His amazing grace. Grace is everything outside hell!

****

Matthew 27:29 - "And then twisted together a crown of thorns and set it on his head." Without the crown of thorns put on the head of Jesus our crowns of grace we anticipate to wear in heaven would have been invalidated.

****

Why did Jesus say that "My God why have you forsaken me?" Jesus said these words so that you and I might not ever say the same words. Jesus turned death into a mere shadow. It is better to be run over by the shadow of the tuck than the truck. The reason is because the shadow is harmless. Jesus allowed death to run over Him so that the shadow of death can run over us. Jesus was forsaken by God so that we might be united with God eternally. After Jesus died on the cross the veil was torn. Now we can approach the Most Holy Throne with boldness. Never shall we ever cry: "My God, why have you forsaken me?"

****

Isaiah 53:10 - "Yet it pleased the LORD to bruise him". God delighted in the suffering and death of His Son. The suffering of Jesus is compared to an expectant pregnant woman that is experiencing labor pains that end in the joy of the birth of a baby. The death and resurrection of Jesus are the birth canal through which the church was born. The Son shares in the joy of the Father for the newly born baby (church). Jesus delights in His throne because on it there is a place for the redeemed (Ephesians 2:6; Romans 8:17). He rejoices in His royal robes since they cover the nakedness of His people (Revelation 19:8). He delights in His resting and calls us to enter it (Matthew11:28; Hebrews 4:3). He delights in His joy and He desires that it remains with us in its fullness (John 15:11) He delights all the more in His glory and He calls us to share it (John 17:22; John 15:11). "Both the one who makes people holy and those who are made holy are of the same family. So Jesus is not ashamed to call them brothers and sisters" (Hebrews 2:11).

****

Matthew 27:29 – "And when they had platted a crown of thorns, they put it upon his head, and a reed in his right hand: and they bowed the knee before him, and mocked him, saying, Hail, King of the Jews!"

Mark's Gospel records that Jesus was mocked as a king 3 times. To the Roman soldiers, the title of King was laughable because their allegiance was to the mighty Emperor Caesar. Satan always offers an alternative choice to counteract the ultimate provision of God. The greatest sin is refusing to acknowledge the rightful Kingship and Lordship of Jesus Christ, and to refuse to bow down to the only One that came to atone for our sins (Savior).

****

These are the seven sayings of Jesus on the cross: "Father, forgive them, for they do not know what they do" (Luke 23:34); "Truly, I say to you, today you will be with me in Paradise" (Luke 23:43); "Jesus said to his mother: "Woman, this is your son." Then he said to the disciple: "This is your mother" (John 19:26-27); "My God, my God, why have you forsaken me?" (Matthew 27:46 and Mark 15:34); "I thirst." (John 19:28); "It is finished" (John 19:29-30); "Father, into your hands I commend my spirit" (Luke 23:46).

****

John 20 - Now on the first day of the week Mary Magdalene went to the tomb early, while it was still dark, and saw that the stone had been taken away from the tomb. Then she ran and came to Simon Peter, and to the other disciple, whom Jesus loved, and said to them, "They have taken away the Lord out of the tomb, and we do not know where they have laid Him." The visibly empty tomb created an even deeper emptiness in them. They were desperate, frustrated, discouraged and disappointed. But Jesus made His presence known to them that He is alive! The empty tomb turned into their place of hope.

****

Somebody asked that, "Do you believe that no person has ever suffered as Jesus did at the crucifixion?" If you mean physical torturing the answer is no. From the time of the arrest of Jesus to

His body being placed in the tomb was less than a day. According to historical accounts, crucifixion has been known to last for three days. The crucifixion of Jesus was rushed because of the pending Sabbath holiday in the evening. In some incidents of crucifixions, the victims stayed at the cross for days such that their body parts were devoured by scavengers while still alive. In fact, the physical suffering of Jesus might be even less than that of some of His followers who are tortured by ISIS today for His name's sake. I grew up in the neighborhood of the barrack commanded by one of the notorious thugs of Idi Amin called Juma Butabika. I used to walk through the army barrack daily on my way to school, and I saw graphic images of people being brutally tortured to death. Like making the victims stand barefoot on sharp broken pieces of bottles till they bleed to death. Some soldiers smashed the fingers of their victims with hammers, one by one, till the whole palm was fingerless in bid to extract the forceful confessions from them.

The uniqueness of the suffering of Jesus depends on the fact that the sins of the whole world were put on the only sinless person on the earth. When the sins of the world were put on Jesus, for the first time, God turned His face away from His Son. He cried that, "My God, my God, why have You forsaken Me?" (Matthew 27:46). For the first time ever, Jesus lost connection with His Father. Jesus was judged for our sins. All religions believe that God is Holy and Just. Ironically, when God lets sin go unpunished He becomes unjust! Christianity is the only faith that plainly explains how God justifies a sinner and He remains the Just God. Ask a person of another religion what will happen to their sins when they face the justice of God? They have no answer to it except following their religions blindly. It is Jesus and only Jesus that can turn away the righteous judgment of God against sin from a sinner to Himself. We (believers) put our faith at the same place (cross) where our sins are, and we are saved.

****

John 12:32 - "And I, if I be lifted up from the earth, will draw all men unto me." This sounds like one of the resolutions of prosperity that we make and that we are determined to keep at all costs. Yet, it was not a fancy place that Jesus was talking about. Jesus was talking about the Roman cross. He was delighting in hanging on that rugged cross to bring the lost world back to the Father. He was not ashamed of it. He went bragged about it that, "I have brought you glory on earth by finishing the work you gave me to do" (John 17:4). Praise our Savior!

****

When Jesus said that "It is finished", He fired the high priest and the priests from their jobs and sent them home because there was no more need of animal sacrifices. The payment for our sins was made in fullness at the cross. The resurrection is the receipt to prove that the wages of sin were paid in full. When Jesus Christ was crucified the stroke of God's righteous anger against sin (judgment) fell on His Son instead of on the whole world (Isaiah 53:8). We deserved God's wrath against sin but Jesus took it on our behalf (Romans 6:10). Jesus died for our sins once for all, for all men that believe, for all time and eternity (Hebrews 7:27; 9:12, 26, 28; 10:1-18). He died for our sins, once for all, so that we might die to our sins daily.

****

Answering a question about the alleged documentary film on the Discovery Channel, projecting that the tomb of Jesus was supposedly located somewhere, a liberal religious leader said that, "Even if they found the bones of Jesus, it wouldn't change his faith as a Christian because the spirit of Jesus is already in heaven." He missed the point! The Bible says that without the bodily resurrection of Jesus Christ, the Christian faith becomes null and void (1 Corinthians 15:14). Jesus gave up His spirit on the cross but the same power that raised Him from death works in us to regenerate us.

****

John 10:18 – "No man takes my life from me, but I lay it down of myself. I have power to lay it down, and I have power to take it again." Jesus is the only person that has ever chosen to die. What about thousands of people who commit suicide? These people do not choose to die because it is appointed for every person to die as per God's judgment against sin. When they commit suicide they simply choose the timing of their death. No one can resist the natural death of the corrupt bodies. Even the redeemed will have to die, and put on new incorruptible bodies. The Bible says that the corrupt bodies (flesh/blood) cannot inherit the kingdom of God (1 Corinthians 15:50). Jesus chose to die on our behalf in order to defeat death and to make way for us to live eternally in the presence of God. Choose Jesus, choose life!

April: Overcoming Temptation

Psalms 118:6 - "The LORD is on my side; I will not fear: what can man do unto me?" All the attributes of Christ, as truly God and truly man, are at our disposal. His divine power and Godhead subservient to our salvation. His omnipotence, omniscience, omnipresence, immutability, and infallibility are all combined for our defense. It is from this prospective that Paul bragged: "What, then, shall we say in response to these things? If God is for us, who can be against us?" (Romans 8:31).

****

Hebrews 4:15 – "For we do not have a high priest who is unable to empathize with our weaknesses, but we have one who has been tempted in every way, just as we are—yet he did not sin." Jesus was truly God and truly man. We must acknowledge His humanity in order to follow Him effectively. He was tempted like any other human being but He never sinned. There is a story of a billionaire that went to one village in the jungles to teach the natives how to work. He put aside his credit card and decided to toil like any one of the poor natives to survive. He inspired many natives to work and to succeed. Jesus put aside His heavenly card aside and became like any one of us and overcame the temptation to prove that we too can make it.

****

Hebrews 10:25 - "Not forsaking the assembling of ourselves together, as the manner of some is; but exhorting one another: and so much the more, as you see the day approaching." Go to church this weekend. One of the shallow reasons that people give for not going to church is that it is boring. Boredom is an emotional feeling often used by Satan to incite us to do other things which we are not supposed to do. If the church is boring most probably the problem is not with the church but it is with you. When you are filled with the Holy Spirit, your heart will click whenever the Word is read and spoken (Acts 2:37). The sooner you learn that the Holy Spirit was given to make the boring life interesting, the better off you'll be!

****

Satan is the personification of evil and the architect of treachery. The Bible teaches that the devil – as he works his craft against us – personifies wiles. He is the master of wiles. In order to be ready for this adversary, we must be knowledgeable of his methods and tactics. The Scriptures tell us of the great ability of Satan to tempt us, enumerates his wiles, and then provides antidotes against his deceptions. The good news is that the Lord is able to defend us and to keep us from the evil one. "Now unto him that is able to keep you from falling, and to present you faultless before the presence of his glory with exceeding joy, To the only wise God our Savior, be glory and majesty, dominion and power, both now and ever. Amen." (Jude 1:24-25).

****

The essential condition of man subsisted in three concentric circles. The innermost was his spirit; the inner, his soul; and the external, his body. With his spirit, man lived and moved in the love of God. The body stood, by means of the soul, under the potential influence of this light of love, and was thence expecting its glorification. By sin, all this has now become reversed. Consequently, the spirit was blunted and it became the servant instead of the master. Regeneration reverses the curse of sin. To be born again (regeneration) is to acquire the new nature of Christ (spirit) and allowing the spirit its rightful position to guide and to lead. The love of God within us motivates to keep His statutes or commandments.

****

What is the sin unto death, according to 1 John 5:16-17? Sin is breaking God's commandments. There are many specific ways of sinning but all of them fall into two ways: the sins of commission and the sins of omission. All sins fall under one or the other. The first, sins of commission, is a category of sin describing the things we did and shouldn't have. For example, I committed (commission) a sin when I lied and I shouldn't have. The second, sins of omission, are the category that encompasses the sins of not doing what we should have. We don't think as much about the sin of omission even though it is as pernicious and destructive as anything we could commit. For example resolving that you should have testified because you knew he was innocent, but you didn't out of fear. When we know the right thing to do and don't do it, that's a sin (James 4:17). All sins leads to death when they are not repented. A sin unto death is the unrepentant spirit; it is deliberately continuing in sin in spite of the conviction of the Holy Spirit. It is the sin that you continue loving to do. We are called to repent to Jesus Christ who has the power to forgive and to clean us of guilt.

****

In our humanity, the desire for God's ways can be so weak, and the desire to sin so strong. The good news is that when we fail, He readily picks us up again by His love. The Word of God is the two-edged sword that can separate us from our human instincts. The Bible says that "For the word of God is quick, and powerful, and sharper than any two-edged sword, piercing even to the dividing asunder of soul and spirit, and of the joints and marrow, and is a discerner of the thoughts and intents of the heart." (Hebrews 4:12). In the Old Testament tabernacle, the double-edged sword was for the priests; it was their sharp blade that they used to sacrifice with. The piercing of the sword is painful. In the same way in our spirituality in order for the Word to bring conviction, it must involve pain and sacrifice; it must be offensive to the natural man and the desires of the flesh. The Word of God (sword) painfully cuts off the flesh (corruption) to present our bodies as living sacrifice before God (Romans 12:1).

****

Somebody asked me to explain "Lead us not into temptation" (Matthew 5:13). We know from James 1:13 that God does not tempt us to sin. If He did, He would be acting contrary to His holy nature, and against His desire for us to be holy as He is holy (1 Peter 1:16). The word "temptation" refers to testing and can also refer to trials. It is a prayer asking God not to remove His hedge of protection over us as in the case of Job (Job 1:10). It is a prayer to God not to allow the trials to triumph. God allows us to go through trials in form of testing our faith because progress is made when we are resisting hardship.

****

Matthew 26:35 – "Jesus said to him, "Truly I say to you that this very night, before a rooster crows, you will deny Me three times." Peter said to Him, "Even if I have to die with You, I will not deny You." Peter thought that he is the rock as his name projected. He thought that he can persevere temptation by his own strength. But he was wrong because Jesus is the Rock that cannot be shaken. Satan attacks us at our strongest point. We overcome Satan by trusting in Jesus Christ and allowing Him to fight on our behalf.

****

Paul instructed us in this way: "Put on the whole armor of God, that you may be able to stand against the wiles of the devil" (Ephesians 6:11). Paul was referring to the armor of YHWH: "He put on righteousness as a breastplate, and a helmet of salvation on his head; he put on garments of vengeance for clothing, and wrapped himself in zeal as a cloak" (Isaiah 59:17). In fact, even the Old Testament high priesthood garment has its foundation in the armor of YHWH. Paul begins by instructing us that, "Finally, be strong in the Lord and in his mighty power" Then he goes on to describe various pieces of armor: "Stand firm then, with the belt of truth buckled around your waist, with the breastplate of righteousness in place, and with your feet fitted with the readiness that comes from the gospel of peace. In addition to all this, take up the shield of faith, with which you can extinguish all the flaming arrows of the evil one. Take the helmet of salvation and the sword of the Spirit, which is the word of God" (Ephesians 6:13-17).

****

Somebody asked me to explain John 14:30. Jesus had submitted himself to God, and although the Devil would try Him, there was nothing for the Devil to use to gain an advantage. This was what Jesus was referring to when He said, "...the ruler of this world is coming, and he has nothing in Me" (John 14:30). The Bible says that, resist the devil and he will flee from you (James 4:7). The only way to actually resist Satan is to submit yourself fully to God.

****

James 2:14-26 – "Faith without works is dead." The word "dead" is the word "nekros" the same word that God uses to describe the pre-salvation condition of a Christian. The word carries with it the meaning of "useless, lifeless, and void. Yes, God saves us when we cannot save ourselves, and God helps the helpless. However, our faith must be proven by our works. Today decide to pray with your heart, hands and legs. Swing into action believing God to bless the works of your hands. Remember that, "Inaction will cause a man to sink into the slough of despond and vanish without a trace." Don't anticipate to be blessed without presenting something to bless. God does not bless idleness. The Bible says that idle hands are the workshop of the devil (Proverbs 16:27). Basically, idleness is alignment out of the will of God and flawed understanding of the Scriptures.

****

"Be ye holy; for I am holy" (Leviticus 11:44; 1 Peter 1:16). God declared His character in both the Old and the New Testaments (covenants). He gave the Ten Commandments (Moral Law) to reveal His character but no man was able to keep all of the Ten Commandments without a possibility of breaking one of them. Finally, He gave His Son Jesus Christ to make His character accessible to man by faith. God does not dare us to do what He Himself does not dare to do. Therefore, when God says that "Be holy; for I am holy" He is not making a suggestion; He is instructing us to be holy, with severe consequences for those who dare not be.

****

Christians are not sinless but they are blameless before God because of the grace of God. If you are a follower of Christ, people are going to bring all kinds of accusations against you purposely to tarnish your reputation and most probably to bring you down. Child of God, make sure that there is no evidence in your life to support their false accusations. Don't be conformed to the pattern of the world lest they use it as evidence against you (Romans 12:2). Just give them massive evidences to convict you guilty for being a Christian.

****

Romans 8:18 – "For I reckon that the sufferings of this present time are not worthy to be compared with the glory which shall be revealed in us." Paul had such a great calling but his calling was not spared from massive sufferings. Jesus said concerning Paul that, "I will show him how much he must suffer for my name" (Acts 9:16). Paul persevered knowing that the future glory by far outweighs his current sufferings. He used the term "reckon" which is a bookkeeping business language. After balancing his books, the balance sheet showed that he is at gain as opposed to a loss; he is not in red.

Habakkuk prophesied the future glory: "For the earth will be filled with the knowledge of the glory of the LORD as the waters cover the sea" (Habakkuk 2:14). Today we experience the glory of God in its limited form but when Christ comes to consummate His kingdom we will experience and enjoy the unlimited presence of God. The whole universe will be God's temple. The Bible says that "Look! God's dwelling place is now among the people, and he will dwell with them. They will be his people, and God himself will be with them and be their God" (Revelation 21:3-4). The blessed hope is that there will be a new heaven and a new earth where the righteous will dwell in the perfect environment and in perfect communication with their God (2 Peter 3:13). Are you numbered among the faithful ones who are going to experience such incredible glory? Jesus alone qualifies us to be in God's glory. Habakkuk prophesied that the just shall live by faith (Habakkuk 2:4). Paul, when inspired by the Holy Spirit, emphasized the doctrine of justification by faith. He quoted Habakkuk 2:4 in three of his Epistles (Romans 1:17; Galatians 3:11; Hebrews 10:38).

****

According to Eric Metaxas, the danger of the fallen nature is that we have desires, which as James 1:15 tells us, "gives birth to sin." We have the willingness to break the rules to get what we want even though we've been warned of the consequences. We have the predilection for rationalizing our actions, even when we've been caught. And finally, we have the elation that accompanies the sense that we've gotten away with something.

It's hard to imagine a better illustration of what Christians mean by "original sin," what C.S. Lewis described as the "bent" in our natures. That's why Moore's prescription, conversations about ethics at work, probably won't help, especially if, as Moore concedes, cheating is part of human nature. That's not to deny that sound moral education wouldn't help. But ultimately, the answer to original sin, the bent in our natures, is a new nature. As Paul told the Corinthians, "Therefore, if anyone is in Christ, he is a new creation. The old has passed away; behold, the new has come."

****

1 Corinthians 3:13 - "Every man's work shall be made manifest: for the day shall declare it, because it shall be revealed by fire; and the fire shall try every man's work of what sort it is." According to the economy of God, your own virtues, like the virtues of any other person that is not born again are going to be reduced to ashes. The works of Jesus Christ through you are the only ones that are going to prevail the testing of fire. The ministry is about blessing others with what God has treasured inside you. Quit bragging that you are doing something for the Lord because it is the Lord doing something in you and through you. Christ will manifest Himself unto such as love Him, and co-operate with Him in obedience to His statutes. Next time before you decide to participate in anything, first ask yourself this simple question: "What would Jesus do in this situation?"

****

We are fighting with such assured victory without a possibility of losing. Effectual grace calls deep-dyed sinners to sit at the table of mercy. Pebbles from the brook are turned by grace into jewels for the royal crown. Worthless dross He transforms into pure gold. Redeeming love has set apart many of the worst of mankind to be the reward of the Savior's passion. My hope is in Christ, hope which will not disappoint. "It is grace that has brought me safe this far, and grace will lead me home!"

****

Satan causes frustrations by reminding us of the past. Never dwell in the past. "We are products of our past, but we don't have to be prisoners of it" ~ Rick Warren

****

There is a saying, "Do not free a camel of the burden of his hump; you may be freeing him from being a camel." Likewise, we cannot escape temptation because it is part of our spiritual warfare. Never expect not to be tempted. God asked Satan if he considered His servant Job. Hence, God brought Job to Satan's attention, not because Job was in sin, but because Job was the greatest servant of God on the earth at that time (Job 1:6-12; 2:3-6). "Jesus Christ was led away from human society into the wilderness and was tempted by the devil. If you will tell me when God permits a Christian to lay aside his armor, I will tell you when Satan has left off temptation".

****

Temptation will surely come but decide before temptation comes that you will not sin. Daniel made a resolution long before he was at the king's court that he will not be polluted by the paganism at the king's court.

****

Pride made the devil to be the devil. God hates pride: "Every one that is proud in heart is an abomination to the LORD" (Proverbs 16:5)

****

Whenever temptation comes, God provides a way out. Always see that way out (exit) as an opportunity to run away as fast as possible before you sin.

****

1 Corinthians 10:12 – "Wherefore let him that thinketh he standeth take heed lest he fall." Arrogance leads to falling. Never think that you are too smart or too strong to fall!

****

Your passions can be overcome by even greater irresistible passion. Overcome temptation by even greater power of righteous.

****

The biggest challenge is your perception of people's perception of you. I made a resolution to please God in order to please the people. "I'd rather stand with the Word of God and make man mad than to stand with man and make God mad!" ~ Willard Obryan

****

Never take God for granted. It is true that God is more eager to forgive than we are to seek forgiveness. That's true regardless of whether we've sinned little or greatly. And it's true Christ died for all sins, past, present, and future. And it is true God will forgive anyone who truly repents and asks for forgiveness. But it is a dangerous thing to presume upon the grace of God and deliberately sin while saying, "God will forgive." A person with such attitude abuses the grace and is not a qualifying candidate for the grace because his or her repentance is not sincere. Remember that the same God that extends grace also says that, "Be not deceived; God is not mocked: for whatsoever a man soweth, that shall he also reap (Galatians 6:7).

****

1 Samuel 17:45 – "David said to the Philistine, "You come against me with the sword, spear and javelin, but I come against you in the name of the LORD Almighty, the God of the armies of Israel, whom you have defied." Here is our moral lesson: "Focus on God and the giant you are facing will stumble; focus on the giant, and you will stumble."

****

Know that God will sustain you and will not forsake you. Know that you are forgiven. When God saves He does not forgive on an installmental plan but He absolutely forgives all of your sins (the past, present and future) unconditionally.

****

When you want something and you can't stop taking it or using it even if you wanted to, it's called addiction. The urge is too strong to control, even if you know that what you want is harmful to your life and character.

****

Somebody asked "My husband says that I am addicted to the Internet. I just love the Internet and cannot do without it. Is it possible that I am addicted?" Excessive computer use which interferes with daily life may be akin to addiction. You can tell that you are addicted to something when that particular thing controls you. That is when that particular thing dictates to you when to use it instead of you deciding when to use it. Something that you cannot let go obviously controls you. Addiction has harmful cognitive and psychological effects. However, you can fight it spiritually especially by praying and fasting. In your case, I am not talking about abstaining from food but fasting by occasionally taking a day or two days without going on the Internet.

****

Somebody asked "Is addiction demonic?" The answer is No. Addiction is psychological and biological due to weak will or moral character. Demons are entities; they are fallen angels with capabilities to occupy space, scheme and seduce. A born again Christian can be addicted, and can be oppressed by demons but he or she cannot be possessed by demons because Jesus cannot share the same house with demons (Mark 3:27). Demons can easily possess a non-believer although not all vice conducts are demonic. Like any other bad habit of the flesh (old corrupt nature), addiction can open way to demonic possession. The good news is that Jesus can deliver you from addiction and demons. Deliverance from demons is part of the package of salvation. "But if I drive out demons by the finger of God, then the kingdom of God has come upon you" (Luke 11:20).

****

There is nothing more provocative than the seductive culture of today. It is not uncommon to come across something that is provocative in an unsettling way. The visual seduction, in particular the sexy outfits of some ladies is astounding. Given the fact, there is no excuse for you to be victimized. If you are truly a man of God, seduction should accomplish just one thing: It should arouse the male in you but not the man in you. Remember that Christians are like a moon that has no light of its own but reflects the light of the sun. Likewise, we are supposed to reflect the light of Christ. A life lived outside Jesus Christ is not life at all.

****

Life is a challenge involving dealing with people, people like you and me. Impart as much as you can with your spiritual being. Do it to those who are on the road with you, and accommodate those opposed to you without compromising your values. Remember that life is better when you are happy but life is best when other people are happy because of you. Never underestimate the impact you can have on the lives of others. God can use even your dark days to light someone's path.

****

James 4:6 - "God opposes the proud but shows favor to the humble." The Greek word "opposes" is to resist or to range in battle against. God is at war with the proud because the proud heart has no room for the grace. Pride views things from the human prospective (self) as opposed from the divine prospective. God never ceases to remind us that He is God, and we are not.

****

Somebody asked me to explain "Thou shalt not take the name of the Lord thy God in vain" (Exodus 20:7). The Israelites of the biblical times never verbalized the name of God. They believed that no mouth was clean enough to pronounce the name of God. In the Hebrew manuscripts, they used the letters YHWH (English Jehovah) to represent the secret name of God. Also, in the Hebrew culture, the term "taking the name" was used in reference to a wife taking on the name of the husband in marital relationship. When a bride dishonored her body it was considered to be dishonoring the family name of the husband (taking the name in vain). Marriage is used to describe the relationship between God and Israel in the Old Testament (Ezekiel 16:8-14) and between Jesus Christ and the Church in the New Testament (Revelation 19:7-9). We take on the name of our Bridegroom (Jesus), to honor it by manifesting His holy life. Any sinful act committed by a confessing believer dishonors the name of Jesus. It is taking His name in vain.

****

2 Timothy 2:22 - "So flee youthful passions and pursue righteousness, faith, love, and peace, along with those who call on the Lord from a pure heart." This scripture is probably one of the most concise bits of advice reminding us how we should engage in the fighting against lust. Commit it to memory. Chew on this verse daily. Let your mind marinate in it. Character formation depends on making wise decisions. The world is a slippery place whereby all of us are vulnerable. "Mock not the fallen, for slippery is the road ahead of you." Take precaution and resolve to stay away from slippery places in order to avoid falling down.

****

The glory of God is the human being that is fully alive, filled with the Holy Spirit.

****

God never asks us to do what we can't do. He equips us to do what He asks us to do. "My job is to take care of what is possible and trust God with the impossible." Ruth Graham-Bell, daughter of Billy Graham

May: Apologetic

1 Peter 3:15 - "Always be prepared to give an answer to everyone who asks you to give the reason for the hope that you have. But do this with gentleness and respect". God requires us to be ready with answers as presented to us in the Scriptures and to give them to those in need of them with a good attitude.

****

How do we know that the Bible is the Word of God? The Bible has been proved historically accurate regarding people and places reported to have existed and lived in biblical times. The Bible has been proven accurate by history and science. For example, God commanded Moses that, "On the eighth day the boy is to be circumcised" (Leviticus 12:3). Science says that when a baby is circumcised on the seventh day he will bleed to death because he has not yet developed vitamin K. In 1935, Professor H. Dam proposed the name "vitamin K" for the factor in foods that helped prevent hemorrhaging in baby chicks. We now know vitamin K is responsible for the production (by the liver) of the element known as prothrombin. If vitamin K is deficient, there will be a prothrombin deficiency and hemorrhaging may occur. On the eighth day, the amount of prothrombin present actually is elevated above one-hundred percent of normal—and is the only day in the male's life in which this will be the case under normal conditions.

****

Isaiah 66:1, "Heaven is my throne, and the earth is my footstool." When the Bible speaks of God's "throne," the emphasis is on God's transcendence, dignity, and sovereign rule. The fact that His throne is in heaven further emphasizes the transcendent nature of God's existence. God does not have to leave His throne in heaven in order to be on the earth. He can be in heaven and on earth at the same time. Given the fact, God is not everywhere and in everything but He can be wherever He chooses to be. Certainly, every created being and thing stand before God for accountability. He gives abundant mercy to the souls that repent, and no mercy at all to the souls that reject repenting. There is no repentance outside Jesus Christ.

****

Ijaz Ahmad asked that, "Do you really believe the New Testament is the inspired word of God?" It is not possible to believe in the Old Testament and not believe in the New Testament because it is one Word with one central message of redemption. The New is in the Old Concealed, the Old is in the New Revealed. One of the reasons Jesus was revealed is to fulfill the Law by rightly interpreting the books of the Law. He is still doing the same work through the Holy Spirit. Thus to understand God's cosmic plan of redemption, we must hold all things in the Old Testament in the light of Christ and the teaching of the apostles.

It seems you are skeptical about the Canonization as opposed to inspiration of the New Testament. Canon means to measure. The first steps in the formation of a canon of authoritative Christian books, worthy to stand beside the Old Testament canon, which was the Bible of our Lord and His apostles, appear to have been taken about the beginning of the second century, when there was evidence for the circulation of counterfeit collections of Christian writings in the Church. The Bishops who canonized the Scriptures sorted out the counterfeit manuscripts that were not originally written by the Apostles. In the same way, we have counterfeit currencies today. For your information counterfeits are modeled after the original. There can be no counterfeits without the existence of the true original copy.

I want to emphasize that all Scriptures are inspired because they were written by men when moved by God. Biblical inspiration may be defined as God's superintending of the human authors so that, using their own individual personalities (and even their writing styles), they composed and recorded without error His revelation to man in the words of the original autographs. Inspiration means that "the Holy Spirit of God superintended the human writers in the production of Scripture so that what they wrote was precisely what God wanted to be written.

****

The meaning of the truth should be self-evidence as in the case of the Scriptures. The Bible is a living book that is relevant to all times. Because it is alive, it has the ability to change lives. God change lives. The Bible has opened up its secrets concerning the timeline of history. Everything the Bible declares has the full authority of God Himself. For all the negative things we say to ourselves, God has a positive answer to it. No wonder the Bible is still the No. 1 seller of all time, with an estimated 6 billion copies sold. You have got everything you need at your fingertips to take the world in your stride. Choose to live the purposeful life guided by the Holy Spirit through the Scriptures.

****

Somebody asked this question: Do you believe that the story of Jonah staying in the belly of the fish for three days is literally true? Answer: I believe the story of Jonah is true because the Bible is the written Word of God. As one professor said that, "Even if the Bible said that Jonah swallowed the whale I would have believed it." The story of Jonah is not a parable because the parables do not specifically mention the names of the people. Jonah is a historical figure. Jonah is first mentioned in the Bible in 2 Kings 14:25 from where we learn that Jonah's father was Amittai and that he was born in Gathhepher, which I understand is in Galilee, not far from Nazareth. He lived during the reign of Jeroboam II (786–746 BC). Jesus quoted the story of Jonah: "For as Jonas was three days and three nights in the whale's belly; so shall the Son of man be three days and three nights in the heart of the earth" (Matthew 12:40).

****

We are facing a culture that does not see truth as absolute - that says all paths lead to God, and that disdains the rigorous intellectual pursuit of the things of the Lord. Such darkened thinking resists the light of God's Word, and it influences the church in ways that hinder our ability to shine forth the Lord's truth. The threats of anti-intellectualism, relativism, and postmodernism are real. Christians are exhorted to proclaim Christ as the way, the truth, and the life. We should move away from a low view of truth to a view that places truth front and center in the Christian mission. The false messages of the age reduce our humanity to the products of cosmetic chemical accidents. The cultural context we live in sees humanity with no intentional origin and with no noble destiny involving integrity.

Indeed, we are living in the world that has lost its story. Reality is dwindling whereby everyone has a right to their own version of reality. Your reality might not be my reality when we are all true in spite of the contradiction. The only absolute is that there is no absolutes! Accuracy has been replaced by feelings and advocacy; it is not about what is true but what I want to be true. According to the deception of our age, history depends on one's opinions. We have a situation whereby everyone sees history through their own lens, and all are valid in spite of the contradiction. Isaiah lamented concerning this generation that truth has stumbled in the public square. Where are we heading to? Historians say that out of the 22 civilizations that appeared in history, 19 collapsed when they reached the immoral decay the USA is at today.

****

Recently, a young white American girl called Rachel Dolezal surprised the TV audience on CNN by these words: "Those Are My White Parents, But I "Consider Myself Black". I want to say that it is not surprising to me because this is the consequence of the society that embraces no absolutes. In the secular world, the decisions of the people are motivated by feelings instead of facts. People can decide their gender and race depending on their feelings as opposed to the instincts of natural realities!

John 1:1 - "In the beginning was the Word, and the Word was with God, and the Word was God." The Word is the pre-existence of Jesus. God (unchangeable) put on human flesh to dwell among us. Jesus is God with us. God has revealed Himself to us as God/man through Jesus Christ. The Word of God (Bible) is God/man too. God has spoken to us in His Word through real men when moved by God in the way we can understand Him. "For no prophecy ever originated because some man willed it [to do so—it never came by human impulse], but men spoke from God who were borne along (moved and impelled) by the Holy Spirit" (2 Peter 1:21).

****

Jesus is God-man. Likewise, the Bible is God-man. It was inspired by God and written by man. The Bible has opened up its secrets concerning the timeline of history with accuracy. The Bible speaks to all people of all races, gender and age. There were two races in the old covenant – Jews and Gentiles, and there are two races in the new covenant – born again believers and unbelievers. The Bible is relevant to all times and to all people; it knows no generation gap. It speaks to all people regardless of their race, gender and age. Everything the Bible declares has the full authority of God Himself. The author of the Bible is the teacher as well. You have got everything to take the world in your stride. It is your choice either to live a purposeful life in accordance to the Word of God or ignore it at your peril!

****

The theory of Relativism states that because of the enduring difference in perception and consideration, no truth is absolute and points of view do not bear ultimate validity! It is impossible for each of us to be right in our own ways, different from others, yet all of us be right!

****

Throughout the Bible, we find God portrayed as the Father figure. This portrayal, however, is surprisingly rare in the Old Testament. The old covenant involved the Law. Rules without relationship equal to rebellion. Jesus made it possible for God to be our Father (John 20:17). The teaching of the Fatherhood of God takes a decided turn with Jesus, for "Father" was his favorite term for addressing God. It appears on His lips some sixty-five times in the Synoptic Gospels and over one hundred times in John. God chose to be a parent because a parent can never resign from being a parent. The best love of all is that of our heavenly Father! What a blessing it is that He loves us! He fills the hole in our hearts with a love that can't be matched!

****

Jesus is not just a name given to our Lord but it stands for His purposes. Joshua (Ἰησοῦς) meaning salvation (σωτηρία) of the Lord (YHWH). It is given to our Lord because "He saves His people from their sins." The rulers of this world have often called themselves great, conquerors, bold, magnificent, and the like. But the Son of God is content to call Himself the Savior. He is the Suffering Servant that saves by His own blood. We are bond- slaves of Jesus. He extends to us opportunities to believe in Him and to suffer for His name's sake.

****

Somebody asked when the Bible says in Col. 1:15 that Jesus is the firstborn of all creations, does it mean he is a created being? In order to understand the term 'firstborn' look at these parallel scriptures: Exodus 4:22 "And thou shalt say unto Pharaoh, Thus saith the LORD, Israel is my son, even my firstborn". God also said in Jeremiah

31:9, "For I am a father to Israel, and Ephraim is my firstborn." So who is God's firstborn—Israel or Ephraim? In this case, the term firstborn does not apply to numerical sequence but to significance. It means that he has the first place or position in everything. Similarly Christ, as "the firstborn of all creation" (Col 1:15), is not only prior to it in time, but above it in power and authority. "All things have been created through him, and unto him" (Col 1:16). He is the One who has been appointed by God to be in authority over all things (Colossians 1:13-23; especially verses 15, 18). The term firstborn therefore has two main meanings. The first is more literal, referring to the fact that this son is the first son to be born of his father. The second meaning refers to the rights and authority of a person, because they are the firstborn. Our Lord is the "firstborn" in several ways, most prominently the first person to experience resurrection. Resurrection means overcoming death and never to die again. All of us who are born of God are patterned after Christ's nature.

****

Our culture is inundated (obsessed) with the following adage: "Nobody is perfect". We say it over and over, intriguingly, without evaluating the remuneration of not being perfect. By virtue of the statement, we acknowledge the need to be perfect, and our incapability to be perfect. It means that the concept of "original sin" is not alien to us. God created a perfect man in His image. The corruption of sin separated us from the holy God. We cannot enter the presence of God because those holy gates forever bar the pollution of sin, guilt and shame. God demands that we be perfect as He is (Matthew 5:48). But in reality, we cannot regain our lost holiness by any natural means. Therefore, in order for holiness to be ours it must come from beyond us - In this case, it must be granted to us by the holy God. Faith is trusting in God's abilities other than our own abilities to be perfect. The Bible says that "But without faith it is impossible to please Him, for he who comes to God must believe that He is, and that He is a rewarder of those who diligently seek Him" (Hebrews 11:6). We are perfect in Jesus Christ (Colossians

1:28). When God chose His elects, He chose Christ and all His people were chosen in Him. We are new creations born of God in the perfect image of Christ.

****

The deception of Islam is to convince the Muslims that God will accept them in His presence (heaven) depending on the magnitude of their good deeds. Their holy book (Quran) teaches that God will weigh your deeds, and if the good outweighs the bad, He will let you into heaven. The truth is that God is allergic to sin regardless of its size. Sin is an abomination to the holy God. Remember that it is just one sin that made Adam to lose fellowship with God, and to be kicked out of the Garden of Eden. God will not accept anything less than 100% perfectness. The same perfectness cannot be naturally earned but it is granted by God's grace through Jesus Christ and it is received by faith.

****

Somebody asked that, "Do you believe that there is one way to God?" Yes. God made one way to be born in this natural world by the union of a man and a woman (sperm and the egg). He also made one way to be born in heaven by our union with Christ (regeneration by His Spirit). Jesus is not just one of the ways to heaven but He is the only way to God. Jesus said that, "I am the way and the truth and the life" (John 14:6). I am – In the Greek language, "I am" is a very intense way of referring to oneself. It would be comparable to saying, "I myself, and only I, am." Jesus used the definite article to distinguish Himself as "the only way." In this case, a way is a path or route for His disciples to where He came from and where He was going (heaven).

****

God can do all things that do not contradict His morality and nature. These are things that God cannot do: 1) God cannot sin.

2) God cannot cease to be God. 3) God cannot create another God because the second God cannot be God but a created creature. God is self-existence and cannot be created.

****

Somebody asked that: "How do you tell a genuine Christian?" If you want an answer from the biblical prospective it is found in the Gospel of John. "By this shall all men know that ye are my disciples, if ye have love one to another" (John 13:35). Christians are not identified by being fanatic but by the Agape love which the world cannot afford to duplicate because it is spiritual. For example accepting to be offended without a possibility of reiterating. "If someone slaps you on one cheek, turn to them the other also" (Luke 6:29). There are things which are unique to us: Loving our enemies is abnormal to the people of the world. Forgiving and not taking revenge is considered to be a cowardly act by the people of the world. Yet these are the very distinguishing marks which identify us with Christ. A Christian wearing labels and tags but who has no agape love becomes a case of false advertisement.

****

The real powers lie in your willingness to look beyond what you were told. For as long as you keep searching, everything becomes - in a quick flash - super-achieve able, but you become as its cost, the 'MAD Prophet'; a threat to the TRUE holders of the actual events. You consequently become rechristened to "mentally imbalanced with borderline schizophrenia", so that those whom you tend to attract to the center of your 'troubling' knowledge may become doubtful in your system. "But if there is one thing the 'crazy ones' will forever achieve for willing to look beyond what they are told, is a lousy change that will outlive their moments- outlive their times" ~ A. W. Uduak

****

Ani Williams says that "I'm not anti-education; neither am I against the intellectual advancement that schools readily offer (although never functional in real time and never comes in handy against the challenges of real life)." He goes on to say - This is what I am: a rebel against the status quo that all men must be found attentive and always present in class if they desire success. But real success is found running amid the lines of innovation and dedication - a discipline of those who expand their minds beyond the confines of the convention of education, and challenge the confronting menaces that rise against the soul of humankind, with their natural mental capacity and creative disposition to question the usual order of events. Thus, my verdict: Classes dull the mind; they destroy the potential for authentic creativity. (Ani Williams)

****

The secularists want nothing more than a world free from the constraints of Christian morality. Gobry warns them that they had better consider—or rather remember—what that world looks like. These days, of course, Christianity takes the fall for things that cramp people's style: monogamous marriage, chastity, the sanctity of life, and the nuclear family, to name but a few. But in their rush to dismantle these irksome rules, modern secularists would do well to heed G. K. Chesterton's warning about knocking down a fence before knowing why the fence was put there in the first place. Pascal-Emmanuel Gobry explains, "Today it is simply taken for granted that the innocence and vulnerability of children make them beings of particular value, and entitled to particular care...[but] this view of children is a historical oddity." It is from the same prospective that Erick Metaxas points out that it's important we understand what a civilization truly free of irksome Christian rules looks like—especially if we hope to make the case for why some fences need to stay put.

****

Does the government has the mandate to legislate morality? The government has the responsibility to enforce the laws of the country as portrayed in the constitution. The government has three long arms (the executive, parliament and judiciary) to enforce the laws of the country. All laws declare one behavior right and one behavior wrong. But morality is not just what is right for man but what is right for the Moral God. This is the very definition of morality. When we say that morality cannot be legislated, we intend to mean that legislation cannot change hearts. Which is true, changing hearts is not the purpose of the laws. God alone can transform the hearts of men. The moral laws (Ten Commandments), which portray the morality of God are written in the hearts of all men, and cannot be legislated by any man. Given the fact, the civil laws encourage a certain behavior by citizens agreed on by the state. That is why the Bible instructs us to be law abiding citizens. Therefore, legislation cannot be divorced from morality. All laws (Moral/civil) constitute to morality. The question is not then can the government legislate morality, but whose morality does it legislate? The people are the government. The citizens should, therefore, stand up and fight for the right morality as projected by the Scriptures.

****

We need not to stutter or to stammer when declaring the truth. Stammering is different from stuttering but both conceal the true meaning of the truth spoken. Stutterers have trouble with the letters while stammerers trip over entire parts of a sentence. Jesus neither stuttered nor stammered when hammering home the truth. Likewise, we need to love the truth and speak the truth with love. I mean without being judgmental and without the possibility of compromising. The world interprets tolerance as compromising. But Christianity teaches that tolerance does not mean compromising.

The sour truth is that sexual immorality is an abomination to God. Sexual immorality involves any sexual encounter outside a married couple (a husband and his wife). The Bible says that "Or do you not know that the unrighteous will not inherit the kingdom of God? Do not be deceived: neither the sexually immoral, nor idolaters, nor adulterers, nor men who practice homosexuality, nor thieves, nor the greedy, nor drunkards, nor revilers, nor swindlers will inherit the kingdom of God. And such were some of you. But you were washed, you were sanctified, you were justified in the name of the Lord Jesus Christ and by the Spirit of our God" (1 Corinthians 6:9-11).

****

The past weeks have been marked by strenuous efforts by the evil forces of darkness: "Adultery is legalized in South Africa by the Constitutional Court. Gay Marriage is legalized by the U.S. Supreme Court. As if that is not enough, Germany's National Ethics Council has called for an end to the criminalization of incest between siblings after examining the case of a man who had four children with his sister. Lastly, Japanese court rules "Adultery is OK if it's for business purpose" All in one week! Then the following week Kenya legalized polygamy marriage. These are typically what we call the last kicks of a dying horse. A dying horse's last kicks may be vigorous and dangerous but they don't go on for very long and they get weaker before the animal finally succumbs.

****

Yes, the world can legalize whatever they like just like they have legalized homosexuality in USA and bestiality in some states. So civil laws when they are in contradiction to the Scriptures are considered to be worldly. They definitely don't ascertain right from wrong, but just what the natural man wants. Yes, homosexuality is socially destructive, naturally inconvenient, unfruitful, repugnant and spiritually rebellious. Soon these satanic people will legalize pedophilia and marriage to dolls... "Because of this, God gave them over to shameful lusts. Even their women exchanged natural sexual relations for unnatural ones. In the same way, the men also abandoned natural relations with women and were inflamed with lust for one another. Men committed shameful acts with other men and received in themselves the due penalty for their error. Furthermore, just as they did not think it worthwhile to retain the knowledge of God, so God gave them over to a depraved mind so that they do what ought not to be done" (Romans 1:26-28).

****

Delivering his annual report to the nation (State of Union), President Obama said that, "He and his family decided to embrace homosexuality after reading the scripture saying that "'Love your neighbor'". I want to say with due respect to our president that he took the scripture out of context to mean what he wanted to mean. Jesus said that "'Love the Lord your God with all your heart and with all your soul and with all your mind.' This is the first and greatest commandment. And the second is like it: 'Love your neighbor as yourself (Matthew 22:37-39). Jesus used the word "first" not in terms of sequential order but in terms of significance. The love of God compels us to love His ordinances. God dictates to us how to love others without a possibility of compromising His values. Loving a neighbor means to reprimand them when they are messed up so that they don't go to hell.

The Bible is unequivocal about Homosexuality. It is wicked, unacceptable and the epitome of utter rebellion against God. It is a badge of high moral decay in our society. It shouldn't be glamorized but condemned and demonized. The following scriptures call homosexuality an abomination to God (Genesis 19; Romans 1:26-27; 1 Corinthians 6:9-10; 1 Timothy 1:10).

****

Did you know that four of the Supreme Court judges that voted the legalization of gay marriage are Jews? Today, Tel Aviv — which the government of Israel is now pushing as one of the most gay-friendly cities in the world — and gay tourism is booming. Prophecy is into play that the Antichrist will be Jewish: He will sit in the temple (2 Thessalonians 2:4). He will be homosexual - "Neither shall he regard the God of his fathers, nor the desire of women, nor regard any god: for he shall magnify himself above all." (Daniel 11:37)

****

59:14–15 - "Our courts oppose the righteous, and justice is nowhere to be found. Truth stumbles in the streets, and honesty has been outlawed". This scripture is prophetic concerning our generation. The culture we live in considers God as the problem instead of the solution. The culture of today is eroding God instead of engaging Him. Christians are seen as intruders and intolerant. We are accused of enforcing our morality on others. Yes, it is very intolerant to say that Jesus is the way the truth and the life and that no one can get to God except through Him as Jesus Himself said in John 14:6. If what Jesus said and did is true, then Christianity isn't intolerant. It is simply true and it is the world that is intolerant of that truth. Ironically their accusations against Christians become complements before God as long as we preach the same message as Jesus. Jesus was intolerant of ignorance when He taught the people the truth (Matthew 5). Jesus was intolerant of hatred when He said: "love your enemies" (Luke 6:27). We are called to emulate Jesus. As Pastor Tony Evans says, "Discrimination against sin is legitimate discrimination." The homosexuals have come out of the closet, we need to come out of the closet too and express our values without fear!

****

Almost one month since the USA Supreme Court redefined marriage to include same sex couples, last week, the United Nations (UN Human Rights Council) passed the Protection of the Family resolution. The resolution, approved by a vote of 27 to 14, urges member states to adopt laws and policies that support the family values—yes, the family—definite article. It calls the family, "the natural environment for the growth and well-being of all its members and particularly children." While the White House was splashing rainbows on government buildings to celebrate our un-defining of marriage and family, the global community was reaffirming God's created definition. Not surprisingly, the mainstream liberal U. S. media ignored the story. Sharon Slater of Family Watch International called the vote an "unprecedented," "tremendous victory for the family." And not surprisingly, progressive and pro-LGBT organizations wasted no time in condemning it. One group known as the Sexual Rights Initiative bizarrely warned that recognizing the natural family would "perpetuate patriarchal oppression, traditions, and harmful practices..." But sad to say it was the 14 dissenting nations—including most of Western Europe and the United States—that really pulled out the stops to defeat this resolution.

Erick Metaxas says "Folks, if there's a wrong side of history, the United States of America is on it right now—at least when it comes to this issue. Thank God that despite bribery, bullying, and blackmail from the West, 27 nations voted to protect the family." Were it not for the enthusiastic support of China and Russia—major powers that spent the latter half of the last century trying to eradicate the natural family—this resolution may have failed. China and Russia learned the hard way how destructive anti-family policies are. Also, both countries have seen a rapid growth of Christianity in recent years. Thank God for the work of the missionaries.

****

Every person regardless of their religious affiliation have their world view. We (Christians), our world view is determined by our faith. We are called to hold on our values and fight every inch of the way without the possibility of compromising. As Chuck Colson wrote, "We're certainly not going to conform—Lord help us!... The church will have to hold its ground and refuse to knuckle under." The challenges are real and they come to us dressed in different forms like bioethics, political correctness, radical Islam, persecution, judicial usurpation, and many other issues we're facing today. It is appropriate to say that the church is facing a new Dark Ages. Our only hope is in Christ - the rock of our salvation. On this unshakable Rock, we stand. Be sure you put your feet in the right place, then stand firm.

Christ will carry you through all storms raging around; you will stand firm if He is the rock of your salvation. May God make you an epitome of success in all areas of your life.

****

From the worldly prospective, life seems to be a meaningless string of random incidents. Myths, philosophical systems and scientific theories have something in common – they can define but not negate the principle of randomness in the world. Power, money and love, however much we get of them, we simply end up in a condition of emptiness. There's a lot of randomness in the daily decisions that we make. Resist the randomizing forces of nature. Never allow the randomness of the world to lead you into randomness to God. Self-esteem is that assurance within you that God is at war on your behalf against the odds of life, and He is watching over you.

****

Genesis 4:1 – "And Adam knew Eve his wife, and she conceived, and bare Cain, and said, I have gotten a man from the LORD." The word 'knew' in this verse is the Hebrew word 'yada'. It is the same word used in Genesis 3:5 - "For God knows that in the day you eat from it your eyes will be opened, and you will be like God, knowing good and evil." Intimate knowledge in and out involves commitment and devotion. To know is basically to discover knowledge. Adam knew Eva and she conceived and bare Cain. Cain was a menace to the family of Adam. The reason is because, at the moment of conception, Adam had no communication with God. Human sexuality can only be known (discovered) by knowing the God that created sex.

****

Somebody asked "Doesn't the Bible say that when Adam sinned we all sinned? Why should God punish us for Adam's fault?" Answer: The Bible does not say what you are saying. Adam alone is responsible for the first sin of partaking of the forbidden tree. God is never going to judge you for partaking of the forbidden tree or the first sin committed by mankind. However, because all of us come from Adam, we are born with the corrupt nature (the original sin) that causes us to disobey God (sin). We have intents to sin even before we commit the actual sins. The Bible says that "Wherefore, as by one man sin entered into the world, and death by sin; and so death passed upon all men, for that all have sinned" (Romans 5:12-21). As I said, God will judge us for our individual sins (breaking His moral laws) as opposed to the first sin committed by Adam. We are sinners by nature unless we are redeemed by God. Here is the justice of God: By the negligence of one man (Adam) we all became vulnerable to sin, and by the righteousness of one man (Jesus) we are all vindicated when we repent: "For if by one man's offence death reigned by one; much more they which receive abundance of grace and of the gift of righteousness shall reign in life by one, Jesus Christ" (Romans 5:12-21).

****

Somebody asked me to explain Matthew 5:28. "Did Jesus mean that anytime I look at another woman (that I am not married to) differently I commit adultery?" Answer: Jesus said that "But I say unto you, That whosoever looketh on a woman to lust after her hath committed adultery with her already in his heart" (Matthew 5:28). Look at the context and you will discover that Jesus was defining the character and nature of sin. Sin is one of the saddest but also one of the most common phenomena of human life. It is a part of the common experience of mankind, and, therefore, forces itself upon the attention of all those who do not deliberately close their eyes to the realities of human life. Also, Jesus said that "You have heard that it was said to those of old, 'You shall not murder; and whoever murders will be liable to judgment.' But I say to you that everyone who is angry with his brother will be liable to judgment" (Matthew 5:21-22). Jesus basically defined sin in intents as opposed to actions. Adultery is full grown lust of the heart. Murder is full grown bitterness (hatred) of the heart. In real life, there is no man that has never looked at a woman lustfully. In the same manner, no one has never been angry. Sin is the reality of our fallen nature. Our actions are the manifestation of the corrupt and deceitful hearts. Jesus meant that everyone needs the Savior because every person is a sinner by nature even without committing a specific sin. Unless redeemed, we are all doomed because we are sinners by nature.

****

A liberal religious leader was asked to comment on the allegation that aired on the Discovery television show projecting that the tomb of Jesus where he was supposedly buried was located somewhere with his name on it. He replied that, "Even if they found the bones of Jesus, it wouldn't change his faith as a Christian because the spirit of Jesus is already in heaven." First, the name Jesus (Joshua) is one of the most popular name given to many Jewish people. The liberal leader missed the point! The Bible says that without the bodily resurrection of Jesus Christ, the Christian faith becomes null and void (1 Corinthians 15:14). Jesus gave up His spirit on the cross, His body was buried in the tomb, and on the third day, He was raised from death. The same power that raised Him from death works in us to regenerate us. The empty tomb is one of the evidences of the resurrection. The secular world has been toiling in vain to disapprove the Bible. If the dead body of Jesus was laying somewhere, they could have happily produced it as evidence to disapprove the authenticity of the Scriptures. Remember that the Jewish religious leader tried to fabricate the stolen body hypothesis posits that the body of Jesus Christ was stolen: "They told the soldiers, "You must say, 'Jesus' disciples came during the night while we were sleeping, and they stole his body.'" (Matthew 28:13).

****

Somebody asked, "Is it true that God loves me the way I am?" The right answer is that God loves you in spite of who you are in anticipation of changing you into what He wants you to be. God's standard of love is in Jesus Christ (John 3:16). Everybody outside

Christ will be discarded in eternal hell (pit of fire) because they are dented or unwanted.

****

Somebody asked that "If God loves unconditionally why did he chose to love Jacob and hate Esau?" The scripture says that "Just as it is written: "Jacob I loved, but Esau I hate" (Romans 9:13). God is not just loving but 'Love' is His very essence. The right interpretation of the above scripture is that God loved less Esau. The same word was used when Jesus said: "If any man come to Me and hate not his father and mother, and wife and children, and brethren and sisters, yea, and his own life also, he cannot be My disciple" (Luke 14:26). Hate, in this case, means loving less. Love is a two edged sword that cuts both sides; it cuts away the bad in order to preserve the good. Authentic love hates evil. God loved Jacob because from him came the twelve tribes of Israel and our Messiah. But from Esau came the hostile tribes of the Edomites. Herod the Great was an Edomite and during his reign, he played a key role trying to kill Jesus as a child and not forgetting his persecution in allegiance to Rome. The omniscient God looked into the descendants of Esau and He despised him.

****

Somebody asked "What did Jesus meant in John 1:18, when He said that, "No one has ever seen God, but the one and only Son, who is himself God and is in closest relationship with the Father, has made him known". Didn't Adam and Moses see God face to face?" Answer: Only Jesus stood face to face with God and knew the Father intimately. He stood face to face with the Father. No man except Jesus has ever seen God in His fullness. Jesus came to reveal the Father whom He knows best. Jesus said that "Don't you believe that I am in the Father and that the Father is in me?" (John 14:10). The very thing that reveals God conceals Him. In the Old Testament, there was temporarily a visible manifestation of the presence and glory of God called theophany. This may be in natural phenomena such as cloud or fire, in human form or in prophetic visionary experience.

Theophany is the manifestation of God that is tangible to the human senses. In its most restrictive sense, it is a visible appearance of God in the Old Testament period often, but not always, in human form. Some would also include in this term Christophanies (pre-incarnate appearances of Christ) and angelophanies (appearances of angels). In the latter category are found the appearances of the angel of the Lord, which some have taken to be Christophanies, reasoning that since the angel of the Lord speaks for God in the first person (Gen 16:10) and the human addressed often attributes the experience to God directly (Gen 16:13), the angel must therefore be the Lord or the pre-incarnate Christ. In the New Testament, Jesus revealed the fullness of God to mankind, but He was God veiled in human flesh. Jesus said that "Anyone who has seen me has seen the Father" (John 14:9). Jesus is the ultimate and only revelation of God to mankind. He said that "I am Alpha and Omega, the beginning and the end, the first and the last" (Revelation 22:13).

****

Somebody asked me "Do you still call Jesus the Son of God?" Answer: I will never doubt that He is whom He says He is. The term Son of God has two specific meanings. When the title is used concerning Jesus it is capitalized "Son of God" because it is in reference to His deity – same nature/character with God. Also, the term 'son of God' was used in reference to Israel because of her status as adopted members of the household of God: "When Israel was a child, I loved him, And out of Egypt I called My son" (Hosea 11:1). The nation of Israel was a theocracy ruled by God. This is an affirmation of the faith that God, the Creator of the universe, the Ruler of the world, has rescued the Israelites from captivity, and He is the absolute King. Also, the Scriptures call Adam 'son of God' (Luke 3:38). Likewise, Jesus is called the 'Second Adam' (1 Corinthians 15:45). This time, the title 'Son of God' is in reference to His perfect obedience to God the Father. Adam failed the testing. Jesus came to clean up the mess of Adam. Jesus embodies everything God created Adam and - all humans to be – and in Him alone we find the image of God and our original and full being: "Hereby know we that we dwell in him, and he in us, because he hath given us of his Spirit." (1 John 4:13). In Christ, born again believers are adopted into the family of God. We are children of God.

****

Somebody asked me to comment on the newly released picture of Jesus by advanced science/technology. I don't believe that Jesus wanted us to know Him by His physical appearance. I visited some African American Churches that have the picture of Jesus as a real Black (Negro) man. Then we have this popular image of Jesus we see in movies with blue eyes and very long curled hair. I don't think any of us has the real picture of Jesus. Jesus did not wear long hair as projected. In the first century, Jewish men, in particular, Rabbis wore their hair short and brushed forward at the forehead. It was considered very unseemly to wear one's hair long. It is from the same prospective Paul instructed men to cut their hair short, "Does not nature itself teach you that if a man wears long hair it is a disgrace for him" (1 Corinthians 11:14).

The Bible gives us the required information about Jesus: He was conceived of the Holy Spirit and born of a virgin (Luke 1:34-35). We might cast a comparative glance at the scriptures which have the passages that speak of Christ's 'racial' lineage. He was a Semite (Jewish) sprung from the tribe of Judah (Hebrews 7:14). He was from the house of David (Romans 1:3). We are related to the blood of Jesus and His nature as opposed to His physical appearance. Paul taught that we do not now think carnally of Christ himself, who has now left the world, and, therefore, he must be thought of spiritually by us (2 Corinthians 5:16). I think it is idolatry to have any of these images, supposedly to be of Jesus, engraved in our minds and worship them as the real Lord Jesus Christ.

****

Somebody sent me this message: "I am not a Christian but I respect all religions. I love my Moslem religion very much. I practice all my religious obligations as prescribed by the Quran. I believe we are all going to be rewarded by God in accordance to our beliefs". Answer: God is not going to ask you about your religion but He is going to reject you because of your sins. We go to God in the sinless image and nature of Christ. I want to say that the truth does not depend on what we believe but on what God says. Remember that God judged the world by the floods during the times of Noah. Noah's Ark is the typology of our salvation. There was one Ark symbolic of one way of salvation. There was also one door to the Ark symbolic of one door to heaven. Jesus said that "I am the way, and the truth, and the life. No one comes to the Father except through me" (John 14:6). Also, Jesus said that "I am the door" (John 10:9-16). He did not say that I am one of the ways or one of the doors. I believe what He said. I know the Moslems calls Him just a prophet. The good news is that they don't call Him a false prophet. Therefore, His Word is yes and amen.

****

God gave His promises from the prospective of love and grace; therefore, it is quite certain His Word will be fulfilled. Faith connects us to the promises of God. Faith views each promise in its connection with the promise-giver.

****

The commandments of God are part of the Word. In his new book, "Ten Commandments: Still the Best Moral Code," the writer makes the case that these core principles of morality underlie not just the Mosaic Law as understood in Judaism and Christianity, but civilization itself. This articulation of right and wrong and our resultant duties, inscribed on tablets by the hand of God, literally sets in stone the moral law already written on the tablets of our hearts. It's what legal scholars and jurists for millennia have recognized as the underpinning of good personal ethics and civil legislation.

****

"Know that a man is not justified by observing the law, but by faith in Jesus Christ. So we, too, have put our faith in Christ Jesus that we may be justified by faith in Christ and not by observing the law, because by observing the law no one will be justified" (Galatians 2:16). This passage reveals that the Law cannot justify or make righteous any man in God's sight, which is why God sent His Son to completely fulfill the requirements of the Law for all those who would ever believe in Him. God wrote the Moral Law on the heart of every person, and He gave it in written form to Moses on two tablets of stones. The Ceremonial laws were given to teach us the work of Jesus Christ. To know what our Messiah fulfilled on our behalf.

****

Luke 18:11 - "I thank you that I am not like other people--robbers, evildoers, adulterers--or even like this tax collector." It is within our human instinct to see sin in the lives of others rather than in our lives. The Pharisees considered themselves to be holy by claiming to strictly observe the Law, and by comparing themselves to others. The Gospels portray the Pharisees as absolutely evil. RC Sproul says concerning the Pharisees that, "It may well be in the calculus of evil that the only character faring worse than a Nazi is the Pharisee. These were the original black hats. In each of the Gospel accounts they are the no-accounts, the very foil of Jesus Himself."

Often we condemn the Pharisees even when we harbor the same attitude. Many confessing believers still claim salvation by their good works apart from faith in Christ. Some have a tendency of ascribing to others every conceivable sin that they think themselves not guilty of. They may have to confess to this sin or that, but at least, they tell themselves, "We aren't like those guys." The Bible does not instruct us to determine our righteousness by comparing ourselves with others. God revealed His morality to us in the Moral Law as the only yard stick to measure our holiness. Given the fact, none of us can observe all of the Ten Commandments without a possibility of breaking one of them during our lifetime. Ironically, breaking one means breaking all because God demands 100% perfection; He will not accept 99%. For this reason, we are called to run to Jesus Christ to save us from the wrath of God (eternal death) being the consequence of breaking God's commandments. "Without the shedding of blood there is no forgiveness; without shedding of blood, there is no remission of sins" (Hebrews 9:22). Obedient to God's commandment is the evidence of those saved by the grace.

****

One atheist demanded to know, "How did the donkey talk in the Bible?" I told him I didn't know. This is which he wanted to hear, so he could scoff back at me: "Then how can you believe it?" Clearly he wanted to keep the discussion on ridiculous ground. I want to pause and ask, which is more nonscientific: An animal to speak or humans to evolve from animals?

****

Has God's power diminished since then, now that He has grown so much older? No, God is all powerful and immutable. Jesus told us that all things are possible with God (See: Matt. 19:26). Jeremiah affirmed that there is nothing too difficult for Him (see Jer. 32:17). No person or force can stop Him from fulfilling His plans (see 2 Chron. 20:6; Job 41:10; 42:2). Through Jeremiah God asks, For who is like Me.... And who then... can stand against Me? (Jer. 50:44). The answer is no one, not even Satan. Speaking through the prophet Isaiah, the Holy Spirit said, Do you not know? Have you not heard? The Everlasting God, the Lord, the creator of the ends of the earth does not become weary or tired (Is. 40:28). Paul wrote that God is able to do exceeding abundantly beyond all that we ask or think (Eph. 3:20).

****

Whenever part of the truth is preached and half of the truth ignored, the half-truth preached become untruth. The biblical truth is that He is God of love and God of wrath. He extends grace to the humble sinners who repent but He judges the proud hearts of the sinners who reject His grace too.

****

"Open theology is anti-Christian. I guarantee there will be more heresies in a person's repertoire than openness theology in the thinking of "open" theologians" ~ Sproul

****

"The LORD trieth the righteous: but the wicked and him that loveth violence his soul hateth. Upon the wicked, he shall rain snares, fire and BRIMSTONE, and an horrible tempest: this shall be the portion of their cup." (Psalm 11:6) The word theion translated "brimstone" is exactly the same word theion which means "divine". The ancients had used brimstone for religious purifications, such as in Homers Odyssey, which it is written; 'Bring hither fire, and hither sulphur bring To purge the palace' (Homer, Od. xxli. 481 f.).

****

GENESIS 1:20 – "And God said, Let the waters bring forth abundantly the moving creature that hath life, and fowl that may fly above the earth in the open firmament of heaven." This is a very scientific chronology of the account of creation in Genesis! After plant life was caused by God to exist at the dusk of the third day and the sun to give light unto the earth immediately at the dawn of the fourth day, marine creatures were brought forth at the dusk of the fifth day! What a wonderful scientific narration, not found in any other book on earth! Here's an excerpt describing the Earth before as "barren landscape" quoting researchers from Pennsylvania State University - The earliest evidence of land plants and fungi appears in the fossil record around 480 million years ago. Before that, the Earth's landscape was believed to consist of barren rocks, home to bacteria and possibly some algae. But some have argued that it is quite possible for land-dwelling plants and fungi to have been around much earlier, but their primitive bodies were too soft to be preserved as fossils in rock. If atheists attempt to acid test the Bible through science, then, we can conveniently say we should check science through biblical truths instead.

****

Somebody asked that if gambling is sin why did they cast lots over Jonah; why did they cast lots to choose the replacement of Judah? Answer: Casting lots was a legitimate method used by the Jews of the Old Testament and by the Christian disciples prior to Pentecost to determine the will of God. Lots could be sticks with markings, stones with symbols, etc., that were thrown into a small area and then the result was interpreted. "The lot is cast into the lap, but its every decision is from the LORD," (Proverbs 16:33). There are many instances of casting lots in the Bible. Some people equate "casting lots" in the Bible to gambling. But I don't agree with them. Casting lots was more of a form of decision making (like drawing straws or flipping a coin), whereas gambling really is a form of thievery. The intents in the Bible of casting lots were clean but the intents of gambling are not. I compare it to two people going to the same beach with two different motives. One with a motive of having cool air and the other with a bad motive of looking at the half-naked bodies of the ladies. In this case, the evil act is not going to the beach but the motivation. Here is a reason why Gambling really is a form of thievery: Legitimate business is a win situation. If I sell you a widget for a dollar, you get the widget and I get the dollar. We both win. Nobody can win at gambling without another losing. Many of the losers are those least able to afford it. The person who gambles and wins has the motive of getting something from another for nothing: thievery. The Bible says "Woe to him who increases that which is not his" (Habakkuk 2:6).

****

Is casting lots not gambling? The Scriptures cite many instances of people casting lots, and it seems to be used when important decisions needed to be made. In the Bible, the practice was used in a variety of circumstances, including (1) the selection of the scapegoat (Lv 16:8-10); (2) the allocation of the tribal inheritance in the Promised Land (Numbers 26:55, 56; Jos 14:2; Judges 1:3; etc.); (3) the determination of the families who had to relocate to give a proper distribution of the populace or of those warriors who had to go to war where only a percentage was required (Jgs 20:9; Neh 11:1); (4) the order of the priests and their duties (1 Chr 24:5-19; Neh 10:34); (5) the determination of an offender (Jos 7:14-18; cf. Proverbs 18:18).

God never specifically condemned the casting of Lots in the Bible. Leviticus 16:8, "And Aaron shall cast lots for the two goats, one lot for the Lord and the other lot for the scapegoat." 1 Chronicles 25:8," And they cast lots for their duties, all alike, the small as well as the great, the teacher as well as the pupil."; Psalms 22:18, "They divide my garments among them, and for my clothing they cast lots."; Matthew 27:35, "And when they had crucified Him, they divided up His garments among themselves by casting lots."

Acts 1:26, "And they drew lots for them, and the lot fell to Matthias; and he was numbered with the eleven apostles." After Judas killed himself, the disciples cast lots to see who would be his replacement. The lot fell to Matthias, but this was before Pentecost. Since the New Testament does not have any instance of Christians casting lots to discern the will of God after Pentecost, we conclude that after the arrival of the Holy Spirit we do not need to rely on that method, but instead must rely on the ministry of the Holy Spirit and the further revelation found in the New Testament. Gambling is a sin because it takes away from the poor to make another person rich. Gambling is addictive too.

****

Somebody asked that, "Why do Christians judge others when the Bible says we should not judge others?" I want to say that the word judge has two different meanings when used in the Scriptures. The first meaning is to condemn. The one sitting on the throne (God), alone, has the right to condemn. The second meaning is discerning or weighing. The Bible gives us the right to weigh. Jesus gave us the spiritual gift of discerning (1 Corinthians 12:10). The scripture most probably confusing some people is: "Judge not, that ye be not judged" (Matthew 7:1-3). When you read this scripture within the context, it instructs us to use the right judgment, and not to judge others for the same things we are guilty of: "Why do you look at the speck of sawdust in your brother's eye and pay no attention to the plank in your own eye?" Certainly, we are called to judge the words of the prophets: "Let the prophets speak two or three, and let the other judge" (1 Corinthians 14:29). We are called to discern (judge) the spirits, and know the true believers: "By their fruit you will recognize them" (Matthew 7:16). I think love is clearly depicted by our will to uplift others, especially in their areas of weakness. Any weighing and judging should be aimed at edifying our brothers. Regarding the lost world, since there is a very vivid line between good and evil, we have the mandate and integrity to tell the lost world that they are heading the wrong direction - purposely not to judge them but to let them be convicted by the Holy Spirit.

****

Several people have been asking me about the "Illuminati" infiltration of Christianity. Illuminatis are in all sects including Christian religions. They are in for the money and how much they can get out of rich patrons. It is for the same reason why some preachers and gospel artists aim at mega churches just for pure publicity stunts. Given the fact, not all mega-churches are in this category. There are some good mega churches established by the finger of God. Unfortunately, several powerful preachers and gospel singers like Billy Graham, Joel Osteen, Joyce Meyer, Michael Smith, Hillsong band, Casting Crown, Third Day Band and many others have been branded as "Illuminati". I am not saying that it is true, and I am not denying it. I don't want to judge. However, certainly false teaching is our greatest challenge and threat to the Church.

The Bible warns that the spirit of the Antichrist is already here in the world (1 John 4:3). It is the spirit of deception. Given the fact, we must be careful not to label pastors to be Illuminatis on the mere basis of symbolism. The Bible warns us that, "Your enemy the devil prowls around like a roaring lion looking for someone to devour" (1 Peter 5:8). We should deny Satan a chance to use this opportunity to pounce on us. Let us judge the teaching or the doctrine instead of focusing on symbolism. Is it possible that some Christians/Bands are not aware of the symbolism in the graphics they're using? Some writers do not design the covers of their books and CDs. In fact, some Christian writers and Christian artists use secular people to design the covers of their books and CDs. They might not be aware of what's going on in the editing and designing of these covers. I appeal to all believers to be on offensive by searching for the truth in the Scriptures instead of going on rampage defensive searching for who is wrong. God did not give us the Spirit of fear but of power, love and sound mind (2 Timothy 1:7). Fear can be spiritually damaging. Let us focus on the positive instead of the negatives. I am not trying to defend the culprits. The Bible says that "The discerning heart seeks knowledge, but the mouth of a fool feeds on folly" (Proverbs 15:14).

****

Kazibwe Edris posted: *"Since there are roughly twice as many Christians as Moslems in the world, it may initially seem strange that Muhammad has been ranked higher than Jesus..... Jesus his existence was highly added on by people who couldn't even prove he ever existed. BTW if you know anything about history the Romans kept records of every execution and Jesus' doesn't appear anywhere. We know Mohammed existed, he never claimed to be of celestial origin."*

Answer: Jesus is a historic figure and truth. His story is given even in the secular books. For example Flavius Josephus (A.D. 37 – c.

100) was a Jewish historian born in Jerusalem four years after the crucifixion of Jesus of Nazareth in the same city. Because of this proximity to Jesus in terms of time and place, his writings have a near-eyewitness quality as they relate to the entire cultural background of the New Testament era. But their scope is much wider than this, encompassing also the world of the Old Testament. His two greatest works are Jewish Antiquities, unveiling Hebrew history from the Creation to the start of the great war with Rome in A.D. 66, while his Jewish War, though written first, carries the record on to the destruction of Jerusalem and the fall of Masada in A.D. 73. In Antiquities 18:63—in the middle of information on Pontius Pilate (A.D., 26-36)—Josephus provides the longest secular reference to Jesus in any first-century source. Later, when he reports events from the administration of the Roman governor Albinus (A.D. 62-64) in Antiquities 20:200, he again mentions Jesus in connection with the death of Jesus' half-brother, James the Just of Jerusalem. These passages, along with other non-biblical, non-Christian references to Jesus in secular first-century sources—among them Tacitus (Annals 15:44), Suetonius (Claudius 25), and Pliny the Younger (Letter to Trajan)—prove conclusively that any denial of Jesus' historicity is maundering sensationalism by the uninformed and/or the dishonest.

As Lukwago mentioned that, "Do you know that the name Jesus Christ (Isa Massiya) is even mentioned more times than the name Muhammad in the Quran?" Jesus knows the way to heaven because He has been there. How can Muhammad guide his followers to the heavenly places where he has never been? According to the Quran, when Muhammad was about to die he said to his followers that he didn't know what will happen to his soul after death! But the resurrected Jesus said, "I go to my Father." Mohammed influenced the world by the sword. Jesus influenced the world by the Word. His legacy cannot be weighed as per now because He is still alive. The legacy is for dead people like Muhammad!

****

The destiny of every person on the universe depends on one man (Jesus Christ). The choice of heaven and hell depends on believing or not believing in Jesus. Jesus has revolutionized every life on the planet since his own life. He is the only man to claim to be the Son of God himself (which I personally believe) and still have a majority of the world believing it but people today still don't deny the fact that he existed. The gospel (good news) has created a religion that is still going strong 2000 years later and is, in fact, the largest religion in the world. Do you know that Islam is not more than 1400 years old religion? Unlike Mohammed that preached Jihad (holy war), Jesus preached a philosophy of love, acceptance and understanding. Jesus proved that He is from God by multiple miracles and wonders, and He is still performing miracles. The greatest being transformed lives. By the way, Muhammad performed no single miracle.

****

Did you know that the word "Jerusalem" occurs 806 times in the Bible - 660 times in the Old Testament and 146 times in the New Testament but it is not mentioned even one time in the Quran? God said that "And unto his son will I give one tribe, that David my servant may have a light always before me in Jerusalem, the city which I have chosen me to put my name there" (1 Kings 11:36). David is a type of our Lord Jesus especially in his role as King over Israel. In Jewish thought, the Messiah was known as the 'Son of David' and this is firmly established in the New Testament in various passages. In fact, the last description of Jesus in the Bible is in Rev 22:16, where Jesus Himself declares that He is a descendant of David. God repeatedly said that "In Jerusalem I will put my Name" (2 Kings 21:4). When God identifies Himself with something, He does not propose that it is His, He imposes ownership that "It is mine". We cannot separate Jerusalem from the God of Israel. No wonder the eyes of the whole world are set on this tinny nation Israel!

****

Somebody asked, "Why didn't Adam and Eva see that they were naked before they sinned?" There are two parallel answers to this. Some scholars believe that Adam and Eva were covered by the glory of God before they sinned. The same glory departed after the fall. Another answer is that before treason, Adam and Eva had no sin conscience. Gen. 2:25 says they were both naked and not ashamed. Without sin there cannot be guilt and shame. Most probably compared to the toddlers (infants) in their state of innocence they are not ashamed to walk naked. Spiritual deficiency is the root cause of our physical deficiency. Jesus died to restore to us the kind of relationship Adam and Eve had with God the Father before sin.

****

Somebody asked, "Which is the greatest sin?" Answer: Sin is the breaking of the commandments of God. All sins are equally offensive to God. However, pride is the mother of all sins. Pride is the first sin that was committed in heaven. Also, pride influenced the fall of man on the earth. The serpent appealed to the ego of Eva. The serpent basically told Eva that you shall be like God, and you won't need God to boss you around! Pride is the evidence of the depravity of man. Pride is manifested in our ego. Almost all sins (wars, rape, divorce, arguments, selfishness, controlling others, and etc.) are influenced by our ego or pride. "The ego is the false self-born out of fear and defensiveness." The ego embraces self-love and no virtue or truth outside "self". People reject God's plan of salvation because of the flaws of their own egos. Surrendering to Christ is exchanging our ego with His grace.

****

Passivity separates men from boys. Real men avoid passivity. Adam was consumed by passivity. "If Adam was a Chinese we could have been in the Garden of Eden. Instead of being consumed by passivity, he could have consumed the snake!"

****

Acts 17:6 - "And when they found them not, they drew Jason and certain brethren unto the rulers of the city, crying, These that have turned the world upside down are come hither also". This world operates contrary to the divine plan. What people consider to be normal is actually abnormal. People will applaud you even when you make blunders or suggestions which are morally corrupt. The worldly people cannot tell when something is upside down, wrong-side up because they are in spiritual darkness. The believers, being the custodian of the truth, have the mandate to speak against the evils of the world. Unfortunately, whenever they try to set the record straight they are ridiculed. They are falsely accused of turning the world the wrong-side up. Yet we have the answer to this darkened world. The answer to the perishing world is neither in the academicians nor in the politicians but in the gospel. Right is immutable because right depends on the immutable character of God. "Wrong is wrong even if everyone is doing it; wrong does not cease to be wrong because the majority share in it."

****

Josh Magara asked: "Do you mean to say that without God we cannot have morality or know bad and good?" The answer is definitely yes. Without God the truth becomes relative depending on a particular group of people. For example, a cannibal is justified by the norms of his society because it is acceptable by the people within his circles. A terrorist is justified to kill in the name of his book and is applauded by his religion as a hero. A gay person is applauded by the values within his cultural setting, and etc. In such situation, every person becomes right in their own ways, and no one has the integrity to enforce their values on others. The holy God alone has the integrity to enforce His morality over all creations. He sets the absolute standard (truth) for all of us to embrace.

****

Is it biblical for the Catholics to worship visible images? The Bible says that "Thou shalt not make unto thee any graven image, or any likeness of anything that is in heaven above, or that is in the earth beneath, or that is in the water under the earth. Thou shalt not bow down thyself to them, nor serve them: for I the LORD thy God I am a jealous God"

(Exodus 20:4). The Bible forbids worshipping anything other than God. The Bible itself claims ultimate authority over any other dogma. Anything that is not biblical even if it is in the form of remembrance it should be rejected. If it is not sanctioned by the Scripture it is falsehood at its best! Remember the Nehushtan (a bronze serpent on a pole which God told Moses to erect to protect the Israelites who saw it from dying from the bites of the "fiery serpents" which God had sent to punish them for speaking against God and Moses. King Hezekiah later instituted a religious iconoclastic reform and destroyed "the brazen serpent that Moses had made; for unto those days the children of Israel did burn incense to it (2 Kings 18:4). A wrong theology produces a wrong doctrine and hence a wrong belief.

****

Somebody asked that, "What is wrong when the Catholics confess their sins to their priests? Doesn't the Bible tells us to confess our sins to one another?" The scriptures you are referring to is James 5:16. The scripture instructs us to acknowledge our faults to each other, in bid to induce peace and brotherly love. A righteous person, a true believer, justified in Christ, experiences restitution vertically with God and horizontally with the neighbor. The scripture adds, "The effectual fervent prayer of a righteous man availeth much". Jesus instructed that "Therefore if you are presenting your offering at the altar, and there remember that your brother has something against you, leave your offering there before the altar and go; first be reconciled to your brother, and then come and present your offering" (Matthew 5:23-24). Confessing our sins involves acknowledging breaking the laws of God - for sin is the breaking of the Moral Law (1 John 3:4). The Ten Commandments reveal the righteousness of God, and the commandments belong to God. It is from the same prospective,

David, after committing the sin of adultery with Bathsheba lamented that "Against you, you only (God), have I sinned" (Psalm 51:4). All sins must be confessed to God with the prior objective to be forgiven. Remember that in the Lord's Prayer Jesus instructed us to ask forgiveness for our sins from our Father (Matthew 6:12). When Jesus died on the cross, the veil of the temple was ripped opening the way for all of us to approach God in repentance without guilt.

****

The Pope has condemned religious fundamentalism. How dangerous are extreme and radical views? It can be dangerous when an interpretation of religious doctrine excludes views differing from its own. However, there is the positive side of it. Religious fundamentalism becomes beneficial when applied by the right religion. Paul was as fanatical before and after he was converted to Christianity. Religion is like a knife in the hands of the surgeon. The same knife can be of benefit when it is in the hands of a good surgeon, and fatal when in the hands of a bad surgeon.

****

The toll from a stampede at Mecca is rising to 769. Iran was most affected. By Saturday, 136 Iranians were dead while 344 are still missing. Nobody with sanity rejoices at the death of another human being. However, I am here to set the record straight and to warn those who are still living. The stampede occurred when the pilgrims were rushing to throw three stones at the devil in defiance and in steadfastness to Allah. According to Islam, Satan is believed to inhabit a pillar shielded by a wall. The truth is that Satan is an entity that dwells in the hearts of all men as opposed to the concrete wall. The Pilgrims were ambushed by Satan because they ignorantly ignored Satan's primary dwelling place and influence. Satan cannot be ignored.

Satan is spiritual and is much powerful than any human being apart from Christ. The only person Satan is afraid of is Jesus. This reminds me of this biblical event: "Seven sons of one Sceva, a Jewish chief priest, were doing this. And the evil spirit answered and said to them, "I recognize Jesus, and I know about Paul, but who are you?" And the man, in whom was the evil spirit, leaped on them and subdued all of them and overpowered them so that they fled out of that house naked and wounded" (Acts 19:15-16). Saudi Arabia has rushed into criticizing African Pilgrims, labeling them as ignorant of the rules required to be followed by all Pilgrims. The reality is that all Pilgrims were ignorant of this simple truth: We don't fight Satan with stones (rocks), we stone Satan by Jesus Christ the Rock.

****

According to John Byamukama, Islam states that Muhammad had similarities with Prophet Moses but when you look into the Bible and Quran Moses of the Bible is much different from Muhammad. Moses asked for forgiveness for his people from God and God forgive them, Exodus 32:11-16. Muhammad can't ask for forgiveness for anybody and Allah forgives him or her Quran 9:80. Allah tells Muhammad that even if he asks for forgiveness for his people 70 times Allah will not forgive them. This seems to be the reason why Muslims and Allah have been asking for Muhammad's forgiveness and sending blessing for many years without any proof that he receives them.

****

Question: If witch-doctors have no power how did the witch identify King Saul and how did she bring the ghost of Samuel? Answer: The scripture you are talking about is 1 Samuel 28:11–15. King Saul was rejected by God. He was now clearly a troubled man who desperately wanted counsel regarding what he should do next. It is at this point in his life he seeks to contact the prophet through a woman who had a 'familiar spirit,' a witch of the city of Endor. Saul walked in foolishness again by seeking out the very resource (a medium) he had previously removed from the land. By divine law, mediums and spiritualists were banned from Israel (Deut. 18:11), and Israel was not to be defiled by them (Leviticus 19:31). According to the scripture, the witch invited Samuel who was deceased. The passage does not give us any reason to believe it was anyone other than Samuel, who is described by the medium as "an old man wearing a robe" (v. 14). Obviously, age and clothing do not exist in the realm of the spirits of those who have died, but God miraculously gave Samuel such appearances as would enable Saul perceive who the spirit was. The message Samuel gave Saul was completely accurate. God allowed the witch of Endor to summon the prophet Samuel in order to give King Saul the news of his coming defeat and death. The main thing is the message as opposed to the messenger. Remember that God can even use a donkey to deliver His message. This does not mean that it is genuinely possible for witches or mediums to speak with the dead, only that God allowed it in this one exception. Given the fact, witch-doctors have supernatural powers because Satan is a spirit with supernatural capabilities. Read 2 Thessalonians 2:9. Unlike the miracles of God, the miracles of Satan do not edify. For example, the witch-doctors can predict the negatives of your life as opposed to the positives of life. The reason is because Satan, their master, plans the evils of life. It is not a big deal for Satan to reveal his nasty plans to his agents or worshipers. Certainly, Satan cannot foretell your good future otherwise he would not have crucified Jesus because it was akin to shooting himself in the head (1 Corinthians 2:8).

****

Explain Ezekiel 1:10: As for the likeness of their faces, they four had the face of a man, and the face of a lion, on the right side: and they four had the face of an ox on the left side; they four also had the face of an eagle. In this vision, Ezekiel saw four faces: the face of a man, the face of a lion, the face of an ox and the face of an eagle. Now, these four faces were the ensigns of the tribes of Israel. The lion was the ensign of the tribe of Judah, the ox was of Ephraim, the man was the ensign of the tribe of Reuben and the eagle was of Dan. Judah, the Lion, camped on the east, opposite Ephraim, the ox, on the west. Dan, the eagle, camped to the north, opposite Reuben, the man, to the south. Now, things get even more interesting! These four faces represent the four sides (if you will), of the person of Jesus Christ our Lord. In the Gospel of Matthew, Jesus Christ is figuratively portrayed with the face of a lion. He is the Lion of Judah, the Messiah of Israel, and the King of kings. In Mark, Christ is figuratively portrayed with the face of an ox, that is, that is, as a Servant. In Luke, Christ is portrayed as a man, the "second" Adam. In John, Jesus is figuratively portrayed with the face of an Eagle, the Son of God.

****

What does the word "profane" mean? "It means the God of the Bible is the God of glory... He is weighty, He is heavy, He is preeminent, He is significant. Profanity is when we treat Him lightly and inconsequentially, and just dismiss Him, and make sport of Him... and fun of Him." We're not supposed to avoid God's name but we are called to honor it and not to abuse it and never to use it maliciously. We're to use God's name in a way that honors Him. "Hallowed be His name" (Matthew 8:9).

1 Peter 2:9 – "But you are a chosen people, a royal priesthood, a holy nation, God's special possession, that you may declare the praises of him who called you out of darkness into his wonderful light." The history of redemption reveals God calling a people out of the world to be a holy people. God has called His people in both the old and new covenants to be a kingdom of priests and a holy nation. All nations belong to God but His people are uniquely His possession. We are priests, and Jesus is our Great High Priest. As priests, we are mediators of God's grace to the lost world. We are priests called to intercede for others. A holy nation and peculiar people, vessels of honor set apart to serve at the altar. Our holiness is deeper than of the vessels used at the altar because we are called to be moral. A cup might be set apart (holy) and yet not moral. Doing the opposite of our calling is taking God's name in vain. It is profanity.

****

Simon asked that, "Why did God create human races?" Theologians trace the origin of human races to the sons of Noah. Thus, the biblical evidence seems to argue for the total destruction of all of humanity, except for the eight people in the ark. This would necessitate the races deriving from Noah's three sons and their wives. The names of Noah's three sons were Japheth, Ham and Shem. White people are believed to be direct descendants of Japheth. Black people are believed to be direct descendants of Ham. Jewish people are believed to be direct descendants of Shem. The differences among humans can possibly be explained by natural selection, evolution due to the environment, cultural preference, and small isolated populations.

Given the fact, the Bible addresses only one human race. All human beings are direct descendants of Adam. God created man from dust and breathed into his nostrils life and man became a living soul. The judgment of sin brought about different languages and races. Sin brought corruption towards humanity and our social and physical world. Spiritually, after the fall of man, there are two races before God: The race of the redeemed and the race of the lost world heading for destruction. There is no racial superiority before God. Our bodies (white, brown and black) came from dust and will return to dust. Our lost image of God in Adam was redeemed through Christ (the Second Adam), and it is spiritual in nature.

****

How many times the word 'hell' appears in the Scriptures? It would depend on the translation being used. She'ol, in the Hebrew Bible, is a place of darkness to which all the dead go, a place of stillness and darkness cut off from life and from the Hebrew God. In the oldest manuscripts available, the Hebrew word Sheol appears 65 times. The King James Version translates this Hebrew word Sheol, 31 times as "hell," 31 times as "grave," and 3 times as "pit." So in the "Old Testament," the KJV version uses the word "hell" 31 times, but it interesting to note that the same Hebrew word Sheol was also translated into two other words, "grave" and "pit." In the

"New Testament," the King James Version translates the Greek word "Hades" in all 10 places it occurs, as "hell." The King James Version also uses the word "hell" or "hellfire" when translating the Greek word "Gehenna" 12 times. Other Bible translations translate the Hebrew word Sheol and Greek word Hades in different ways, some don't use the English word "hell" at all, instead transliterating the Hebrew and Greek words directly as "Sheol" and "Hades." Jesus Mentions Hell and Destruction in 46 Verses!

****

Jesus Mentions Hell and Destruction in 46 Verses! In the "New Testament," the King James Version translates the Greek word "Hades" in all 10 places it occurs, as "hell." Hell is mentioned often not to turn the gospel of love into a "gospel" of fear, damnation and punishment but to emphasize the mission of Jesus. Without the existence of hell, there would have been no need of the Savior. Hell is symbolic of the biblical dumping pit (Gehenna), outside Jerusalem, where the fire burned day and night to get rid of the garbage from the city. God created hell to purge of the world of the unwanted corrupted souls. The cross of Jesus is the barricade intended to prevent us from going to hell. Here, love embraces justice. Here, the innocent Son of God took upon Himself your guilt, was judged for your sins and died in your place so that you might take on His innocence and be born in His very nature that is not subject to corruption.

****

Acts 26:14 – "And when we were all fallen to the earth, I heard a voice speaking unto me, and saying in the Hebrew tongue, Saul, Saul, why persecutes thou me? It is hard for thee to kick against the pricks." Saul, when, obsessed with false religious convictions thought that he was serving God when in the actual sense his actions projected deep resentment of God. We are all religious one way or the other but religion is potentially capable of derailing and torpedoing generations and destinies with fanatically fabricated ideologies and doctrines. Begin by questioning everything you ever been taught in the light of the Scriptures, you may find some grains of falsehood injected into the core of your being and which has been affecting the momentum of your destiny. Remember that the truth does not come from our heads to the Bible but it comes from the Bible to our heads.

****

Jesus said that Abraham though physically dead, he is still living: "I am the God of Abraham, and the God of Isaac, and the God of Jacob? God is not the God of the dead, but of the living" (Matthew 22:32).

Uncle Jonathan responded to the above posting: *"No person is in heaven. These people (Abraham and other heroes of faith) are actually dead, but they died with the FAITH of Jesus [Revelation 14:12, 13] and so they were SURE of resurrecting in the FIRST Resurrection. Revelation 20:4-7. John 5:24-29. Jesus Himself said He had to go and prepare a place for His people then come back for them. John 14:1-4. Abraham has not yet received what he wanted. Hebrews 11:13-19. The Apostles said the saints are still dead. Acts 2:29. 1Thess. 4:13-18. Revelation 3:21; 4:1-11. They could not be alive UNTIL the Judgment is over, when Christ then receives his Kingdom. Luke 19:12-27. Hebrews 9:27. Jesus said He was to come exactly as He went. Visibly. Acts 2:9-11; 3:19-21. The one who came at Pentecost was the Holy Spirit. John 14:15-26. Matthew 24:24-30. When He comes the 2nd time, there will be wailing. Revelation 6:14-17. The Church of Christ was to go through 7 stages before Christ comes to His Temple. Rev. 1-3; 3:20, 21. Isaiah 59:20. 2 Thess. 2:1-15."*

My answer: True, Jesus will return in person to take His bride (Church). The Holy Spirit is the third person of the Godhead. Let us begin by studying the doctrine of trinity. The Christian doctrines of the trinity (from Latin trinitas "triad", from trinus "threefold") defines God as three consubstantial persons, expressions, or hypostases: the Father, the Son (Jesus Christ), and the Holy Spirit; "one God in three persons". The three persons are distinct, yet are one "substance, essence or nature". In this context, a "nature" is what one is, while a "person" is who one is. Three distinct persons yet one

God in a non-separateable manner. The Spirit proceeds from both the Father and the Son. The Holy Spirit is referred to in Scripture as both the Spirit of the Father (Mt 10:20, Rom 8:10-11, 2 Cor. 1:21-22, Eph. 3:14-16) and as the Spirit of the Son (Rom 8:9, Gal 4:6, Phil 1:19, 1 Pt 1:11). The Holy Spirit is the presence of Jesus Christ in all believers. Jesus promised that He will be with us up to the uttermost ends of the earth by His Spirit (Acts 1:8).

John 5:24-29: Jesus Himself said He had to go and prepare a place for His people then come back for them. John 14:1-4. Remember that Jesus said that in His Father's mansion there are already many places; more than we can occupy. The preparation has nothing to do with heaven but has everything to do with us here on earth. Jesus went to heaven so that He can send the Holy Spirit to prepare us for heavenly places. The audience of Jesus whom He was addressing were Jews of His time in the Bible Land (Palestine). Jesus indeed came for them and for all believers on Pentecost. Pentecost is Jesus coming to indwell His body (the Church). We are the spiritual body of Christ (Ephesians 1:22-23).

The name of Jesus Immanuel means God with us (Matthew 1:23). For we were all baptized by one Spirit so as to form one body-- whether Jews or Gentiles, slave or free--and we were all given the one Spirit to drink (1 Corinthians 12:13). Through His Spirit, we have fellowship with the Father and the Son. This is the Church that is spiritual that is not built with bricks and stones (1 Peter 2:5). Yes, we shall in future occupy a new city (Jerusalem) coming down on the earth after we acquire the glorified bodies when Jesus comes for His bride to put an end to this age of corruption. We shall be reunited with our beloved ones who died in Christ. But as per now the body of Christ consists of the living saints on the earth and those departed souls in heaven.

The physical death does not mean extinction. The soul continues to live after death. In the story of Lazarus and the rich man the memories of the rich man were still untouched. Jesus said in the same story that Abraham replied to the rich man that "Son, remember that in your lifetime you received your good things while Lazarus received bad things" (Luke 16: 25). The word 'remember' is appealing to the subconscious that never lost its data even after death. God's breathe in us (His image) was corrupted but never dies. It continues in eternity. Our Savior extended to us the choice to choose where to spend eternity: either in the presence of God or separated from God forever.

****

Explain Matthew 11:13 – "For all the prophets and the law prophesied until John". It has been preached that the Moral Law was no longer binding after John the Baptist died. This is an absurd suggestion in view of the verse which follows it, which completely contradicts that understanding, and is a failure to rightly divide the scriptures on this subject. Just look at what Jesus said elsewhere: "Till heaven and earth pass, one jot or one stroke shall in no way pass from the law, until all is fulfilled" (Matthew 5:18). Matthew recorded the verb "prophesied" which Luke missed out. John the Baptist is the last Old Testament prophet (although he appears on the pages of the New Testament). He introduced the Messiah in the present: "Behold, the Lamb of God, who takes away the sin of the world!" (John 1:29). All prophets and the law until John - meaning that all prophets and the ceremonial laws were given to prepare the people to receive the Messiah. All of the prophets prophesied about Jesus who was to come in future, who began His ministry in the days of John the Baptist. They prophesied where and how He would be born (Micah 5:2), that He would be born of a virgin (Isaiah 7:14), when He would be born (Daniel 9:25), how He would die (Isaiah 53), and many other details of His life, and that is all this scripture (Luke 16:16) is saying. Jesus warned us that after He ascends to heaven, many false prophets will come in His name claiming to be sent by God (Matthew 7:15). Also, "For many will come in my name, claiming, 'I am the Messiah,' and will deceive many" (Matthew 24:5).

****

End of May Memorial Month:

In the USA, Memorial Day is set apart to honor those who fought for our freedom. We celebrate the freedom we are enjoying and at the same time we shed tears for those who perished in the liberation wars. It is a combination of joy and mourning. Memorial Day, unlike some other recognized holidays, is a secular day for all Americans. The holiday arises from values from our common nationality but that need not arise from or be rooted in any individual's deeply-held beliefs.

****

"On the eleventh hour of the eleventh day of the eleventh month of this year in the twenty-first century, we pause to honor our veterans on this Veterans Day and remember that first of the great world wars, which ended the eleventh hour of the eleventh day of the eleventh month of 1918. To those who served, we thank you."

****

Sometimes you will never know the true value of a moment until it becomes a memory.

****

Memorial Day is for those who gave up everything so that others could enjoy everything. It is the incessant turmoil of the world, the constant attraction of earthly things that takes the soul away from Christ. "While memory works to preserve a poisonous weed, it allows the rose of Sharon to wither. Let us charge ourselves to tie a heavenly forget-me-not around our hearts for Jesus our Beloved, and whatever else we let slip, let us hold tight to Him" ~ Alistair Begg.

****

The bitterest tears shed over graves are for words left unsaid and deeds left undone ~ Harriet Beecher Stowe

In Memory of Those Who Passed On

In spite of the abundant resources available to demonstrate a current and accurate scientific opinion regarding death from fright, death is still scaring as ever. Modernism has invented pain killers to allow peaceful death. Today we have cosmetics and finest clothes to make a dead person look nice and less scaring. There are funeral directors to make the burial ceremony presentable. Then beautified graveyards in form of park yards. In spite of everything, death is still as scarring as ever.

****

"Death leaves a heartache no one can heal. Love leaves a memory no one can steal."

****

In memory of aborted babies. Smith said: "Since 1973" -- when the U.S. Supreme Court handed down its landmark decision in the Roe v. Wade case -- "well over 54 million babies have had abortion forced upon them." Now, he said, this "perverse proposal" for "after-birth abortion," or killing a newborn in all cases where abortion is permissible, has emerged. Given the fact, the pro-life are not losing the battle. Russel Moore pointed out, the ultrasound itself has become a symbol of the pro-life movement. Seeing children in utero on that black-and-white screen isn't just an experience millions of parents cherish—it's also one that's convinced countless others not to have abortions. In fact, close to 80% of abortion-minded women who see their baby on ultrasound choose life. Ultrasound has been God's technological gift to the pro-life movement and a threat to the abortion industry's bottom line.

****

To all heroes of our faith: "To such men as this, the church owes a debt too heavy to pay. The curious thing is that she seldom tries to pay him while he lives. Rather, the next generation builds his sepulcher and writes his biography – as if instinctively and awkwardly to discharge an obligation the previous generation to a large extent ignored."

****

The Church is planted and watered by the blood of the martyrs. How the Apostles Died:

1. Matthew: Suffered martyrdom in Ethiopia, Killed by a sword wound.

2. Mark: Died in Alexandria, Egypt, after being dragged by Horses through the streets until he was dead.

3. Luke: Was hanged in Greece as a result of his tremendous Preaching to the lost.

4. John: Faced martyrdom when he was boiled in huge Basin of boiling oil during a wave of persecution In Rome. However, he was miraculously delivered from death. John was then sentenced to the mines on the prison Island of Patmos. He wrote his prophetic Book of Revelation on Patmos. The apostle John was later freed and returned to serve As Bishop of Edessa in modern Turkey. He died as an old man, the only apostle to die peacefully.

5. Peter: He was crucified upside down on an x-shaped cross. According to church tradition, it was because he told his tormentors that he felt unworthy to die in the same way that Jesus Christ had died.

6. James: The leader of the church in Jerusalem, he was thrown over a hundred feet down from the southeast pinnacle of the Temple when he refused to deny his faith in Christ. This was the same pinnacle where Satan had taken Jesus during the Temptation. When they discovered that he survived the fall, his enemies beat James to death with a fuller's club.

7. James the Son of Zebedee was a fisherman by trade when Jesus called him to a lifetime of ministry. As a strong leader of the church, James was ultimately beheaded at Jerusalem. The Roman officer who guarded James watched amazed as James defended his faith at his trial. Later, the officer Walked beside James to the place of execution. Overcome by conviction, he declared his new faith to the judge and Knelt beside James to accept beheading as a Christian.

8. Bartholomew, also known as Nathaniel was a missionary to Asia. He witnessed for our Lord in present day Turkey. Bartholomew was martyred for his preaching in Armenia where he was flayed to death by a whip.

9. Andrew: Was crucified on an x-shaped cross in Patras, Greece. After being whipped severely by seven soldiers they tied his body to the cross with cords to prolong his agony. His followers reported that, when he was led toward the cross, Andrew saluted it in these words: 'I have long desired and expected this happy hour. The cross has been consecrated by the body of Christ hanging on it.' He continued to preach to his tormentors for two days until he expired.

10. Thomas: Was stabbed with a spear in India during one of his missionary trips to establish the church in the Sub-continent.

11. Jude: Was killed with arrows when he refused to deny his faith in Christ.

12. Matthias: The apostle chosen to replace the traitor Judas Iscariot, was stoned and then beheaded.

13. Paul: Was tortured and then beheaded by the evil Emperor Nero at Rome in A.D. 67. Paul endured a lengthy imprisonment, which allowed him to write his many Epistles to the churches he had formed throughout the Roman Empire. These letters, which taught many of the foundational Doctrines of Christianity, form a large portion of the New Testament.

Perhaps this is a reminder to us that our sufferings here are indeed minor compared to the intense persecution and cold cruelty faced by the apostles and disciples during their times For the sake of the Faith. And ye shall be hated of all men for my name's sake: But he that endureth to the end shall be saved. Please pass this on to encourage other Christians who are persecuted for their faith.

****

According to Chuck Colson, our story begins in the year 135 A.D. The Roman emperor Hadrian had just subjugated Judea after the Second Jewish Revolt. Hadrian was determined to impose Roman religion upon the Judeans. After destroying the Jewish synagogues in Jerusalem, he then turned his attention to the Christians.

What better way to squelch this upstart religion than to obliterate its holy places? The site of Christ's crucifixion and resurrection was known and venerated by Christians at the time. So Hadrian concealed the site under a massive concrete platform and built a temple to the pagan god Zeus on top of it. Like Watergate, this was a cover-up.

Nearly two centuries later the tables turned: The emperor Constantine converted to Christianity. He decided to build a magnificent church in Jerusalem to commemorate Christ's crucifixion and resurrection, and he insisted that the church be built upon the actual site. When

Constantine's architects arrived in Palestine, Christians pointed them to Hadrian's temple, which marked the very spot.

The builders set to work demolishing the pagan temple. Sure enough, underneath they found the ancient quarry called Golgotha, and nearby, the remains of the tomb of Christ. Today, the Church of the Holy Sepulchre in Jerusalem's Old City still marks the actual site of the crucifixion and resurrection of Christ.

You see, the early Christians knew their faith was rooted in historical events. So they built churches throughout the Holy Land for precisely that reason—to mark the actual historic locations.

****

Mark 8:36 – "For what shall it profit a man, if he shall gain the whole world, and lose his own soul?" No one can have enough of this world. Even if there was one, they couldn't be able to keep it to themselves. One person compared this world to a huge tree whereby we can enjoy the fruits and the leaves but we cannot eat the whole tree. Therefore, settling for this world is fatal; it is giving away everything and gaining nothing.

Over one hundred years ago, the king of Buganda (Mwanga), killed the Christian converts in bid to secure his kingdom. Today, Mwanga is no more and none of the people he wanted to rule is still alive. One hundred years later Idi Amin appeared on the scene as the personification of evil. Like every egomaniac, Idi Amin behaved as if this world revolved around him. He persecuted the Church and slaughtered Christians in shoves, but today he is history. He was called home to confront the creator of the souls he destroyed. His notorious acts earned him fame at the expense of His soul. As one writer insinuated "A life without fame can be a good life, but fame without a life is no life at all".

The shocking truth is that there is a time when every person who has ever lived in this universe was not (never existed) but there is no time when every person who ever lived in this universe will be not. Death is just the beginning of endless time after this life. The question is, "Where are you going to spend eternity?" There are only two destinies: Heaven for those redeemed by Christ, and hell for those outside the divine plan of salvation.

The story of the Uganda Martyrs is probably one of the most re-told stories there is in the Uganda Christian faith context. The 45 men that gave their lives in a grandiose show of faith etched their names in history. However, for almost the entire part of that history, it is the 22 Catholic martyrs that have been celebrated the most. What you will not hear of is that there were another 23 or so Anglican martyrs. History tells of the 22 Catholic Martyrs killed between 1885 and 1887 by Kabaka Mwanga of Buganda; 13 of the martyrs were burnt to death at Namugongo.

What history does not tell us is that a decade before the Christian martyrs embraced their end; Muslim men had also met the same fate in Namugongo – perished in a blazing inferno – on the orders of Kabaka Mutesa I, Mwanga's father. History does not give us figures of those martyrs. However, some history books and collaborations put the number between 50 and 70. On June 6, 1920, the Catholic martyrs were beatified by Pope Benedict XV and canonized by Pope Paul VI in 1964. The other two martyrs were speared to death in Paimol, Gulu in the North of Uganda in October 1918. They were beatified by Pope John Paul II on 20th October 2002.

1875 Explorer and journalist H. M. Stanley arrives at the palace of Kabaka Muteesa I, and the Kabaka writes a letter to England requesting for missionaries to be sent to his kingdom.

June 1877 Anglican Missionaries of the Church Missionary Society (CMS) arrive at the Kabaka's Palace and soon start spreading their faith among the natives. Key among them is Alexander Mackay.

1885 - The first martyrs are killed on the orders of Kabaka Mwanga, as the new faith starts to clash with the Kabaka's reign. Andrew Kaggwa is one of the very first killed. 1886 - The famous mass killing of martyrs takes place, the majority of them burned at Namugongo —comprising of the canonized Catholic martyrs as well as several protestant ones.

1888 – 1892 The Buganda religious wars erupt, in form of a three-way struggle between Protestants, Catholics and Muslims for the political control of the country. Protestants win control with support of British Imperial forces, but agreements are made to co-exist with Catholics and Muslims.

1968 the Basilica of the Uganda Martyrs at Namugongo is built and becomes the venue of massive pilgrimages.

****

Somebody asked that "Isn't Jesus the greatest martyr?" I want to say "NO." The martyrs die for their faith. Even though they are ready to die, they are forced to die. Jesus came to this world with the prior intention, knowledge and plan to die for our sins. He said that "For this reason the Father loves Me, because I lay down My life so that I may take it again. No one has taken it away from Me, but I lay it down on My own initiative." I have authority to lay it down, and I have authority to take it up again (John 10:17-18). He willingly offered His life for our sake. Also, Jesus had a prior plan of resurrection so as to make His life available to all: "I tell you the truth, unless a kernel of wheat is planted in the soil and dies, it remains alone. But its death will produce many new kernels--a plentiful harvest of new lives" (John 12:24). Resurrection involves acquiring a new nature of life that will never die again. He is the first person ever to resurrect. He did it not for Himself but to reconcile the sinners to God. He made it possible for the sinners to be adopted in the divine family. For this case Jesus is NOT a martyr; He qualifies to be the true and ultimate Savior, with a capital "S"!!!

****

February 1977 - Archbishop Janan Luwum was killed by President Idi Amin Dada after he criticized the dictator over his terror-bestrewn leadership. 2008 Archbishop Luwum was declared a saint and a statue of him was erected at West Minister Abbey in London, the seat of the Anglican branch of Christianity, making him one of the foremost African icons of the faith.

****

Israel Kyeyune: You reached the climax of your prominence in the 70s, at the worst time of the persecution of the Church. You were a victim of circumstances such that you couldn't escape the clutches of the ruthless dictator Idi Amin. The important thing is that you never gave up on your faith. Your love for Christ will light our way. Your memory will forever be with us.

****

Tribute to my late father Israel Kyeyune: You were the voice that couldn't be shut down. You spoke you minds without mincing words. You were such a great man with Lion's heart, fearless, disciplinarian, caring, a legend, a perfect and honorable gentleman, and a great dad to all. The world cheated us of a great father and grandfather. You left our eyes red-wet; inconsolably heartbroken and with more questions than answers. We will miss you always.

****

10th of January 2016, has been chosen as a date to remember our beloved dad, grandfather, husband and friend – Israel Kyeyune. A house has been built at Degeya in memorial of my late father. This day has been chosen to be observed in honor of him every year since we do not have the exact date of his death and burial place. A memorial service will be held at Degeya on the 10th of January every year (annually) to honor him. Thank God for my mother Milly Muganzi Zake who initiated the idea and invested heavily into it. Special thanks go to my brother Andrew Kazibwe Lwanga, my sister Mabel Kyeyune and all members of the Degeya Project. God bless you.

****

Dr. Kibirige Lwanga: You were enterprising, professional and friendly. You inspired me to spread my wings and to fly. You were such a charming character and comforting. I can hardly forget the rib-cracking jokes you made that sent every person around you into laughter. Death is the greatest of all robbers because it robbed us of such a non-replaceable character.

****

In the mid-1940s, Raphael Lemkin, a Jewish lawyer born and raised in Poland, coined a name for what prior to the 20th century had been unthinkable. He combined the Greek word for "family," "tribe," or "race," and the Latin word for "killing," to describe events like the Nazi extermination campaign against his fellow Jews, Stalin's starvation of millions of Ukrainians, and the Turkish cleansing of their Armenian and Assyrian subjects. Since then the word 'genocide' has been used to describe the deliberate exterminating of one group of people by the other.

****

On March 14th, 2016, the House of Representatives voted 393-0 to declare that the "Islamic State's (ISIS) assaults on religious minorities in Iraq and Syria constitute genocide." Lemkin defined genocide as more than the "mass killings of all members of a nation." Genocide, he suggested, was a "coordinated plan of different actions aiming at the destruction of essential foundations of the life of national groups, with the aim of annihilating the groups themselves." It is the radical attempts to suppress the culture, language, and of course, the religion of the targeted group. The last time Congress declared something genocide was in 2004, specifically Sudan's actions in Darfur.

The fanatical Islamic sect (ISIS) is committing genocide against Christians and other religious minorities. They pledged to mingle the waters of the Mediterranean Sea with the blood of the Christians until the blood flows all the way to Rome. The horrors committed by these fanatic thugs against innocent Christians are beyond sanity. Most probably compared to X-rated fiction movies. The difference is that these horrors are not staged by artists or actors, they are real. The similarity is that as in the case of film acting triumph is reserved for the good guys. Therefore, the action by the House of Representative is a giant step to curb hate and fanaticism in the name of religion, which is always prone to plunge the world into primeval barbarism.

****

On 11th. July, 2015 Saturday night my friend Eddie Hill (Head Huncho) was fatally shot nine times. I did not receive the bad news till Monday afternoon when I went to work. I sweated plasma upon hearing of the sad news. Then followed an obesity of grief that overwhelmed my thin body. My heart was thoroughly and irreparably broken. I had known Eddie for less than a year after he was employed at my workplace. The moment I saw him, there was that magnetic attraction that pulled me towards him. He opened his heart to me, and I immediately started ministering to him. He was a very attentive listener but slow when it comes to heeding and to implementing. Two months ago he surprised me by showing up at my church a couple of times. This momentum was quashed when he was given more overtime hours to work on weekends. He considered it to be a blessing to earn more money but I saw it as Satan's bait to lure him to worldliness. I did not give up on him but continued to minister to him at work whenever I got a chance. About four weeks ago, Eddie approached me at lunch time with what he considered to be the good news. He told me that he has got a short gun for protection. He could tell by looking at my face that I was not pleased by the idea. He went ahead to assure me that he was legal and licensed to carry it. I replied to him that, "Eddie, this gun will not protect you. In case of conflict, somebody is going to shoot at you out of precaution even when you did not have prior intentions to shoot him; and he will make sure that you are dead". I did not intend to be prophetic but unfortunately these prophetic words came to pass last weekend. Funeral arrangements for Eddie are made on Saturday (RIP).

Justice finally served: A judge sentenced a South Bend man to 55 years in prison for a deadly shooting outside a bar last summer. Michael Jones, 41, was found guilty of the July 2015 murder of Eddie Hill. Jones was at Antonio's Bar on Franklin Street in South Bend with his girlfriend until the early hours of June 11. Eddie Hill was also at the bar. The owner of Antonio's says he saw the two men walk outside at around 3 in the morning. Minutes later, he heard gunshots. Hill died of multiple gunshot wounds in the bar's parking lot. After his sentencing Thursday, Jones said he plans to appeal.

General Aronda Nyakairima died on Saturday 9/12/ 2015, aboard a flight from South Korea to Dubai on his way home. Like a snail moving from point A to point B leaves a mark on its path, General Aronda Nyakairima has, in the same way, left a mark in this world. He rose through the lowest ranks of the army, to the top as Chief of Defense Forces (CDF) and for the last two years, as Minister of Internal Affairs. Born a gentleman, served as a gentleman and rested forever a gentleman and with integrity. He confessed to be a born again believer. Will forever miss you and your legacy will leave on.

****

Somebody asked that: "I am angry at God. Why should God allow the good people like Pastor Kawesa to die so soon?" We are all grieving the death of the three pastors. However, according to the words of Jesus, there is no good person in the eyes of God because of the pollution of sin. Jesus said that "No one is good except God alone" (Mark 10:18). Therefore, the legitimate question to ask is why does God allow good things to happen to bad people. God's judgment against sin decrees that the day you shall sin you will surely die (Genesis 2:17). It means every moment we breathe in and out, it is because of the amazing grace of God. Actually, God does not cause death but sin caused death to mankind. God gave His Son to overcome death (John 3:16). God sees us in the victory of His resurrected Son because He is not limited by time. To Him the past and the future are in the present. God sees His children (born of God or born again) in His glory seated at His right hand in Christ. Death was reduced to the means of crossing over to God. God may allow death to take its course for some good and bad reasons. For good reason, He may call us home when our callings expire. It is better to go when your communication with God is still good. We don't know whether these people would be strong tomorrow as they were today when they passed. The bad reason is when God calls you home to reprimand you. I want to end by saying that it is biblical to mourn the death of our beloved ones and at the same time to celebrate their lives. But we have no moral integrity to question God's action. Faith trusts God even in the very things which we don't understand.

****

Tamale Mirundi said that the Baganda have a proverb that says, *'Ekirya atabaala, kyekirya n'asigadde eka,'* (meaning that death is everywhere). Another proverb says that *Awafiira omuzira, tewaba nsitaano* (the brave don't die in big battles); this was evident in the death of [South Sudan president] John Garang, Jonas Savimbi of Angola, Col John Charles Ogole, Maj Gen James Kazini and Alexander the Great.

****

According to Alistair Begg, although Christ prays that His people may eventually be with Him where He is, He does not ask that they may be taken at once away from this world to heaven. He wishes them to stay here. Yet how often is the weary pilgrim heard to pray, "Oh, that I had wings like a dove! I would fly away and be at rest." Jesus Christ does not pray like that; He leaves us in His Father's hands until, like shocks of fully ripe corn, we shall each be gathered into our Master's garner. Jesus does not plead for our instant removal by death because our earthly journey is needful for others even when daunting for us. He asks that we may be kept from evil, but He never asks for us to be admitted to the inheritance in glory until it is time.

****

Postings on Life / Death

The central message of the cross is death. We are redeemed by the substitute death of Jesus on the cross. The Jewish way of execution was by stoning. The cross was the Romans' way of executing those convicted of capital offenses. The Romans didn't invent crucifixion. That probably happened in the Medes and the Persians era. The Romans actually got it from the Phoenicians but they perfected it. Several hundred years even before the Romans and their culture existed, the Bible predicted that the Messiah would be crucified. Psalms 22 was written nearly 800 years before the Romans perfected the art of crucifixion in execution. The significant of the cross is that - it is the wooden Altar upon which Jesus sacrificed Himself to pay the wages of our sins. The wages of sins is death. He paid the same wages on your behalf in full. His death becomes your death the moment you invest your faith in His finished works at the cross. The resurrection of Jesus is the proof that He defeated death. Jesus made this profound statement: "Now that the dead are raised, even Moses showed at the bush, when he calleth the Lord the God of Abraham, and the God of Isaac, and the God of Jacob. For he is not a God of the dead, but of the living: for all live unto him (Luke 20:37-38).

****

US airstrike has taken out the notorious ISIS terrorist known as Jihadi John, who beheaded hostages in gruesome propaganda videos. The real name of the man said to be ISIS' chief killer of foreign hostages is Emwazi. According to Saleh, the former counselor to the hostages, who recently defected from the group and fled to Turkey, the hostages were reportedly encouraged to become Muslims and given Arabic names to help them feel more relaxed among the militants before they were beheaded. People like Jihadi John, Hitler, Idi Amin and many others in this category are the embodiment of evil. However, neither God nor do we rejoice in their death (Ezekiel 18:23). We are instructed only to rejoice in the death of the born again believers because Jesus overcame death on their behalf. Life is sweeping by; we are all on our last cruise. The mighty fall and go under but the broken in Christ will never go under but soar with the harnessing power of the resurrection to help them ascend.

****

John 11:26 - "And whosoever lives and believes in me shall never die. Do you believe this?" Those who live without Christ are dead even though they are not aware that they are dead. They simply exist but they are not living. But the dead in Christ are living. Sin brought about corruption and death. The entire human race is subject to depravity. But there are different degrees of corruption. Some are eviler than others but they are all equally dead in their sins. Eternal life is in Jesus alone. Want to live before you die and to live after you are dead? Accept Jesus Christ as your personal Savior and Lord of your life. Choose to die to your old nature now: "I have been crucified with Christ and I no longer live, but Christ lives in me. The life I now live in the body, I live by faith in the Son of God, who loved me and gave himself for me" (Galatians 2:20). Let it die and let Christ live in you!

****

Revelation 6:10 – "And they cried with a loud voice, saying, How long, O Lord, holy and true, dost thou not judge and avenge our blood on them that dwell on the earth?" According to this scripture the martyred saints are in the presence of God. They are not screaming impatiently for delayed justice but they are making a statement that vengeance is of God. "Repay no one evil for evil," and verse 19-20, "Beloved, never avenge yourselves, but leave it to the wrath of God, for it is written, 'Vengeance is mine, I will repay, says the Lord.' (Romans 12:17). When we are persecuted, we are not supposed to retaliate with violence. On the contrary, we must pray for our enemies and dispense grace to them. "If your enemy is hungry, feed him; if he is thirsty, give him something to drink; for by so doing you will heap burning coals on his head" (Romans 12:20). We are ministers of the transforming grace, the humble faith and the Christ-like love for Christ's sake. Forgiveness does not mean that the sins of the oppressors will not be revisited. Justice will certainly take its course but by the Just God. He says "Vengeance is mine; I will repay".

Both the cross and hell stand for the justice of God. At the cross judgment was extended to the innocent Son of God to save you. God judged His own Son by nailing Him to the cross for the sake of justice so that you might be saved from His wrath against sin. When we think about salvation, we think of it as an operation of divine grace alone but salvation is a matter of divine justice too. Those who reject God's offer will certainly pay the wages for their own sins in hell. This is a place where God judges a sinner without a possibility of redemption.

****

My Uncle Jonathan Zake responded to the above teaching in this way: *"It is their SOULS, not themselves, that are under the ALTAR. The altar is the Earth, where the Lamb of God was slain. Not in Heaven. Revelation 6:9. Exodus 29:39-46. M91055:1. The altar of sacrifice was outside of the Holies. The altar of incense [represents the Prayers of God's people] was the one in the first apartment. It's only their Prayers, their cries, that are in Heaven, not themselves. If they had been in Heaven, they would NEVER have cried! No one cries in Heaven. Not even in the earthly sanctuary!"*

My reply: Thanks, Uncle. Please check your concordance the word CRYING is numbered 2896 - it means calling loud as opposed to crying in pain. When one considers that Stephen saw the heavens opening to receive him as he was being martyred (Acts 7:54-59), it is only reasonable to conclude that he went to be with the Lord. Remember that Stephen called on the Lord and said, "Lord Jesus, receive my spirit!" (Acts 7:59). Elsewhere, we see in the Scriptures that Moses and Elijah were present at the transfiguration, speaking with the Lord in Matthew 17:1-4. We read in the Scriptures about "the whole family in heaven" (Ephesians 3:14, 15) and that we are citizens of Heaven (Philippians 3:20). And again in Luke 16:22 we are told that Lazarus was "Carried by the angels into Abraham's bosom." Ecclesiastes 12:7 plainly states, "Then shall the dust return to the earth as it was: and the spirit shall return unto God who gave it." Biblically, the soul is dismantled upon death, and the spirit returns to God our Creator. 2nd Corinthians 5:8 plainly speaks of one's spirit being "absent from the body"..."to be present with the Lord." Jesus said that whom He regenerate will never die: "Jesus said unto her, I am the resurrection, and the life: he that believeth in me, though he were dead, yet shall he live; And whosoever liveth and believeth in me shall never die. Believest thou this?" (John 11:25, 26).

Philippians 3:20 says, "For our conversation is in heaven; from whence also we look for the Savior, the Lord Jesus Christ." The Greek word for "conversation" means "CITIZENSHIP, A COMMUNITY." Thus, every believer is already a citizen of our Heavenly home. There is a community in Heaven where we are being expected. When we die, there will be a heavenly family awaiting and welcoming us. I can say with confidence that the souls/spirits of just men made perfect are in heaven now in the presence of Jesus, while the church and assembly of the firstborn are now, at present, made to sit in this same heavenly place by faith in Christ Jesus. "But ye are come unto mount Zion, and unto the city of the living God, the heavenly Jerusalem, and to an innumerable company of angels, To the general assembly and church of the firstborn, which are written in heaven, and to God the Judge of all, and to the spirits of just men made perfect, And to Jesus the mediator of the new covenant, and to the blood of sprinkling that speaketh better things than that of Abel." (Hebrews 12:22-24).

****

There is a doctrine of error teaches that the soul sleeps after death. An example that disproves soul sleep is that he Bible says that "And the LORD said unto Moses, Behold, thou shalt sleep with thy fathers" (Deuteronomy 31:16). But Moses and Elijah appeared with Jesus on the Mount of Transfiguration. Moses had not been resurrected as yet, for the first resurrection has not taken place, but he was present in soul/spirit on the mountain in the Feast of Tabernacles.

There is an account for both the living and the dead; the quick and the dead, since the Gospel of Jesus Christ has been preached and heard by all in the earth; for this is the light that lighteth every man that cometh into the world. "Who shall give account to him that is ready to judge the quick and the dead. For this cause was the gospel preached also to them that are dead, that they might be judged according to men in the flesh, but live according to God in the spirit." (1 Peter 4:5, 6)

Physical death means very little, for the believer has already passed from death unto life, and will never die; his/her spirit being ever present with the Lord. Death never means never existing or sleeping; never extinction until a future resurrection of the just and unjust, for both are held in comfort or in torment depending on where the tree falls; whether in God or separated from God.

Death does not mean extinction. The soul continues to live after death. In the story of Lazarus and the rich man the memories of the rich man were still untouched. Jesus said in the story of the rich man and Lazarus that Abraham said and to the rich man that "Son, remember that in your lifetime you received your good things, while Lazarus received bad things" (Luke 16: 25). The word 'remember' is appealing to the subconscious that never lost its data even after death. God's breathe in us (His image) was corrupted but never dies. It continues in eternity. The choice is yours to choose where to spend your eternity.

****

The doctrine of annihilation being burned up and never existing again is false since the worm dies not and the fire is not quenched. The body only dies and goes back to dust from whence it came, while the soul/spirit does not go to the dust, but to the appropriate place according to one's life in judgment; that is, to be present with the Lord, or in Hades being tormented until the final second death is pronounced and executed by the Lord at the white throne judgment. The soul/spirit is immortal with eternal life if in God; or dead in trespasses and sins, and will continue in consciousness whether in heaven or hell. The choice of life and death is ever present in this age; chose life that ye may live. Who would choose death knowing these truths? Once you are reunited with God by Christ, nothing can separate you from Him; not even death.

****

Jesus did not need to die in order to live eternally because He was very God and very man. He died for us so that we might live eternally in His presence. "For we know that if our earthly house, this tent, is destroyed, we have a building from God, a house not made with hands, eternal in the heavens" (2 Corinthians 5:1). Paul specifically says that the body (earthly tent) dies but not the soul. He says that knowing that when this earthly body is destroyed, there is another body: "a building from God, a house not made with hands, eternal in the heavens." This is an assurance of the spiritual body upon resurrection. Verse 1 is introduced by that simple phrase that is filled with meaning: "we know!" Paul writes of that which we can know here in 2 Cor. 5:1. This is the knowledge enjoyed by those who walk by faith, not by sight. The philosophical speculation of men supplies no strength!

****

J. Nakyeyune wrote: *"I remember in Christian Religious Education, we used to give reasons as to why the dead are not dead, but my late dad makes me dispute all the reasons I gave. Which dad quietly rests in his grave watching all kinds of injustices done to his daughters. You die and indeed die completely. As regards my dad, the dead are indeed dead. I challenge him to prove me otherwise by taking an action on this or else he'll remain completely dead to me. 19 years of no father, not even a disguising figure of one. I want back my daddy...... if indeed the dead are not dead, reveal yourself now or take me with you dad"*

Reply: Sister, death dismantles the soul whereby the bodies return to the soil from where they came. Those who received the resurrected life of Jesus Christ cannot die again; they were raised in Christ and their spirits are alive in the presence of God. Jesus said that, "And whosoever liveth and believeth in me shall never die. Believest thou this? (John 11:26). The souls of those who died without Christ are locked up in hades (Luke 16:19-31). God can do anything that does not defy His character; but he said that it is not His way to send the dead people back to the world to minister to the living: "But Abraham said, 'They have Moses and the Prophets; let them hear them.' 30 But he said, 'No, father Abraham, but if someone goes to them from the dead, they will repent!' 31 But he said to him, 'If they do not listen to Moses and the Prophets, they will not be persuaded even if someone rises from the dead.'" Be careful because there are demons operating in this world that might visit you disguising as your father. Satan never gives up on us, and he is sneaky and cunning. There is real life forever in the presence of God for those who are in Christ, and life in hell for those outside Christ. Please don't gamble with your life. Apart from Christ, there is nothing fulfilling in this life, no matter what you get!

****

Luke 23:46 - "Jesus called out with a loud voice, "Father, into your hands I commit my spirit." When he had said this, he breathed his last." You see! The Spirit returned to the Father; the body was at the cross; the soul went to paradise. After being made alive, He went and made proclamation to the imprisoned spirits ---- (1 Peter 3:19). According to Peter, sometime between His death and His resurrection Jesus made a special proclamation to "the spirits in prison." Acts 2:31

says that He went to "Hades" (New American Standard Bible), but "Hades" is not hell. Our Lord yielded His spirit to the Father, died, and at some time between death and resurrection, visited the realm of the dead where He delivered a message to spirit beings. This is proof that His soul was not dead asleep but was conscious.

****

The Bible clearly states that Jesus rose bodily from the grave. His spirit returned from the Father to his soul which returned from the pit, and both rejoined his body which rose literally from the dead. Jesus is fully alive in body, soul and spirit, now and forever. In Revelation, Jesus declared, "I am He who lives, and was dead, and behold, I am alive forevermore. Amen. And I have the keys of Hades and of Death." (Revelation 1:18). Not only is Jesus fully and bodily alive, He ascended bodily into heaven (Luke 24:51) and He will return in the same, glorified human body (Acts 1:11), in fulfilment of all the prophets on the Day of the Lord. You can choose not to believe the Scriptures, but they have been proven true repeatedly and you will weep on the day Jesus returns if you can't believe in His resurrection now. Choose life, choose Christ!

****

Does the soul/spirit have consciousness after death? Yes, for the soul/spirit of man does not go back to dust, for neither soul nor spirit come from dust, but from God. For the righteous, the inner man which is fashioned after Christ Jesus lives forever is incorruptible and cannot die. "But let it be the hidden man of the heart, in that which is not corruptible, even the ornament of a meek and quiet spirit, which is in the sight of God of great price." (1 Peter 3:4). The inward man is the spirit of the man that is immortal. "For I delight in the law of God after the inward man." (Romans 7:22).

The inward man knows through the spirit, not the intellectual natural thinking of the mind: "For what man knoweth the things of a man, save the spirit of man which is in him? Even so the things of

God knoweth no man, but the Spirit of God." (1 Corinthians 2:11). The real person is not the fleshly outward appearance of the body but is the inward man. For which cause we faint not; but though our outward man perish, yet the inward man is renewed day by day." (2 Corinthians 4:16). This inward man which is immortal is activated and strengthened by the Holy Ghost: "That he would grant you, according to the riches of his glory, to be strengthened with might by his Spirit in the inner man." (Ephesians 3:16).

The soul cannot be destroyed by any natural means as Jesus spoke in the following: "And I say unto you my friends, Be not afraid of them that kill the body, and after that have no more that they can do. But I will forewarn you whom ye shall fear; Fear him, which after he hath killed hath power to cast into hell; yea, I say unto you, Fear him." (Luke 12:5). Man cannot but kill the body, for the soul only can God cast into hell (Gehenna) where everlasting shame and contempt is. The consciousness of the soul is present after the death of the body proved by Lazarus and the rich man; both for the righteous as well as the wicked.

****

Uncle Jonathan Zake asked, *"If the dead are alive then what is death? And why a resurrection? And why does the Bible say that the wages of sin is Death? Romans 6:23."*

My reply: Death is two ways. One way is spiritual death due to sin, meaning separation from God. Every person is born separated from God because of the corruption of sin. Those living on earth without Christ are dead people walking but the dead in Christ are living. Jesus said that "Very truly I tell you, whoever hears my word and believes him who sent me has eternal life and will not be judged but has crossed over from death to life" (John 5:24). Eternal life is in the present regeneration as opposed to future. Look at John 3:16. John 20:31: But these are written, that ye might believe that Jesus is the Christ, the Son of God; and that believing ye might have life through his name. The Bible says "For in him we live, and move, and have our being" (Acts 17:28) Look at this scripture: "In His great mercy He has given us new birth into a living hope through the resurrection of Jesus Christ from the dead" (1 Peter 1:3). Elsewhere Jesus said that "My sheep listen to my voice; I know them, and they follow me. I give them eternal life, and they shall never perish; no one will snatch them out of my hand" (John 10:27-28). Hearing His voice is to heed to the calling and receiving eternal life. The significance of salvation is that we are united to Christ in His resurrected life; not even death can separate us from Him! Eternal life is not just a statement made about us; it is the reality working within us; it is the real experience of the soul. It is not something we do but what God does to our souls.

The physical death is the separation of the soul from the body. Remember that we became a living soul after God breathed His life in the clay or dust of the earth. Upon death, the body returns to the soil. According to science, the 59 elements found in the human body are all found in the earth's crust. God is triune (Father, Son and Holy Spirit). Man is a triune being because he is created in the image of God. "I pray God your whole spirit and soul and body be preserved blameless unto the coming of our Lord Jesus Christ" (1 Thessalonians 5:23). Regeneration is the spiritual transformation in a person, brought about by the Holy Spirit - that brings the individual from being spiritually dead to become a spiritually alive human being. The Bible says that, "And God raised us up with Christ and seated us with him in the heavenly realms in Christ Jesus" (Ephesians 2:6). Jesus said that unless we are born again (or "born from above"), we will not see the kingdom of God (John 3:3).

Yes, there is the future resurrection of the body but the spiritual regeneration (rebirth) takes place here on earth when you receive Jesus Christ. Believing is receiving Jesus Christ (John 1:12). The Bible says that "This is how we know that we live in him and he in us: He has given us of his Spirit." (1 John 4:13). Jesus said that whom He regenerate will never die: "Jesus said unto her, I am the resurrection, and the life: he that believeth in me, though he were dead, yet shall he live; And whosoever liveth and believeth in me shall never die. Believest thou this?" (John 11:25, 26). The future promise of our resurrection involves new bodies: "But if the Spirit of him that raised up Jesus from the dead dwell in you, he that raised up Christ from the dead shall also quicken your mortal bodies by his Spirit that dwelleth in you" (Romans 8:11)

****

Somebody asked "Did God predetermine when a person should die in this life?" Answer: The Bible says that "Then the LORD said, "My Spirit will not contend with humans forever, for they are mortal; their days will be a hundred and twenty years" (Genesis 6:3). God predetermined the average life expectancy of man to be 120. However, our free-will determines how long we live within the limitation of our predetermined life expectancy. God instructed that "Walk in obedience to all that the LORD your God has commanded you so that you may live and prosper and prolong your days in the land that you will possess" (Deuteronomy 5:33). God gave to us the physical laws, the Moral Law, the civil laws and the diet laws to be obeyed for our benefit. Our lifestyles involve the choices we make daily - like how we live, where we live, what we do, what we eat and etc. The same things determine how long we live in this world. Yes, God can call you home any time according to His sovereignty but most times it is our lifestyle that determines how long we stay alive. The psalmist said that "So teach us to number our days that we may get a heart of wisdom" (Psalm 90:12).

****

Somebody asked "Why did God choose a curse of labor pain for all women? True, as much as ladies love babies, they hate the labor pains. Every curse pronounced against mankind (in the third chapter of Genesis) targeted sin in the world where Adam and Eva dwelt as outcasts after they were expelled from the Garden of Eden. God first cursed the serpent that permitted its body to be used by Satan. God then imposed pain and sorrow upon Eva prospectively. Finally, God did not directly curse Adam but instead "cursed the ground for his sake" [Genesis 3:17-19]. All of the curses were intended to implement God's judgment of death: "For in the day that you eat of it, you will surely die" (Genesis 2:17).

Death is God's way of eradicating sin from the face of the earth. God cursed Adam with death (not Eva) because all human races have the blood of Adam (not of Eva). The same blood passed on to us from Adam was corrupted by sin. Since life is in the blood, God's curse towards life was directed against the blood of Adam and passed on to us from Adam. God cursed the ground because the food that sustains life comes from the ground. Concerning pain in labor, life comes into the world through the labor of a woman. The pain and sufferings involved are symptoms of the reality of death. The climax of pain and suffering is death. We are born in pain and we enter this world crying because this world is not where we belong. We were forced into this corrupt world by sin.

Ironically, nobody wants to die, and at the same time, nobody wants to live eternally in this world full of sufferings. Death is imminent and is a process of living in the corrupt bodies too. Every single day we grow up in this world reduces one day from our lifespan. We basically grow into death. The good news is that in our second birth (new birth) there is no pain and death. Pain and death were swallowed up in the body of Jesus Christ at the cross. The Bible says that, O death, where is thy sting? O grave, where is thy victory? (1 Corinthians 15:55). We have a new nature that is immune to death: "The first man Adam was made a living soul; the last Adam was made a quickening spirit" (1 Corinthians 15:45).

****

A butterfly lives only for 14 days but still flies joyfully capturing many hearts. The fact that life is short does not hinder it from capturing the attention of many with its beauty. Don't let the pains and problems of life make the beauty of life to fade. So give life your best, and live and beautify other people's lives. "The mystery of human existence lies not in just staying alive, but in finding something to live for."

****

"The purpose of life is not to be happy. It is to be useful, to be honorable, to be compassionate; to have it make some difference that you have lived and lived well."

****

When you are ready to die for the first time, then you are ready to live forever. A true believer is never afraid to die. He acknowledges that Jesus neutralized the power of death at the cross. Death becomes a bridge to walk over to eternity.

****

Death is a great equalizer, neither respecting the rich nor the pauper, king nor subject. The fabric of dust is made for all regardless of one's status. Certainly, death is one thing that none of us can avoid, so in that regard, we're all the same. Only a fool puts his trust in the earthly riches.

****

"One of the best feelings in the world is knowing that your presence and absence both mean something to someone."

****

"When life gives you a hundred reasons to cry, show life that you have a thousand reasons to smile."

****

The death of anyone diminishes me for I am part of humanity so said the great poet John Donne

****

The dead cannot cry out for justice. It is a duty of the living to do so for them.

****

African cultures never speak ill of the dead! Not knowing our last moments makes us try our best to sympathize with the loss of persons who could have wronged us in the past. Only sad souls would hurl abuses at the dead who cannot defend themselves.

****

In Memory of the living heroes

He never called himself Jesus but people prefer calling him Jesus to calling him Dr. Tom. You see, "Dr. Tom," is the only physician stationed permanently in the war-torn Nuba Mountains. According to Erick Metaxas, the people of Sudan called this missionary Jesus: "Jesus Christ has been spotted in Sudan's Nuba Mountains" -- and that's according to a Muslim! We've all heard the phrase, "Like father, like son." While it's not always true, fathers and sons tend to resemble one another, and often sons and their dads end up with similar personalities, doing the same things. It's true in the spiritual realm, too. Jesus claimed a close family resemblance to the heavenly Father, saying, "Whoever has seen me has seen the Father," and, "Whatever the Father does, the Son also does." The Lord also said that Christians have the same opportunity to glorify God by their deeds in full view of a watching world: "let your light shine before others so that they may see your good works and give glory to your Father who is in heaven."

In the case of Dr. Tom Catena, a 51-year-old Catholic missionary from Amsterdam, New York, some unlikely people are watching, and they are indeed glorifying our heavenly Father. You see, "Dr. Tom," as folks call him, is the only physician stationed permanently in the war-torn Nuba Mountains. The New York Times calls it the site of "the worst ethnic cleansing you've never heard of." The remote region of half a million people is a frequent bombing target of Sudan's Islamist government, which is trying to crush a rebellion by Christians and animists in the nation's far-south. At last count, the hospital has been bombed 11 times. When he isn't dodging Sudanese bombs or mosquitoes carrying malaria, Dr. Tom removes shrapnel from women's flesh, amputates arms and legs of wounded children, removes appendixes, and even delivers babies—all for $350 a month.

One of those observing Dr Tom's Christ-like service in this forgotten land is a Muslim named Hussein Nalukuri Cupp, who, seeing the family resemblance, stated simply, "He's Jesus Christ." A rebel commander, meanwhile, says, "People in the Nuba Mountains will never forget his name. People are praying that he never dies." Even more amazing—and I say this with tongue firmly planted in cheek—is the response of a serious liberal journalist who realizes that the world needs Christians—and he isn't afraid to say it. That journalist is Times columnist Nicholas Kristof, who is doing what no other "mainstream" journalist would dare—helping the world to see the huge sacrifices that evangelicals and serious Catholics make around the world, doing God's work quietly and humbly. "There are many, many secular aid workers doing heroic work," Kristof says. "But the people I've encountered over the years in the most impossible places—like Nuba, where anyone reasonable has fled—are disproportionately unreasonable because of their faith."

Indeed. God isn't "reasonable" when it comes to the suffering of human beings made in His image. Here's what Dr Tom says about his work: "For me, it's a privilege to be in a position where I can offer my services to people. I don't see it as a hardship. I've been given a lot in this life. Let me go and try to do something with it." Amen. As Jesus also said to His children, for those to whom much has been given, much will be expected.

June: Celebration of family

Words are devalued in our culture—people use words very casually. They'll say to one another, "Well, that wasn't what I meant by that," or "You understand that in a way that is different from me." Devaluation is not limited to the words we use only but it is consuming the institution of marriage that makes up the foundation of our social fabric. It is unfortunate that today we take our vows casual. I mean the words we use at weddings (vows) and the covenant that we make when we call another person to the marriage relationship. The family is the highest institution on earth, and marriage is a covenant with lifetime contract. Part of the task of the legal profession is to make sure that, when the couples confess or make vows it is equivalent to writing down something in a contract, that what is said is what is meant. Precision is important.

I want to explain the most common words used when we are marrying. I begin with commitment. According to Alistair Begg, Well, when you think about committing your life to another person—to another stumbling, bumbling person like yourself—the language is going to be very, very important, especially, if it's going to be a continual reference point for us — There's a phrase that some pastors will use when they begin the vow part of a wedding—where they'll say, "I solemnly charge you." Pastor Alistair says that the phrase can mean something, but unless the context is marked by a genuine sense of solemnity, which actually emerges—not from the phraseology—but from the conviction on the part of the couple and the person conducting the ceremony itself. This is not a cursory thing.

Vows are made before the congregation but to God. It has to do with convictions that are shared in a congregation about what is taking place here—that these folks are entering into a whole new dimension of their lives that they've been living, as singles. So the phraseology of solemnity, and of reverence, and of awe, and all those things is, I think, simply to remind this young couple that—although this is taking place in a very public forum / and friends and family are there, and that's very meaningful—it's actually taking place in view of Almighty God. That it is before God, ultimately, that they will stand to give an account of their response to His Son and their willingness to fulfill their obligations within the framework of marriage.

"Who has a reason forbidding this man and woman to be married?" Anything substantial must be addressed at this moment or else keep quiet forever. The Church wittiness the couples taking their vow must provide accountability. The church is the institution that is sanctioning, blessing, and witnessing their vows as a married couple gets married. I believe it, too, needs to be a body of believers that calls them, regularly, to keep those vows.

"Who is giving away this bride?" Whenever a preacher asks this question, he is asking for somebody that has thoroughly examined the groom and see him fit to take care of the bride. The most suitable person, in this case, is the dad of the bride. He should give away his daughter only with such assurance that he is giving his daughter to the right person.

"To love, to honor and to cherish". The couple who intent to get married should be given the homework to use their dictionary to find out the true meaning of these words. Even when you are still married, I consider it breaking the vows when your spouse ignores implementing the above words in accordance to their true meaning.

Lewis taught us the meanings of love: The first of the four loves is storge - the natural bond of affection that is the product of familiarity. Storge is the love a parent has for a child and vice-versa. The second love is philia, the bond of friendship. For Lewis, friendship was about more than shared interests; it was a spiritual bond. Friendship was about seeing or, at least, caring about the "same truth." For Lewis, "Life—natural life—has no better gift to give" than the bonds of friendship. The third kind of love, Eros, or romantic love. According to Lewis, Eros is what "makes a man really want, not a woman, but one particular woman." And finally, there's agape, or as Lewis called it, charity. It is "wholly disinterested and desires what is simply best for the beloved." While storge, philia, and Eros all have their place, they're prone to selfishness, pride, and possessiveness in and of themselves. It's only in submission to agape, the love of God, that their risks and dangers can be overcome.

Marriage is the biblical mandate requiring all of the four Greek meanings of love. Take away one meaning then the institution of marriage will collapse. In agape, familial affection, friendship, and even romantic love find their highest expression. Agape enables us to love our family, our friends, and our spouses for their own sake and not for what they give us and do for us. There just may be no more abused word in the English language today than "love." Or to paraphrase Inigo Montoya in "The Princess Bride," "We keep using that word. I do not think it means what we think it means."

This is why a man leaves his father and mother and bonds with his wife, and they become one flesh" (Genesis 2:24). The parents of the bride have the right to stop the marriage before the vows are made but not after. The term "What God has united let no man separate" applies to the parents too. Given the fact, the moment you choose a spouse their parents automatically become your parents. The commandment of honoring your parents applies to both your mother in law and father in law.

"Forsaking all others, keeping yourself only unto him" or "…unto her." Even the verb, "to forsake," is a great verb. Alistair says that "forsaking all others"—when we take it in light of what Jesus is saying in the Sermon on the Mount—demands of us an absolutely rigorous commitment to mental purity. I think it means refusing to allow my eyes to wander, my mind to settle on/ my heart to conceive of anyone or anything that will draw me away from my wife. That's what it means to "forsake all others." "Forsaking all others" also means that the husband/wife relationship is primary, beyond the parent/child relationship. If that's not a part of what's going on, it's going to mess up your marriage.

"Forsaking all others"—when we take it in light of what Jesus is saying in the Sermon on the Mount—demands of us an absolutely rigorous commitment to mental purity. I think it means refusing to allow my eyes to wander, my mind to settle on/ my heart to conceive of anyone or anything that will draw me away from my wife. That's what it means to "forsake all others." It doesn't mean that I have fulfilled it, simply by coming home to the same house every night because—if, in my journey to the airport, I am involved in viewing women or viewing printed materials in a way that violate that soul-deep centered commitment to moral purity—then, although I have arrived in the bedroom as I should, the journey to the bedroom has been involved / has been in a whole ton of places that I should never, ever have gone—and I've been breaking my vows.

Mark 19:7-9 – "For this reason a man will leave his father and mother and be united to his wife, and the two will become one flesh. So they are no longer two, but one flesh. Therefore what God has joined together, let no one separate." In order to understand this scripture, we must ask ourselves that "Where was Adam before he was created?" Adam was in God. God breathed man (Adam) out of His nostrils. Hebrew word most logically translated "man" is *ish*. God breathed into the soil (earth) and man became a living soul. The Hebrew word for earth is *adama*. God formed man from the dust of the earth, and on the simplest level, that connection with *adama*, earth, is the basis for man's name. I said God formed (not created) man out of the earth because creating is bringing something out of nothing. Creation is when God spoke something into existence out of nothing. But forming is when He uses the already created substances to form something.

"Where was the woman before God formed her?" Before God formed Eva, she was already created in Adam. The Bible says that "Male and female created he them, and blessed them, and called their name Adam, in the day when they were created" (Genesis 5:2). Also, "In the image of God he created them; male and female he created them" (Genesis 1:27). God created them by His breathe. The word 'woman' means from man. God formed a woman by separating her from a man. We see that Ishah (Aleph-Shin-Hey) is the Hebrew word for woman. She was already in Adam. He did not have to create her a second time but He formed her by divine surgery. God formed Adam by dipping His hands in the already created earth to make them bodies and then breathed in them His spirit and they became living souls with capabilities to function in the physical universe.

The union of marriage rejoins a man and a woman into one - to their original condition as God created them in Genesis 1:27. "---and the two will become one flesh.' So they are no longer two, but one flesh" (Mark 10:8). They were joined by God at creation, separated by God because it is not good for man to be alone, and reunited in marriage as one; therefore, let no man separate them! Spiritually, we are one in Christ (there is no male/no female) - Galatians 3:28.

The two people (male / female) in marriage become one (Echad). There are two Hebrew words translated "one": Yachid / Echad. Duet 6:4: "Hear, O Israel! Yahweh is our God, Yahweh is one [Echad]!" "Echad" is a unified one (team of one), but it is also used of a numeric one as well. Yachid indisputably means an absolute numeric one and is never used to describe God. Elohim is the name used in reference to God in Genesis: "Let US make man in OUR image".

Remember that the earthly marriage is symbolic of the eternal covenant - Jesus the bridegroom the Church the bride. Adam was in

God before he became Adam. We who are born again are in Christ who is very God! We find our way back to God through Christ.

Creation is connected with marriage because when God created Adam, He had in mind multitudes of souls: "And God blessed them, and God said unto them, Be fruitful, and multiply, and replenish the earth, and subdue it" (Genesis 1:28). God created Adam in anticipation of more souls as a result of marriage.

****

Today cohabiting has been approved by many as moral even though the Scriptures strongly prohibit it. Cohabiting is the major cause of divorce because the marriages built on such wobbly foundation cannot survive the storms of life.

****

Scrolling through my sermons on marriage/ communication:

Picking the right spouse is the first, yet the most important step in marriage. I suggest that you involve other people in investigating the person you want to be your future spouse because there is much at stake. Parents should get involved in helping their children to pick their future spouses. Alistair Begg says that, "It's just unthinkable, to me, that we would, in a very short period of time, go from helping our children to pick out their socks to not helping them pick out a mate. That makes no sense at all". Helping involves a process of investment, it implies involvement, and it implies cooperation. There is a need to know the health issues, financial standing, conducts and behaviors of the family of your future spouse. Remember that the person you want to marry might hide something from you but you can discover the same things by looking at the members of his house where he or she is born.

****

The key to effective communication is studying your spouse. Studying is a process without a possibility of graduation because our bodies change and so do our emotion feelings. Know what he or she likes and dislikes. Study his and her body to know how to please him or her. How you communicate with your partner is the most important factor in defining the quality of your relationship. Communicating at a much deeper level involves knowing what to say when to say it, how to resolve conflicts and how you spend value time with your spouse.

****

Six ways to love: Listen without interrupting (Proverbs 18). Give without sparingly (Proverbs 21:26). Pray without ceasing (Colossians 1:9). Share without pretending (Ephesians 4:15). Trust without wavering (1 Cor.13:7). Forgive without punishing (Colossians 3:13).

****

According to Carol Tan, Love isn't always perfect. It isn't a fairytale or story book and doesn't come easy. It is overcoming obstacles, facing challenges, fighting to be together, holding on and never let it go. Love is a short word, easy to spell but difficult to define and is impossible for one to live without it. Love is work, but most of all is realizing every hour, minutes and second was worth because you did it altogether. Love is a two way street that involves two people in relationship. So let embrace God's love and love each and everyone unconditionally.

****

Spiritual connection with your spouse is the most important factor in securing a good marriage. Remember that there will always be somebody that is set to destroy your marriage. They may be your close family members, relative, friends or even neighbors. The reason is because Satan is against the marriage institution.

****

Real men and real women fear God. They embrace the Christian principles with open arms. When Christ is at the center of any relationship, He holds it together (Colossians 1:17).

****

A husband is the head of the house as Christ is the head of the Church. A husband is called to love and cherish his wife. To cherish is to nurture to growth into what God intended her to be.

****

Somebody asked me to explain Genesis 3:16. The scriptures is a curse against Eva: "Your desire will be for your husband, and he will rule over you" This verse causes some puzzlement. It would seem that a woman desiring her husband would be a good thing, and not a curse. Rabbinic Judaism interprets the curse to mean that a woman's desire will be to rule (dominate) her husband but he will rule over her. It is from this prospective Paul instructed that, "Wives, submit (be subject) to your own husbands, as to the Lord. For the husband is the head of the wife, as Christ also is the head of the church, He Himself being the Savior of the body (Ephesians 5:21-32). God has a sense of humor because He gave women power over men, and that power is invested not in physical muscles but in the softness of their tongues. Their persuasive words have power to light fires in the minds of men and to soften the hardest hearts. Persuasive tongue involves knowing what to say and when to say it.

****

Christianity gives women honor and dignity that is unusual in other religions. For example the Muslim book (Quran) instructs women to be treated like commodities. The Quran instructs husbands to beat their wives in case of insubordinate (Surat Al-Nisa 4:34).

****

Genesis 4 - "And Adam knew Eve his wife". The word "know" is intimate knowledge. In Greek it means knowing from the innermost to the outermost. Intimacy is the capacity to love someone after being exposed to his or her weaknesses and strength. It is knowing a person completely. "A person that loves you after knowing you completely loves you truly". It is not time or opportunity that determines intimacy — it is love and disposition. Unfortunately, the world has redefined love to mean lust. The challenge to us (God fearing people) is not to define love but to demonstrate it.

****

Love is the key to reconciliation. The secret of a successful marriage lies in an extraordinary passion to keep the spark alive in your relationship. It is all about two people who are madly in love with each other and who are strongly determined to have a rocking relationship and handle their lives with maturity and understanding.

****

Falling in love is a passive and spontaneous experience but after a few months or years of being together; the euphoria of love dies; it is a natural cycle of every relationship.

****

"Your love has shown me that the most valuable things in life aren't success or what we own but being there for one another. Thank you for understanding me, and being there for me even when I am not at my best."

****

If you are given true love please do not be too adamant to return it to the giver. Don't wait for the giver to retire from giving it out!

****

Love is like a rubber band held at both ends by two people. When one leaves it hurts the other!

****

If a man expects a woman to be an angel in his life, then he must first create heaven for her, because angels don't live in hell.

****

"What we find in a soulmate is not something wild to tame but something wild to run with" ~ Robert Brault

****

We all fall in love and want to be loved. When you fall in love, make sure it's with somebody who treats you exactly how you deserve to be treated. When two people fall in love, their souls also do as well. Nothing pains like loving someone in vain without him or her returning your love. Never force love feelings to someone. You will suffer.....

****

How funny we are: We ignore those who want us…. Want those who ignore us.

****

Love between a husband and a wife is like a candle that lights two other candles and remains burning with light. Love can suffer depreciation but it should never be allowed to quench. Occasionally, there must be a volunteer to run after it before it finally evaporates into thin air.

****

Your spouse is a lifetime friend. Your forever friend that guides you & cheers you. Your forever friend that holds your hand & tells you that everything is going to be okay.

****

Cultivate your relationship to the fullness potential. "You cannot be lonely if you like the person you're alone with" ~ Sandra Gift

****

Value your spouse but spending value time with them. Whom we do life with is as important, if not more important, than what we do.

****

"Time is your most precious gift to give to somebody. You only have a certain amount of it, and no one has enough of it. Once time is invested into someone, it cannot be taken back. That's why the greatest gift you can give someone is your time"

****

Relationship never dies a natural death. It is always murdered by behaviors, attitudes, ego, hidden benefits, arrogance, ignorance and etc.

****

"Never feel self-pity, it is the most destructive emotion there is. How awful to be caught up in the terrible squirrel cage of self"

****

Stress has a serious impact on the mood and attitude of a person. Most times stress is caused by lack of fulfillment and not knowing how to handle failure. Stress makes you believe that everything you need happens now. Faith reassures that everything will happen in accordance to God's perfect timing.

****

Mary came with an alabaster jar of very expensive perfume, made of precious spikenard. She broke the jar and poured the perfume on the head of Jesus. The fragrance of the alabaster perfume filled the whole house (Mark 14:3). Without breaking the bottle the perfume cannot have an impact on the house. Brokenness is the key to peace and harmony in the house. Gentleness and brokenness yield to forgiveness. A broken person initiates reconciliation. A broken heart is the one that God revives. Be broken so that God will not break you.

****

Forgiving is the key to a strong and lasting relationship. People who do not forgive are driven by ego. They are likely to accumulate bitterness that eventually explodes into anger. The anger problem erupts like Volcano. Such have personal conflicts within themselves. It is like sitting on a time bomb that can explode anytime. When a slight incident happens the unconscious conflicts erupt just like a mousetrap. The victim becomes the one who happens to instigate the embedded conflict.

****

Did you know that forgiveness is at the heart of any good marriage or relationship? Robert Quillen affirmed this when he said "A happy marriage is the union of two good forgivers". Have a great week as you ponder how to forgive your partner.

****

Everyone has a skeleton in his or her closet. Focus on cleaning your closet instead of cleaning other people's closets. Many don't want to disclose their weaknesses out of fear of being vulnerable. The good news is that God can turn your mess into a message, and your humiliation into humility. The purposeful living involves embracing the divine plan for your life. Also making life defining decisions and choices out of sincerity and with transparency. Self-assessment involves a process of inventory. Confronting the past rather than ignoring them is the emblem of freedom. Stepping back in your life can sometimes be painful but it is essentially necessary in order for you to move on with precaution. Confront the dark parts of yourself, and work to banish them with brilliance and self-forgiveness. "Your willingness to wrestle with your demons will cause your angels to sing."

****

In a relationship, whether married or still in courtship, there are things you should not tell another person. You never know who will be the Judas over your relationship. There are high secrets you have to keep only to yourself. "If you stop telling your friends everything, your enemies wouldn't know so much". Not all those who say that they are friends are true friends. Even among true friend there should be that place of privacy; we are sacred creatures, meaning we have that separateness - secret places of privacy that should not be interlude by any other person but you. Some of the best moments in life are the ones you can't tell anybody about.

****

Backbiting and back stabbing are relationship killers. The Holy Spirit permits us to censure sin and prescribes the way in which we are to do it. It must be done by rebuking our brother to his face, not by talking behind his back. This approach is manly, brotherly, Christlike, and under God's blessing will be useful.

****

Shield your heart. Think and meditate. There are things which do not qualify to be stored in your data. Such things do not qualify for the tongue. They are not worthy for conversation.

****

There is no such thing as autonomous human being. We were created to depend on God and on each other for our survival. As much as we need other people in our lives, we were created with that sense of sacredness. The word 'scared' also means separated. We need our privacy. Every person has a secret place. Even little children often withdraw to their own place just to be alone. There are things that we consider to be scared, which must be confined to bedrooms in privacy. For example sex; unlike animals and birds that jump on each other's backs at any time and place, we (humans) regard sex and all matters pertaining to intimate sexual relationship (including kissing, seductive moves and words) to be private. Privacy is immanent in all individuals; it is not acquired from outside. No human is exempt from this need of privacy. In fact it is unnatural or vice to behave contrary. The sense of sacredness is the divine image that resides in all. It is a virtue that separates us from the rest of creations. The sense of sacredness is deeper than our feelings and hedonism; it is strong enough to propel us to be rooted into moral aptitude. Personal privacy should only be violated in case people are married in accordance to 1 Corinthians 7:4. Yet, even married couples still need some privacy to a certain degree in order for them to be at liberty instead of bondage. We still need to cultivate a clear and compelling awe for this paradox—this knot of intimacy and privacy—of which our every movement consists.

****

IN –LAWS are members of the extended family. In the book of Ruth 1:16-17, we see this wish done. "Your people will be my people and where you go I'll go". The in-laws usually require special attention. The question is, how do you and I tread on this slippery grounds of the in-laws? The interference of the in-laws into the family affairs must be limited. According to Boniface Muruiki it is God who started the family. Whenever a man marries a wife, brothers and sisters to both comes along. Both of their parents also join the play. Simply, in-laws become a parcel of the Jig-saw. The reality is that, your partner and you came from somewhere before you met and got married. It is hard to assume that the in-laws are nonexistent. My in-laws were brought up together with my wife. There are immediate in-laws and distant in-laws. The ones I have named above are the immediate in-laws. The distant in-laws are not real brothers and sisters or parents, but are just in-laws. Now, in-laws do not have a good press. Only in very few cases whereby you find harmony between married couples and in-laws. But as we may like to criticize them, each one of us should know that he or she is an in-law. If you have not become one, you are on your way to becoming one. So, the way you treat them matters a lot.

****

A disciplined person is considerate of others' feelings and courteous in his or her behavior. He or she puts into consideration the welfare of others in particular when using public facilities like public bathrooms, public telephones, public transportation and etc. Good manners involve self-control, self-discipline, and a series of sacrifices for the sake of others. It is wishing others to be as good as you possibly want to be. The habit of being uniformly considerate toward others will make this world a better place thus making every person equally happy.

****

"Marriage - just like a fair election or a business transaction - is an exchange of TRUST - no more no less" ~ Samuel A. Bakutana

****

Marriage is a 'grow-up' game. The best part about a relationship is when you get close enough with your significant other to begin seeing their traits grow on you. You begin to talk like each other, steal each other's lines, and share each other's sense of humor. You begin to develop inside jokes with each other. You begin to watch TV shows or listen to music that you never thought you would be interested in, all because your significant other likes it. You begin to feel comfortable enough around each other to act in ways that you would never act in front of anybody else because that's a side you only share with your significant other. But nobody else would get it because they would find it weird and odd.

****

Men are different from women. Men don't get bothered by small things and we take life a little easier. "Women pay too much attention to detail - some of you are bothered about how your friend talks to your guy, insecure, paranoid and intolerant, or rather too impatient with others. Ladies also want to be perfectionists whereas men take things easy. It's those small things!" ~ Ivan Okuda

****

I don't see how and why women would want to have their friendships to be like those of men. Men are mostly opportunistic, that's why their "friendships" seem to last, because as long as factors hold constant, there is no need to change a winning formula. Women, on the other hand, act on natural instinct; if she feels you are no longer worth it, she dumps you. This may be triggered by something as small as a suspicion.

****

"If you touch a woman's heart you will get her love. If you touch a woman's mind you will get her interest. But if you touch a woman's soul you will get passion beyond your wildest dreams.." ~ Fred Okello

****

"A beautiful life does not just happen. It is built daily, in prayer, in humility, in sacrifice, in love, in forgiveness, forgetting the past, moving on with the present and focusing on the future. May a beautiful life be yours always".

****

You don't love someone for their looks or their clothes, or for their fancy cars, but because they sing a song only you can hear ~ Fred Okello

****

Every Woman is born as a princess, yet not every woman becomes a queen. Being a queen requires growth, change, evolving, maturing and learning to value, respect and care for yourself and others. It involves being more selfless and more loving than you are. A queen is a woman who knows who created her, and the purpose for which she was created. A queen is a Woman who never stops growing into who she ought to be, she partakes not of drama and childish things. She is a Woman who is strong-minded, intelligent yet humble, soft-spoken and does not justify her weakness but focuses on improving. A queen is everything a princess has the potential to become. Until a woman grows into the queen that she was created to be, she will remain a lost princess. Thanks, Lord for I will grow into a queen of Faith just like Sarah from the Bible.

****

A lasting relationship consists of the 3 C's: Commitment. Communication. Compromise.

****

Commitment is the key to lasting relationship. Emotions are important part of life but love (in marital relationship) goes beyond emotional excitement to the commitment of the will. Commitment is a lifetime conscious decision. There is a story about a man that had breakfast of eggs and bacon. The hen bragged how much it contributed to his breakfast. But the pig said him that I am committed to you because I gave up my life in order for you to have breakfast. Commitment gives up everything in order for this one thing called marriage to work.

****

A habit can either be good or bad. It's not the good things that you do once in a while; it's what you do day in and day out that makes the difference.

****

God is Love. Love, faith and hope, love is the greatest. The reason is because faith will one day disappear, we won't need it when we see Jesus. Hope will also disappear. But love will be there in eternity.

****

No man is worth your tears, but once you find one that is, he won't make you cry.

****

There is always going to be surprises of crisis in your marriage. In such situation seek professional counseling from either the elders or religious leaders or other professional agencies. "It is very encouraging to see people trying consensus and reconciliatory methods while dealing with contentious and provocative domestic issues as opposed to the primitive, violent methods often used these days. Here is a classic example of why we should cherish our cultures."

****

"The depth and strength of a human character are defined by its moral reserves. People reveal themselves completely only when they are thrown out of the customary conditions of their life, for only then do they have to fall back on their reserves" ~ Leonardo da Vinci

****

"A wife's positive attitude can permeate our home like the sweet aroma of freshly picked flowers, or negative attitude can pollute her home like stinky garbage." The Bible says, "A wife of noble character who can find? She is worth far more than rubies. Her husband has full confidence in her and lacks nothing of value. She brings him well, not harm, all the days of her life" (Proverbs 31:10-12). However, "A quarrelsome wife is like a constant dripping on a rainy day; restraining her is like restraining the wind or grasping oil with the hand" (Proverbs 27:15-16). "Better to live in a corner of the roof than share a house with a quarrelsome wife" (Proverbs 25:24). "Better to live in a desert than with a quarrelsome and ill-tempered wife" (Proverbs 21:19). "The wise woman builds her house, but with her own hands the foolish one tears hers down" (Proverbs 14:1).

****

A man asked his father, "Father, how will I ever find the right woman?" His father replied that, "Forget finding the right woman, and focus on being the right man".

****

A man must first find himself, before he finds a woman otherwise he will ruin the life of every woman he comes in contact with along the way.

****

Genesis 4 - "And Adam knew Eve his wife". The word "know" is intimate knowledge. In Greek it means knowing from the innermost to the outermost. It is knowing a person completely. "A person that loves you after knowing you completely loves you truly".

****

Love between a husband and a wife is compared to a candle that lights two other candles and retains its flame. Love can suffer depreciation but it should never be allowed to quench. Among the married couple, there must be occasionally a volunteer to run after it before it finally evaporates into thin air. As long as the flame of love is current there is no discord that cannot be solved.

****

We marry the two people to become one. But it doesn't happen instantly. It takes a decade for the two people in relationship to act as if they are one. Give it time for the deep intimacy to grow.

****

A true spouse that loves you will defend you always even in your absence.

****

The best person to discuss with your problems is the person you are in relationship with.

****

True love is revealed in reconciliation. When you accept someone, you accept their past too. Don't hold it against them later.

****

Love may have brought both of you together in relationship, but prayers will keep and sustain you in marriage forever.

****

Trying to forget someone you love is like trying to remember someone you never met!

****

Despite popular belief, marriage is not about 'give and take', it's about 'give and give----'

****

Conflict is an opportunity to solve issues. In relationship conflict is not a problem but combat is!

****

If you have never been happy when single, you will never be happy even when you are in a relationship because happiness is the decision you make with or without a spouse. If you expect somebody to make you happy, you will always be disappointed.

****

Falling in love is easy. It is a passive and spontaneous experience. At times you don't have to do anything about it; it is something done to you or happened to you. After an extended time into relationship, the euphoria of love fades. The basics of love like communication, touch and romance gradually diminish. If they exist, it is like they are just forced into the relationship. It is the responsibility of the couples involved in the relationship to work on these essentials and polish them to shine. Instead of blaming each other, both of you should take responsibility to work on love. At this point love is not something that just happen to you; it must be worked on in order to make your marriage strong.

****

Difficulties in marital relationships are inevitable. When you are experiencing problems, it means that your spouse is still alive. God's priority is not necessarily to make you happy but to make your marriage holy. God uses the difficulties we encounter to build our characters. Commitment is the key to a lasting relationship. Remember that marriage is a covenant as opposed to a contract. In a contract one can walk away any case of tension but a covenant is a lifetime.

****

It is better to be alone than to be with somebody that makes you feel lonely!

****

"Many men have muscle, but are weak in their minds, hearts, discipline, responsibility, and spirits." ~ Myles Munroe

****

The Bible says that Delilah nagged Samson so much that he gave up and revealed the secret. Men and women all over the world know that nagging is bad. But they have never stopped nagging. "What is nagging? It is a veiled manner of criticism. It eats into the very core of most relationships. It is found in both genders. While women nag their husbands about things they want them to do, husbands, on the other hand, are fact naggers" ~ Boniface Muruiki

****

"Don't walk infront of me, because I may not follow. Don't walk behind me because I may not lead. Just walk by my side."

****

Husbands and wives should learn how to settle their quarrels without delay. There have been situations where couples allow simple disagreement to fester for days. Husband is silently hurting, expecting the wife to speak to him first. Same for the wife, hurting and expecting the husband to play the man. The waiting game leads from one thing to the other. Swing into action to redeem the situation before it escalates.

****

Cellphones, Facebook and Whats-App can bless or break relationships. Used within the proper parameters of marriage or relationship, these can greatly enhance communication between two partners. Unfortunately, many relationships and marriages have failed because of the inappropriate use of cellphones, Facebook and WhatsApp. Protect your relationship/marriage, respect your spouse and don't lead yourself into temptation. Avoid secret communications and intimate conversations and private chatting with people of the opposite sex. Be accountable to one another. Unless you're a paranoia, have an open cell phone policy with your spouse.

****

I say Cheating is a choice, not a mistake...... what is your opinion...........?

****

The reason why other women look attractive is because someone is taking good care of them. The grass is always green where it is watered. Instead of drooling over the green grass on the other side of the fence, work on yours and water it regularly. Any man can admire a beautiful woman, but it takes a true gentleman to make a woman admirable and beautiful.

****

Good Sex profoundly cements the existing relationship between the married couples. Good sex is not a responsibility of a husband alone but it is a responsibility of both couples involved in the intimate relationship. None of the two should demand sex in his or her own way. Taking into account that both of you have different tastes. Everyone should try to make it interesting for the others. No one should have absolute control over the other. It is important to study each other's interests. Good sex may not happen overnight, but as trust increases, so should sex be perfected. On the contrary, bad sex could throw the spanner in the works. Suddenly turning the relationship toxic.

Mathias Wandera says that when it comes to what transpires between the bed sheets, men are always ready, or so it is imagined. They are eager and just cannot wait to get it off. Women, on the other hand, not so much. It is expected more of women to vote "No" when sex is proposed. And it is okay, after all, she has a variety of excuses to fall back to, however trivial. It could be a headache, the kind that only strikes during bed-time. She could also turn down action because, well, "We will wake the children." Never mind that the children are sleeping in their own room, which is literally on the other border of the house. Then, there are the divas whose only concern is to fine-tune their beauty. Love-making is off the cards as long as she just got a new hair-do. "Keep your hands to yourself, you will ruin my hair!" But it could also be the genuine reason of that time of the month (the woman's menstrual cycle), which is totally understandable. Whenever your wife is not in mood of having sex please don't force it and don't get an attitude thinking that you are rejected. There is nothing to break your back over. Just roll up the blanket and live to try another night. That is what men do.

It is simply disturbing how women are rarely able to keep it together the moment a man starts occasionally choosing sleep or a movie over intimacy. Often, girls are raised to believe that when it comes to matters inclined to the master bedroom, men are restless! The widely nursed idea in the female court of opinion is that a man who loves you will always be keen on intimacy.

When a husband shuns his wife's moves to be intimate in bed, she will shudder away from his touch and push herself to the other edge of the bed. Silence will fog over the king-sized bed as she claws into her pillow. And then she will start to cry. She will stop only long enough to lash out at him; "You don't love me." Then she will pick up the pillow to go take refuge on the couch, and there she will cry herself to sleep. That will mark the beginning of a week of silent treatment. She will not speak. Meanwhile, she will embark on an undercover mission as an infidelity spy; going through his phone, pockets and literally tip-toeing through his life to find out that mistress meeting his needs because apparently, as some women seem to have made themselves believe, if he is not looking for the pleasure from home, he must be getting it elsewhere. Unknown to most women, this belief is nothing but a misguided stereotype.

It is simply an assumption that men are always geared up for intimacy. True, we love the physical intimacy and surely there are some men who just cannot keep their hands off their women. But there are times when a man would rather watch a movie, listen to music, stare at the ceiling or just sleep rather than make love. And don't get it twisted. He loves you. Perhaps he even finds you achingly attractive. But he just can't be up for it all the time. Sometimes, he is simply not in the mood.

According to Mathias Wandera, many reasons could make a man call off action for the night, however much he is in love with you. So do not sulk when he makes it clear that he won't be up to play this time round. There are plenty of reasons men may lose interest in the idea of making out. Maybe he is dealing with some issues. Stress and fatigue could be keeping him at bay. Perhaps there is a lot of pressure at work and it leaves no peace of mind for intimacy. Also, he could be nursing an empty wallet. Trust me there isn't a lot of love to give away if you are late on rent, men will agree with me on this.

****

Pastors say that the number one prayer request among ladies is to get a spouse. According to Adeulo Jay, "Husband Scarcity" has become one of the challenges faced by many young girls today. If you go to prayer houses, the majority of the intentions are prayers for a life partner. And this calls for concern. Casting our minds back to the time of our mothers and grandmothers, was there really much of a "Husband Scarcity" problem? Or, maybe there were more men than women then, or there was an adequate corresponding number of both genders. I don't think so. Maybe then, the women had values and were prepared to build a home and not park into a built home. Then, once a young man comes of age and can, at least, feed himself and his wife, he goes out in search of a wife and the woman really appreciates him and helps him to build a future. What am I really trying to say? We created what we now see as "Husband Scarcity" for ourselves. Today, the reverse is the case. Ask an average girl to define her dream husband; you get things like "He has to be tall, handsome, fair, and rich, own a house at least, and be presentable" and then she adds "God-fearing" in order not to sound so worldly. Then, check the number of girls around you and the number of men that meet that standard, and you will see the problem. You hear girls say, "I cannot suffer in my father's house and then go and start suffering with a man."

****

Proverbs 20:15 - "The rod and reproof bestow wisdom, but an undisciplined child brings shame to his mother". Our love for our children should not take away our responsibility to discipline them. Children who are not properly disciplined are among the most miserable of children. Unruly and spoiled children are not the blessings that the Bible says they should be to parents. Correction and training will direct the child so that they will grow up with a respect for authority, and this comes by punishing them when they are rebellious.

****

Isaiah 54:13 - "And all thy children shall be taught of the LORD; and great shall be the peace of thy children". Training involves instructing, educating and disciplining.

****

Somebody asked my opinion concerning this: "I am in love with a girl from a different tribe. It is a taboo in my culture to marry a woman from a different tribe. Also, I am a born again Christian but the woman is not a Christian. But we love each other to death. Should I take a giant step to propose to her?" My answer: Genesis 1:28 – "God blessed them and said to them, "Be fruitful and increase in number; fill the earth and subdue it". God gave this benediction to Adam and Eva before they fall from grace. God intended to replenish the earth with His glory through this holy union between a man and a woman. The corruption of sin temporarily put on halt the divine plan until the dispensation of the grace. We (believers) made in God's image are the chosen ones (remnants) privileged to continue God's sovereign plan on earth. The Holy Spirit works in us through the inspired Word of God.

There are only two races before God: The race of the born again believers and the race of nonbelievers. The two cannot mingle. The Bible instructs us that, "Do not be yoked together with unbelievers" (2 Corinthians 6:14). The reason of this commandment is to replenish the earth with the glory of God and restrict the multiplication of evil on the face of the earth. God demanded that "The first offspring of every womb belongs to me" (Exodus 34:19). The first offspring that opens the womb represents the rest of the offspring that will follow; they all must be dedicated to God. Jesus is called the first of the firstfruits meaning that the rest of the children of God are molded after Him (1 Corinthians 15:23). Christians are also called the firstfruits of God. So God's perfect will is for a believer to marry a believer, and maintain our purity in Christ.

****

Somebody asked "I don't doubt my Christian faith but I occasional struggle with unwanted lustful sexual desires. Do you think I am heading to hell?" I want to say that there is a very vivid line between good and evil. A born again believer is guided by the Holy Spirit to make the right choices between good and evil. Premarital sex is absolutely wrong and so is indulging those involved in it. When principles are set by the Scriptures, they should not be compromised just because some people cannot live unto them. It is possible to resist our desires including sexual desires in the interests of duty and moral principle. Lustful sexual desire is a sin as opposed to a behavior, and cannot be modified but it can be put to death by repenting and crucifying the old nature daily. Given the fact, sexual addiction may not be healed instantly even after accepting Jesus Christ. At times, it takes a process of sanctification and cleansing of the minds.

Mothers' Day:

Mother's Day and how it started as narrated by Alex, Nugubwagye. In 1908, the US congress rejected a proposal to make Mother's day an official holiday, among them (congressmen), making jokes that once they do so they would have to proclaim also a "Mother-in-law's Day". However, due to the campaign efforts of Anna Jarvis, by 1911 all US states observed the holiday, with some of them officially recognizing Mother's Day as a local holiday, the first in 1910 being West Virginia, Jarvis' home state. Later, in 1914, President Woodrow Wilson signed the proclamation creating Mother's Day, the second Sunday in May, as a national holiday to honor mothers. Since then, the world over embraces the day as an important occasion to pay respect and honor to our mothers and wives for giving us life and all their goodness, kindness and sacrifice. Today 10th May is Mother's day let everyone stand up and salute his or her mother. Appreciation is all they need. Thank you, Mum. Bravo to all Ladies. Enjoy your day.

****

This weekend we are celebrating Mothers' Day. Earthly families are a reflection of heavenly families. God is a triune God. Elohim – A Divine Family includes the Father, the Son, and the Holy Spirit. Likewise, God established a family on earth that is triune in nature (Father, Mother, and child), as opposed to same-sex parents. As we are celebrating Mothers' Day, I want to take this opportunity to acknowledge my mother. "God gave me the life, the character, and the grace; Dad gave me the DNA and the tribe; mother nurtured love in me." Mother, your extravagant love reminds me of God's love. It is because of your love I learned to love others. You taught me by example and gave me the responsibility to be responsible. There is an adage: "The Apple Doesn't Fall Too Far From The Tree". It means, "Like mother, like child." Basically, it means children often pick up after their parents. Everything that I am, it is because I am a chip off the old block! Happy Mother's Day to you.

****

Then Jesus said to the disciple, "Behold, your mother!" (John 19:26-27). At this crucial hour of crucifixion, John, the disciple whom Jesus loved needed the comfort of a caring mother. Also Mary, the earthly mother of Jesus needed a son to comfort her. "I surely know that there is no role in life more essential and more eternal than that of motherhood." If your mother is not around, listen to the words of Jesus: "Behold, your mother!" Go ahead and give hugs to all the mothers next to you, and wish them a good Mothers' Day.

****

Dear, God I want to take a minute, not to ask for anything from you but simply to thank you, for my mother. What can I say? What words could I find to express my sincere thanks for the sacrifice made by my mother, so that I could be the responsible person that I am? Home training is paramount in order to exude exceptional and outstanding values! I may not be the best but my mother made me a winner in my own little ways. What can I pay back to her? The only way I can show gratitude is to be a blessing to someone else. Maybe a blessing isn't meant to be re-paid but meant to be passed on. Kind of like the love of God. We cannot repay God for the love and the sacrifice (not to mention the grace). We can only pass along the love of God to someone else. Mother, you are the reason I have high respect for all ladies. May God bless you with more years until the return of our Lord.

****

To my dear mother: Words are not enough to thank you for all that you did for me. You carried me in your womb for nine months and you carry me in your heart forever. You brought me into this world, then babysitting and scooping the filthy and mess I perpetually left behind; you fed me, worked for me, taught me how to walk, protected me from impairment, and picked me up whenever I stumbled. You helped me to make wise decisions - You taught me not to choose my friends for their good looks but to pick my acquaintances for their good characters. They say that a man cannot be too careful in the choice of his enemies but you taught me to turn my foes into friends. Above all, you passed on your faith to me. I want to take this opportunity to say a very heartfelt "Thank you". You are the first lady in my life!

****

Mothers' Day is all women's day because every human being (apart from Adam) is born of a woman. Although not everyone is blessed to have truly good mothers, God created women with the tender and soft heart. In fact, during the colonial era, when a woman committed a crime that is equivalent to murder, she was penalized twice as much as the man that committed the same offense. Women were held to a higher degree of accountability because they are the mothers to all humanity. It is stooping so low when a woman destroys life instead of nurturing it. Also, women were not allowed to participate in violent sports like boxing and wrestling because of their tender hearts. "Women are proof that God is kind, creative, and good." Although some have different opinions regarding traditional gender roles, let all of us be thankful that God loves diversity, complementarity, and difference. Let us celebrate mothers—and all women—who are in our lives.

****

Hope you had a good Mothers' Day. To some of my friends whose mothers are no longer with us: We share the pain. We can still celebrate the lives of the departed ones. I like what George Bernard wrote: "Write your Sad times in Sand, Write your Good times in Stone". In reality, death temporally ends a life, not a relationship. Let us celebrate their lives in their absence believing that they are in better places with the Lord. We should celebrate while believing in the future family reunion; one day we will join them in the eternal presence of God. Certainly, we miss the departed beloved ones and we would rather be with them here on earth, but on the contrary, they would rather have us join them in heaven than be with us here on earth. I am talking about those who died when having the intimate relationship with Christ. They overcame death when they accepted Jesus Christ as their Lord and Savior. Not even death can separate them from Christ.

"Death is not the greatest loss in life. The greatest loss is what dies inside us while we live." We should be worried of our beloved ones, who are still living, who have rejected the saving grace of God. As for the departed ones, who died in Christ, God has taken them from our natural eyes but not away from us since all of us (dead/living saints) are one body of Christ. He has hidden them in His heart, that they may be closer to ours. The sour truth to swallow is that - "Sometimes good things fall apart so that better things can fall together."

****

Mothers play a great role in nurturing and upbringing of a child. Dear mothers, you sacrifice all you can for the sake of the family. You are the pillar and foundation upon which a strong nation is built. They rightly say that when you educate a mother, you educate a nation! The values we grow up cherishing is fostered by you and the love and calm you restore in homes and societies guarantees the peace we all yearn for. It's for this reasons among others that ladies / women must be honored in society. Happy women's Day!

****

According to Ladette Britain, violence among women soars as record 250 are arrested every day. The morality of the society is measured by the morality of women. Women were created with sensitivity because they are the mothers to all humanity. They are supposed to nurture all human nature. The Bible says that "Every wise woman buildeth her house: but the foolish plucketh it down with her hands" (Proverbs 14:1). Given the fact, this is not a woman's world—or a man's world—but God's world! God resents people (male/female), who satiate their desires, and proudly vaunt their power at the expense of the weak, poor and needy.

****

A child is a mother's heart walking outside her body.

****

Each time a woman stands up for herself, she unknowingly stands up for everyone including her mother, your mother, your wife, your sisters, your sister in law and your daughters. The world would not be the same without her. Happy Women's' Day.

****

A woman is a warrior. With a heart and lots of love. So here is a toast. To all the mothers, sisters n wives. You really make the world a better place to be.

****

"There is a kind of strength that is almost frightening in black women. It's as if a steel rod runs right through the head down to the feet" ~ Maya Angelou

****

Saints, never underestimate the power behind a woman of God with a plan and a prayer that is in alignment with God's will for her life ~ Joy Lichtman

****

Depression knows no gender. "When a depressed person has no faith, let your faith count on his or her behalf" ~ Vivian OIkem

****

Fathers' Day

Somebody asked me why I call God the Father. God is the Father of Jesus Christ. The word 'Father' has nothing to do with the natural biological birth but has everything to do with the miraculous supernatural spiritual birth. Jesus came from the Father (John 1:1). In the same way, Adam came from God (breathed out by God from His nostril). The Bible called a son of God (Luke 3:38). The conception of Jesus was activated by the power of the Holy Spirit; He was born of a virgin (begotten Son). Jesus is the Son of God because He is of the same nature (Spirit) and character (sinless) with God the Father. Son of God means to be in perfect obedience to God. Jesus called the Jewish religious leaders sons of Satan by virtue of their allegiance to the devil (John 8:44). We become children of God by receiving Jesus: "But as many as received him, to them gave he power to become the sons of God, even to them that believe on his name" (John 1:12). After resurrection, Jesus, made it possible for His Father to be our Father: "I go to my Father and your Father my God, your God" (John 20:17). By faith, His perfect works were accredited to us. We are children of God by virtue of Christ's obedience.

Children of God are Christ-like. Obeying His commandments is the evidence (not the cause) of our salvation (John 14:15-31; 1 John 5:3). Children of God are spiritually dead to the world of sin, and have abundance life forever in Christ. God is in the business of regenerating (re-birthing) of new natures in Christ as opposed to recycling old natures into new. Jesus instructed us that: "And do not call anyone on earth 'father,' for you have one Father, and he is in heaven" (Matthew 23:9). The Spirit of Christ is the Spirit of our adoption to sonship. And by him we cry, "Abba, Father (Romans 8:15).

****

Hebrews 12:2 - "Looking unto Jesus the author and perfecter of our faith; who for the joy that was set before him endured the cross, despising the shame, and is seated at the right hand of the throne of God." "There were two opposite realities present for Jesus in His own "race"—the joy of being with the Father and of accomplishing what He came for and right alongside, the shame He endured at the hands of sinful men. Joy that pulled him forward...and shame that He despised along the way. Where do you experience those contrasts of joy amidst shame in your life?"

****

By the time a son knows that his father was right he already has a son that thinks he is wrong ~ Evariste Sindiyagaya

****

To all fathers. You are my heroes. Any good father would like to see his children shine in the limelight. Every parent's dream is for their children to be heroes. I want to say with cautiousness that, you don't raise heroes, you raise sons. And if you treat them like sons, they'll turn out to be heroes, even if it's just in your own eyes. "Raising children is an institution where you remain a student until you die. There is no graduation day in this institution. Just when you think you are about to graduate, new assignments, tests, course works and even dissertations come up which you have to complete. Whether you complete them or not, your overall grade is finally and surely revealed by the legacy you leave when you are gone. Good luck fellow students. Happy Father's Day to all of you!

****

I'm always amazed by the lengths a man will go to protect the things that matter to him. The distance between self and purpose is the measure of the strength of a man.

****

Professors Adam Swift of the University of Warwick and Harry Brighouse of the University of Wisconsin, Madison, think they've found the root source of inequality in society: the family. According to John StreetStone, now social scientists have long known that loving families with two parents confer an enormous advantage on children. Evidence shows these kids are more likely to attend college, less likely to suffer or perpetrate abuse, less likely to do drugs or cross the law, and have a higher likelihood of passing on these advantages to their own children. You would think this would make us want good families in our society. But Swift and Brighouse don't think that's fair.

****

Exodus 20:12 - "Honor your father and your mother, so that you may live long in the land the LORD your God is giving you." This is one of the most important commandment, and yet the most ignored by mankind. It is the first commandment to be accompanied by a promise of blessing. Parents give life and they do not stop there, they affect our blessings throughout this world. It is not easy to tell where their influence stops! Honoring your father and mother is being respectful in word and action and having an inward attitude of esteem for their position. Honor them when you are young for your own comfort and benefit, and honor them when you grow up for their own comfort by taking care of them. Then count on God's unlimited blessings!

****

Jesus said that "If you would practice my teaching, imitate my life." But as the life of Jesus is the exact transcript of perfect virtue, He can point to Himself as the paragon of holiness, as well as the teacher of it. The Christian should take nothing less than Christ for his model. Under no circumstances should we be content unless we reflect the grace that was in Him.

What does a child expect from a father? Children expect their dad to love their mother. When you love your wife, or the mother of your son, you are showing him how to treat his mother, his sisters, and all the women he will meet in his life. This will set the foundation for the relationships he will have later in his life. Children want to see how you respond in times of trials. Integrity is standing for what is right when the world is against you. Integrity is accepting your failures gracefully. The best teacher is failure. The best type of failure to learn from is someone else's. When your son sees you fail, and handle the failure well, he sees that it is okay to make mistakes and that mistakes can be great teachers. A boy who is not afraid of making mistakes will grow into a man positioned to accept and conquer great challenges.

Children expects you to be a leader and to lead by example. You are the head of the family; a leader as opposed to a ruler. Your children need to see true leadership in practical sense. A leader is a servant too. When they see you serving, they will understand leadership and will be able to be effective leaders too. I mean effectively leading versus follow his peers. Eventually, as they grow, they will be better leaders in their families, jobs, churches and communities.

A good dad effectively gets involved in the lives of His children spiritually, physically and emotionally. Saw them that you care by spending time with them and cheering them in their daily activities like sports and other achievements. Don't mind being pulled in multiple directions. Do what you have to do. They need your presence in all areas of their lives. Some areas are not suitable for mothers but demand a male character.

Be a cheerleader and motivator. Show much you love them. Say to them or write them a note that, "I love you." "I'm proud of you." "You are amazing." "I know you can do it." "That was an amazing play you made!" "You are a hard worker." "You messed up, but I know you'll bounce back." Be a cheerleader to your children; they need your encouragement. They need to hear these words from your mouth. They need to know and to hear that you love them.

Your children expect you to treat them equally fair without favoritism. Disciplining is a sign of caring. Always discipline them out of love as

223

opposed to anger. When you discipline your son, you set boundaries and expectations. He is going to make mistakes just like you did as a child and just like you do now. But he also needs to know that his actions have consequences. Disciplining him in love will teach him to consider the consequences his actions will have. This will prepare him to think and evaluate the choices he makes both now and in the future.

****

Children, as much as adults wherever they are, deserve our love and affection. It is the responsibility of the parents to give fulsomeness love to their children. However, we should be careful not to overstep. There is this thing called self-esteem. Watch what you say to your kids. Never pull them down by your words, and never spoil them by your words. For example, it is not appropriate to say to your kids that they are better than anybody. Just let them know that they are special to God but they are as good as any other kids. Hope I am helping somebody.

How to avoid Divorce

Bob has two questions. The first is—there are plenty of people that I know who happen to be pagans. They don't have any fear of the Lord, but it looks like they've got a pretty happy marriage, and it's gone the distance. Some people scratch their heads and say: "I hear all you Christians, with all this uptight language, but it sure doesn't seem like the Christians are doing any better job than the pagans are. In fact, I know some pagans do a better job than the Christians are." Where does that come from? How is it that two pagans, with no fear of the Lord, can have a satisfactory marriage?

Well, the fallen man, (whether born again or not), to some extent retains the image of God in them. However, when somebody is not born again, the image of God is blunted by sin. But they are not foreign to morality, except that their natural instincts and desires to please themselves overwhelm the desires to please God. Paul acknowledges that the Gentiles have the law written on their hearts (Rom. 2:15). The morality of God is not foreign to them. They know right from wrong because the morality of God defines sin.

According to Alistair Beg, part of the answer is surely in the fact that marriage is a creation ordinance—that it was given to man as man within the framework of the very origin of society—that it predates if you like / if we can say so—Christianity. God's ideal and God's principles work if applied, even from an external perspective—so that the issue of honesty, the issue of sensitivity, the concerns of communication: of saying, "Please," / of saying, "Thank you," of coming home when you say you come home, of building into one another's lives—these are not the unique precinct of Christianity. These are gifts of the common grace of God. Somebody, who is professing to follow Jesus—who is discourteous to his wife / who is unfaithful to his promises—is obviously going to make a royal hash of his marriage, irrespective of what He has to say. Whereas somebody else, who as yet has never understood the immensity of what is there in the gospel, may actually be a fine, upstanding citizen and a good husband.

Marriage is work in progress. There is always something that needs to work on or to repair. In order to fix your marriage, you need to take inventory regarding your relationship with God. You need to re-arrange your priorities and have God in the first place (above all things). I mean your relationship with God; the two people involved in marriage must evaluate their fellowship with God. Habitual sin breaks up our communication with God. It takes two to tangle. An observation on the fact that it takes two willing people to commit an infidelity, not just one.

Finances: Everyone knows that money problems lead to divorce. Most people think that the stress of living on a tight income is what causes divorce. Sometimes that is true, but typically a tight budget alone does not cause a couple to split. So what types of money issues do cause a marriage to implode? 1) The Financial Roller Coaster: Marriages seem to do better when incomes are stable; extreme highs and lows are devastating to marriages. The Financial Odd Couple-Spenders vs. Savers: Guess who wins in a marriage between a spender and a saver? No one! While common sense seems to suggest that the saver will provide balance to the spender and vice-versa, this is not what occurs in practice. Rather than balance each other out, spenders and savers just come to resent each other's relationship with money.

Control of finances should be in the hands of both parties involved in the relationship. Avoid the Golden Rule: "Whoever makes the gold makes the rules!" Over and over again, family law attorneys watch marriages crumble like packs of cards whenever the major wage earner in the couple (man or woman) attempts to exert solo control over the family income. The irony here is that once the couple divorces over this issue, the controller ends up writing a check every month to the non-wage earning spouse who then spends that money however they choose. If you want to have a long life, let your wife be in charge of your salary, it will be difficult for her to spend it when she's aware of the home needs and bills to pay but if it's in your care, she will keep you asking even when all has been spent.

Different appetites and values: Couples have different areas of interest to invest money. Not surprisingly, different values concerning money lead to conflict. Things like gambling are major causes of conflict. Yet this is the issue that no one wants to talk about. This is a far bigger problem than most people think. Many people who are married to a gambler pull the plug on the marriage because they see it as the only way to prevent eventual financial ruin. The sad part in these cases is that frequently the marriage is "good" apart from one spouse's gambling addiction.

The materialistic mentality is disastrous. Work for the well-being of both of you as couples. Win together and lose together. Work as a team. Figure out ways to leverage both persons strength to win.

****

Conflicts cannot be avoided but they should never be allowed to escalate into violence. Don't ever beat your woman, the pain in her body is nothing to be compared to the wound on her heart and that means you may be in trouble living with a wounded woman.

****

Faithfulness must be proven in actions. Now that you're married, if you live a bachelor kind of life with your wife, you will soon be single again.

****

Never compare your wife to any other woman. Remember that there are ways she's enduring you too and she has never compared you to any other man.

****

Keep the in-laws out of your relationship as much as possible. Yes, you need your parents, but there should be limits of their influence in your marriage. They should not directly control your spouse or your marriage; try to handle issues without always going to them.

****

Forgive yourself. Don't bring into your relationship the past baggage.

Don't let your history hold you hostage. "Holding on to the past mistakes that either you or she makes, is like a heavy anchor to your marriage and will hold you back."

The past cannot be changed, forgotten, edited or erased; it can only be accepted. Accepting yours and your partner's past is one of the healthy steps that you should take towards creating a beautiful present and a bright future together!

****

In case of urgency, separation is recommended. Separating can be a healthy way to avoid divorce. Giving space to your spouse can allow them to think about what they are missing and pull up their socks. Don't wait for the situation to escalate into violence. "Breakups aren't meant for makeups. Sometimes, relationships end in order for you to wake up."

****

No relationship is perfect. Every relationship has ups and downs. The ones who make it through everything are the ones really in love.

****

There is no marriage without issues. Get proper counseling in case of conflicts. Talking to wrong people will make the matters worse. Discussing your marital problems with others makes the matter worse. They are likely to turn a molehill into a mountain.

****

The greatest mistake most people make is to build the relationship based on shallow things: It could be something like physical appearance, expectation, sex or even money. It is important not to build a long-term relationship on shallow things but on sincere love.

****

Never stop courting. Never stop dating. Never ever take that woman for granted. When you asked her to marry you, you promised to be that man that would own her heart and to fiercely protect it. This is the most important and sacred treasure you will ever be entrusted with. She chose you. Never forget that, and never get lazy in your love.

****

Shield your heart. In the same way you committed to being the protector of her heart, you must guard your own with the same vigilance. In order to love others better, you must know how to love yourself. Create a special place in your heart for your spouse where no one must enter except him or her. Keep that space sacred always reserved for your spouse, ready to receive him or her and invite him or her in, and refuse to let anyone or anything else enter there.

****

We fall in love by growing into it. Fall in love endlessly. Where there is love, everything is possible. With love, you can adjust to any situation without frustration. "Choosing love is the only advice you need. If this is the guiding principle through which all your choices is governed, there is nothing that will threaten the happiness of your marriage. Love will always endure."

****

"In the end, marriage isn't about happily ever after. It's about work. And a commitment to grow together and a willingness to continually invest in creating something that can endure eternity. Through that work, the happiness will come."

****

Don't reminisce about your past single life. Things are never going to be the same. You're not the same person you were when you got married, and you will not be the same person in the future. Accept changes as they come.

****

Don't limit your love. Never allow your spouse to look for love outside your marriage. Give it all to him or her. Remember if you don't take care of him or her somebody else will. Tell your spouse how great he or she is. Don't let him or her hear the same encouraging words from somebody else other than you. Always fight to win your spouse's love just as you did when you were courting him or her.

****

Always solve the issues as they come. Never pile up little issues in your heart. Know when and how to address them without being critical. What you focus on will expand. What you save in your heart will never disappear. The only delete button is to solve them as they come. "If you focus on what bugs you, all you will see is reasons to be bugged. If you focus on what you love, you can't help but be consumed by love." See love as opposed to hate in everything. Focus on the good and ignore the bad. Feel that you are the luckiest person to be in the relationship rather than feeling pity of yourself. Never compare your spouse with other people.

****

Accept your spouse as he or she is. Never try to change him or her into what you want. The only person you can change is yourself. Never yearn to change your spouse. Learn to thrive as opposed to surviving. Love your spouse in anticipation that he or she will change by himself or herself. Pray to God to change him or her. Love the person you want her or him to become as opposed to the person he or she is.

****

Learn from the good in your spouse. Accept your mistakes. Be accountable to your spouse. Avoid acting out of emotions. Seek to make your spouse happy. Avoid revenging. Admit that at times life is not going to make sense to you; do not despair. "You are responsible for finding your own happiness, and through that, your joy will spill over into your relationship and your love."

****

Avoid playing the blame game. You will make mistakes and so will she. Try not to make too big of mistakes, and learn from the ones you do make. You're not supposed to be perfect, just try to not be too stupid. Be willing to share your fears and feelings, and quick to acknowledge your mistakes. Never discuss issues when you are angry. Allow time to cool down. Never make your spouse look silly. When discussing issues make sure you are yourself instead of letting something inside your heart to trigger bitterness. Take responsibility for your faults. Always be ready to say that you are sorry. Not sorry because you are caught in mistake but sorry for your acts. We all have the past childhood mentalities intruding in us; never allow them to manifest. Act maturely. Spoil your spouse with love but treat him or her as a mature person. It is ok to be silly but not to act silly. Be silly but don't take yourself so seriously. Laugh. And make her laugh. Laughter makes everything else easier.

****

When your spouse is mad it is not your duty to make him or her more mad. When your spouse is sad or upset, it's not your job to fix it, it's your job to comfort her. Sometimes your spouse does not need a solution but just mere comfort. Hold her; give her a hug with such assurance that everything is going to be ok. Let her know that you hear her, and that she's important and that you are that pillar on which she can always lean. Don't run away from her when she is upset. Stand present and strong and let her know you aren't going anywhere; you are there for her regardless. Don't focus on what she says when she is upset but focus on the cause of turmoil as opposed to what she says. Listen to what she is really saying behind the words and emotion.

****

Make a list of things that you like in your spouse. Study your spouse and the things that turn on the spark of love. Cherish them and use them as your menu to make your spouse feel special every day. Treat your spouse as you would your most valuable client. He or she is.

****

Never think of your past relationship when you are with your spouse. Never compare your spouse to somebody else. Give your spouse the full attention he or she deserves. Give your spouse not only your time but your focus, your attention and your soul. Do whatever it takes to clear your head so that when you are with him or her you are fully there.

****

Be sexually attractive to your spouse. Invest in this area massively. Go out on a date. Show your spouse that he or she is sexually attractive and that you are interested. As for a woman dress up for your husband sexy. As for a man always be romantic. "Carry her away in the power of your masculine presence, to consume her and devour her with your strength, and to penetrate her to the deepest levels of her soul. Let her melt into her feminine softness as she knows she can trust you fully.

****

At times every person needs space. Know when to give your spouse space. Help her with children so that she can have her space too. She needs that space to renew and get recentered and to find herself after she gets lost in serving you, the kids and the world. Take children to the babysitter so that you can have time with your spouse alone without the nagging of the children.

****

Develop trust by being transparent. Never hide anything from your spouse. Things will be worse if your spouse finds out the hard way what you have deliberately hidden from her or him. It takes courage to fully love, to fully open your heart. If you are pretending you will never experience the full dimension of what love can be.

****

Allow room for growth in all areas. Find common goals, dreams, and visions to work towards. Grow together spiritually by attending the same Church. Pray together. People that pray together stay together.

****

Marriage is life, and it will bring ups and downs. Embracing all of the cycles and learning to learn from and love each experience will bring the strength and perspective to keep building, one brick at a time.

****

Life after divorce:

Somebody asked me what I think about the high rate of divorce even in the Church. I want to say that the relationship we normally have at the human level is not what God intended. God intended marriage to be 'a forever relationship.' Jesus said that "What therefore God has joined together, let no man separate" (Mark 10:9). Divorcing may legally end the relationship on the human level but not on the divine level. It is for the same reason Jesus said that "Anyone who divorces his wife and marries another woman commits adultery, and the man who marries a divorced woman commits adultery" (Luke 16:18). Remember that Marriage is an institution created by God (Gen. 2:18-25), and operating on His principles. Jesus showed that the Mosaic Law does not justify divorce, but rather limits it (Matthew 19:3-9).

As bad as divorce can be, and as much as it can bring pain and suffering, there is nonetheless some circumstances where Jesus allowed divorce. Jesus gave adultery as a valid reason for divorce (Matthew 5:31-32). However, even in such circumstances where divorce is permissible, in some instances, the truly biblical course of action would be to rebuke, await repentance, offer forgiveness, and be reconciled (see Matthew 18:15-17).

****

At times, we try to make up for the lost relationship by getting hooked up into a new relationship to make up for the lost one. Never rush into relationship after coming out of another relationship. Give time for healing. Relax, seek viable counseling and join some good single groups.

****

The toughest thing to do is to let your dream go. When the marriage ends please let that dream rest in peace. Never look behind. Remember that it is never safe to drive while looking behind. Stay out of the life of the person you formally married. Never try to follow up the progress of your Ex-wife or Ex-husband'. Wish them well. Do it for your benefit.

****

I came across in the encyclopedia the following quotation containing words from a person whose relationship has hit a rock and they are separated: "We are not enemies, but friends. We must not be enemies. Though passion may have strained, it must not break our bonds of affection. The mystic chords of memory will swell when again touched, as surely they will be, by the better angels of our nature."

****

Amos 3:3 - "Can two walk together, except they be agreed?" (KJV). We cannot walk with God unless we agree with Him. God does not have to agree with us, we must agree with Him. In order for you to be my closest companion, you must not antagonize my relationship with God. My moral compass says it's not OK to be rude to me, lie to me, to steal from me, to cheat on me, to speak disrespectfully to me, to mistreat me or treat me poorly in any way, especially not as a pattern or without explanation or discussion. This is often called setting boundaries, and it gives me the confidence to move forward in a situation or to step back—or even out.

****

Sometimes we tend to be in despair when the person we love leaves us, but the truth is, it's not our loss, but theirs, for they left the only person who wouldn't give up on them.

****

"Stop wasting your time on someone who does not want to be there. If they wanted to be yours you wouldn't have to work so hard to keep them".

****

Don't stress over people in your past. There is a reason why they didn't make it to your future.

****

It is much more difficult to judge oneself than to judge others. If you succeed in judging yourself rightly, then you are indeed a man of integrity.

****

"It is always good to taste one's own medicine to have a lasting lesson." Whenever you pass bad laws don't forget that one day you may receive a full dose of what you prescribed to others!

****

I can still be in love with you without you.

****

A broken heart is when you know you've been hurt, but have no idea how to fix it. A broken heart is when you finally realize that he or she is everything you need and at the same time realize he or she is the one thing you can never have.

July: Freedom / Liberty

Spiritual Liberty:

Our liberty in Christ begins by acknowledging our identity in Christ. The devil is scared stiff of anyone armed with the knowledge of who they are in Christ. Satan knows that a man fully convinced about God's love holds himself with a confidence that poses a huge threat to plundering his sham kingdom. He realizes people assured that their past is crucified live with a boldness that neither he nor his minions can counter. And so, Satan comes as the great identity thief, seeking to conceal or steal your identity in Christ and replace it with his defeated one. He often does it by insisting, "You'll always be who you always were." You've heard one of these arguments: "You were abused by men all of your life; you can't trust any man. You are a victim." Or "You will always be addicted, you can't ever overcome it." Or "You'll always be depressed." Or "You are under a generation curse". God wants you to know this: You are not your past, your feelings or what anyone has ever spoken about you. His Word is your reality.

At the cross, none of the sayings of Jesus is more important or more poignant than, "It is finished" (John 19:30). The Greek word translated "it is finished" is *tetelestai*, an accounting / legal term meaning "paid in full." The eternal debt owed for the sin of mankind was paid in full. When Jesus uttered those words, He was declaring the debt owed to His Father was wiped away completely and forever. Not that Jesus wiped away any debt that He owed to the Father; rather, Jesus eliminated the debt owed by mankind—the debt of sin.

He was paying the wages for our sins. This being the only and final atonement made for our sins.

We (the redeemed), by raising the "shield of faith" in the One (Jesus) who completed the work of redemption and salvation, we can, by faith, live as new creations in Christ. The resurrection is the Father's acceptance of Jesus' finished work on the cross. This is the beginning of new life for all who were once "dead in trespasses and sins" but who are now made "alive with Christ" (Ephesians 2:1, 5). At the cross, the Great Exchange took place (2 Cor. 6:21; Colossians 2:13-15). God looked upon His perfect, precious, and priceless Son as if He had lived the filthy, detestable, sin-stained lives of fallen mankind. No man is perfect to redeem another man apart from the perfect God wrapped in human flesh. Jesus took on Himself our sins in perfect obedience to the Father, and God accepted His works as perfect. And, for those who repent and receive Jesus Christ as their Lord and Savior, God the Father looks upon them as if they had lived His Son's perfect, precious, and priceless life.

****

Ephesians 2:6 – "And God raised us up with Christ and seated us with him in the heavenly realms in Christ Jesus". A believer has two addresses: The first address is in Christ in heavenly places. The second address is Christ in us here in the physical world. In the natural, we are experientially sinners under the grace, yet our positional sanctification is just as perfect as Christ is perfect. Every believer is sanctified in Jesus Christ. Just as much as He is set apart, we who are in Him are set apart (1 Cor. 1:2; Heb. 10:10). The New Testament calls all believers "saints," *hagioi*. We are the "sanctified" or "holy ones." It is from the same prospective Paul wrote that "Therefore, there is now no condemnation for those who are in Christ Jesus" (Romans 8:1).

****

Jesus doesn't change you so that He may love you. He loves you so that He may change you. He loves you so much that He cannot afford to leave you the way you are! The journey to transformation begins with this simple step: When you open up the door of your heart to Jesus, God opens up His door for you to heaven. This makes the spiritual journey easy and exciting!

****

The character of God defines sin. Confession is not adding virtue to virtue but embracing the virtue of that extraordinary figure, Jesus Christ. The standard of human life is no longer a code, but a character of the person of Jesus Christ. The gospel presents boundless opportunity to us. Jesus promised all who seek to find. It is never too late for you to begin again a new life in Christ.

****

1 Peter 2:9 – "But you are a chosen people, a royal priesthood, a holy nation, God's special possession, that you may declare the praises of him who called you out of darkness into his wonderful light." In the Old Testament, although Israel was a theocracy (ruled by God), not all Israelites were priests. The priesthood was limited to the descendants of Aaron (Levitical priesthood). The priestly institution itself was needed only because the sin of the people had not yet been finally dealt with, and an intermediary was required between Israel and God lest His holiness break out and destroy His sinful people (Exodus 10: 24; Amos 5:6). We are the chosen people because our wickedness has been finally dealt with by the death of Jesus on the cross. We are the nation of priests that requires no Levitical mediator between us and the Almighty. Christ in us is God with us (Emmanuel). Having sanctified and perfected us in His Father's sight forevermore through His offering of Himself (Heb. 10:10–14), Christ Jesus has made all who are in Him the priesthood that God always intended His people to be. God wants the Church not to be just a messenger but the message. Jesus willingly descended from

the throne and traded all that He loved and valued so that we might become all that He is.

****

Romans 8:13 – "For if you live according to the flesh, you will die; but if by the Spirit you put to death the misdeeds of the body, you will live." The flesh, in this case, is our Adamic old nature. Believers have the ability to put to death the deeds of the corrupt nature. They do it by living by the Spirit of Christ. Jesus destroyed the power of sin but we have the responsibility to kill the flesh. True Christians have active (not passive) pursuit of holiness. This is most probably the sign that separates true believers from false believers in our local churches.

****

What if all you have is Jesus? No fancy house, no clothes, no electricity, the only property you have is a goat and a dog. Yet Jesus values you by His blood. "Unlike money, the blood of Christ has the purchasing power that is not affected by inflation or erratic swings in the stock market. This power does not fluctuate depending on where you are in the world." Child of God, smile because Jesus loves you! The Bible reminds us that Jesus purchased a people to inherit His own possessions. We understand the nature of possessions involves incorruptible things. We own everything that He owns even the eternal riches! "What's in your wallet?" At that point, dollars won't do. Euros won't count. Silver and gold will be of no service. You better have Jesus. You better have His blood. What's in my wallet? The blood of Jesus! He has purchased me, and I am His and He is mine forever.

****

John 1:29 - "Behold! The Lamb of God who takes away the sin of the world!" The uniqueness of the sacrifice made by Jesus Christ when He died on the cross is that for the first time the sacrifice was made for the whole world. According to the old covenant (Leviticus

16:9-14), on the Day of Atonement, the high priest was required to make sacrifices for his own sins, for the sins of the individual families and for the sins of the nation of Israel (Leviticus 16:9-14). All this while the scapegoat was standing looking eastwards, facing the people, and waiting to bear the sins of all the people to a solitary land. Laying both his hands on the head of this goat, the High Priest now confessed and pleaded for all the people. The scapegoat was then led through the temple's east gate to a waiting priest whose job was to take it to a predetermined spot about ten to twelve miles away. Along the way, there were ten stations with food or drink in case the tired priest needed to break his fast. When the priest came to the final station, he pushed the goat off a cliff. Using a system of signal flags, the priest leading the animal would message back to the Temple that the sins of the people were forgiven. And, tradition has it that when the sacrifice was fully accepted the piece of red wool on the temple door would turn miraculously white, to symbolize the gracious promise in Isaiah 1:18; but it adds that this miracle did not take place for 40 years before the destruction of the second Temple, that is, after Christ Himself completed the final sacrifice.

The animal sacrifices made in the old covenant temporarily covered the sins of the people. The blood of Jesus permanently removed the sins of all people in the world that believe. The blood of the animals is compared to covering your trash in the trash can whereby it keeps the stench out of the house but keeps the trash within the house until the trash man come to pick it up. Jesus is that trash man that carries the trash away from the house eradicating the stench from the house forever.

****

The Bible reminds us that Jesus purchased a people for His own possession (Galatians 3:13-15). Jesus came to retrieve the stolen territory from our enemy and return it to its right owner. We don't have our own life to live anymore except His life. Unlike money, the blood of Jesus Christ has the purchasing power that is not affected by inflation or erratic swings in the stock market. This power of the blood does not fluctuate depending on where you are in the world. The ground at the foot of the cross is leveled; nobody stands at a higher level than the other. "Keep your feet on the ground, but let your heart soar as high as it will."

****

Today is Yom Kippur - meaning "Day of Atonement" according to Leviticus 16. All the sacrifices were to picture the final, perfect sacrifice that God himself would provide in the Messiah (Isaiah 53: 3-12). The primary Messianic ministry is to atone for our sins. At the cross, Jesus said that "It is finished" (John 19:30). Meaning "Paid in full." The ledger is zeroed out. The wages of our sins (past, present and future) were paid in full. God accepts us on account of what Jesus did. The Bible says that "He made Him who knew no sin to be sin on our behalf so that we might become the righteousness of God in Him" (2 Corinthians 5:21). His righteousness was imputed on every sinner that repents. Our sinful life became His, and His sinless life became ours. What a great bargain extended to us! Do you believe?

****

Ezekiel 18:20 – "The soul that sins, it shall surely die." The power of the gospel reverses the decree of sin therefore overruling the power of sin even death. Paul wrote to the Philippians saying that he wanted to know the power of Christ's rising (Philippians 3:10). The greatest evidence of God's reversing abilities is the resurrection. The resurrection declares that no situation is out of control that our God cannot act. The same power that raised Jesus from the dead is at work in our bodies. Life is filled with ridicule, with unexpected and sometimes drastic reverses, but the damage of the heart is irreversible. God alone can reverse the irreversible. He can reverse reputations and realities. Thank God for the blood of Jesus.

****

God opposes the fallen world by the power of His will. The Word of God is the will and covenant of God. We change the world with the unchanging Word. Overcomers are world changers. They are followers of Christ, and they successfully resist the power and temptation of the world's system by the conviction of the Holy Spirit through the Word. They excel by living by faith and by being faithful. Our faith is measured by the measure of the Word of God in us. To be faithful is to live a life full of faith.

****

Ephesians 1:3-4 – "Blessed be the God and Father of our Lord Jesus Christ, who has blessed us with every spiritual blessing in the heavenly places in Christ, just as He chose us in Him before the foundation of the world, that we would be holy and blameless before Him." The natural man is made after Adam but we find our new nature in the Second Adam (Christ). We (born again believers) are spiritual beings. Since we were dead in our sins, and could not go back to God in our corruption, God decided to come to us by His Son so that we might go back to Him through regeneration. God's idea of election is not an afterthought on the part of the deity but a forethought. God chose us in Christ before the foundation of the world. Our identity is in Christ. In Christ God chose us to be His own. He is holy and He makes us one family of holiness and He is not ashamed to call us His brothers and sisters (Hebrews 2:11). Our salvation is rooted in the eternal plan of God. Jesus told Nicodemus unless you are born again or born from above (John 3:7) you cannot see the kingdom of God. Jesus told the Samaritan woman that "God is a Spirit: and they that worship him must worship him in spirit and in truth" (John 4:24). True worshipers are of the same nature and character with God.

****

We come into this world upon birth in agony (while crying), and we leave this world upon death in agony (while crying). The reason is because we do not belong to this world, we are pilgrims. Our bodies and this world are not our home. There is a compatible relationship between this corrupt world and our corrupt bodies. Our bodies came from this earth and return to the earth. Given the fact, the bodies of the redeemed are sanctified by the indwelling Spirit of God (temple). Our citizenship is heaven. We do not need to speculate on where heaven is. Heaven is where Jesus is. Jesus said, "I will come back and take you to be with me that you also may be where I am." (John 14:3).

****

What a friend we have in Jesus! Jesus is a name, which is especially sweet and precious to believers. The Lord has been good to us beyond comprehension. The Song of Solomon describes our experience in this way: "Your name is oil poured forth" (Song of Solomon 1:3). Happy is the person who trusts not merely in vague notions of God's mercy and goodness, but in "Jesus." His name has given to us what money cannot buy - that is, inward peace. When we accept salvation as His free gift, we enter into His rest and His presence now as well as in eternity. He eases our wearied consciences and gives rest to our heavy hearts. If you are tied and wearied He is calling you to come home. Coming home is when your heart becomes His home. There is no greater work of God than bringing you into His presence. As He draws you to Himself, He draws others to you.

****

2 Corinthians 12:9 - "My grace is sufficient for you". The grace of God is the spring from eternity watering this universe without limit to perfect it. There is no sin we commit that cannot be covered by the grace because the prevenient grace preceded our sins. It would be sufficient if the rest of the heavenly springs dried up except the grace. All of creations belong to God but the grace comes from God to us, and it is ours. We came with nothing to this world and we take nothing out of it when we die apart from the grace. The only sin is therefore rejecting the grace. God provides to us by His grace, and we receive from Him with the hand of faith. All of our vineyards are

a portion of the Lord's great vineyard, and we are stewards. However, when we become His, everything He owns become ours. Therefore true prosperity is to become co-heirs with Christ (Romans 8:16-17).

****

What if all you have is Jesus? No fancy house, no clothes, no electricity, the only property you have is a goat and a dog. Yet you are the richest person if you have Christ. Jesus values you by His incorruptible blood. "Unlike money, the blood of Christ has the purchasing power that is not affected by inflation or erratic swings in the stock market. This power does not fluctuate depending on where you are in the world." Child of God, smile because Jesus loves you! The Bible reminds us that Jesus purchased a people to inherit His own possessions. We understand the nature of possessions involves eternal things. We own everything that He owns even the eternal riches! "What's in your wallet?" At that point (eternity), dollars won't do. Euros won't count. Silver and gold will be of no service. You better have Jesus. You better have His blood. What's in my wallet? The blood of Jesus! He has purchased me, and I am His and He is mine forever.

****

Somebody asked me to explain Ecclesiastes 7:2 - "Better to spend your time at funerals than at parties." The book of Ecclesiastes was written for the natural man under the sun. The redeemed are spiritual, and their priorities are eternal things as opposed to material things. According to this scripture, we (the redeemed of God) can now say that our worst days in this world are by far greater than the best days of the people of the world who are not born again. In this case, our mourning now is better than the luxurious partying life of the world.

****

Somebody asked "Could God have loved us if Jesus didn't die on the cross?" According to John 3:16, "For God so loved the world that he gave his one and only Son, that whoever believes in him shall not perish but have eternal life". God did not love us because Jesus Christ died the cross but it is His love for us that motivated Him to give His only Son to die for us on the cross. The love of the Father preceded the cross. This is not the chicken and egg situation in which it is impossible to say which of two things existed first and which caused the other one. The cross is not the cause of God's love but the evidence of God's love. Neither did Jesus twist the hand of the Father by virtue of His death in order for the Father to love us nor did the Father twist the hand of Jesus to die for us. Love. God is Love!

A prominent Old Testament word describing God's grace is 'chesed'. This word speaks of deliverance from enemies, affliction, or adversity. It also denotes enablement, daily guidance, forgiveness, and preservation. In the New Testament grace means God's love in action towards men who merited the opposite of love. God granted us the grace when we least deserved it.

The choice of God to love us is the fountainhead of the transformation of our lives. The Bible says that, "He chose us in Him (Christ) before the foundation of the world, that we would be holy and blameless before Him" (Ephesians 1:3). There is the sheer wonder of being loved from all eternity and being drawn into the presence of our Father by Christ. We are called to live holy because we were chosen in Christ. The evidence that we have been chosen is to live the holy life pleasing to Him. "The greatest invitation the Lord Jesus ever gave to the sinners to come to Him is rooted in the conviction of the Lord Jesus - It is the divine election, divine revelation, and divine illumination that bring the blind, the lost and the dead sinners to faith in Jesus Christ."

****

The communion and union of the Godhead (Father, Son, and Holy Spirit). The triune reflects God that is relational in nature. Everything that God accomplishes on the universe involves the Father, the Son, and the Holy Spirit. Even at the cross when the Son carried on Himself the sins of the world, and the Father turned His face away from the Son, the Father was with the Son spiritually. The spiritual transaction that was taking place at the cross was within the perfect will of the Father. The Apostle Paul described the event in this way: "God [the Father] was reconciling the world to himself in Christ [the Son], not counting people's sins against them. . . . God [the Father] made him who had no sin [God-the-Son] to be sin for us, so that in him [the Son] we might become the righteousness of God [the Father]." (2 Corinthians 5:19, 21).

You see, the Father is united with the Son even in suffering. In the same manner, we are united with Jesus Christ in His suffering and the glory of His resurrection. Paul wrote, "That I may know him, and the power of his resurrection, and the fellowship of his sufferings, being made conformable unto his death" (Philippians 3:10). Our passion and ambition is to know Him and to know Him more. To know Him is to make Him known by suffering for His name's sake. It is our communion and union with Him.

****

Somebody asked this question: "Did Jesus instruct us not to call any person father even our earthly parents? (Matthew 23:9). Is it wrong for Catholics to refer to their priests as fathers?" Answer: It would be confusing for God to give the fifth commandment in Exodus 20; 12: "Honor your father and your mother, so that you may live long in the land the LORD your God is giving you" and then later restricts us from calling our earthly fathers "fathers." Biological fathers are always fathers by virtue of their parenthood. Jesus said in Matthew 23:9 that, "And do not call anyone on earth 'father,' for you have one Father, and He is in heaven." The context of the scripture is not in reference to our biological fathers. At the beginning (Matthew 23:1-12), Jesus is denouncing the Jewish Scribes and Pharisees (religious leaders) for rejecting Him as their Messiah, in particular for their hypocrisy in elevating themselves above others with titles such as "teacher" and "master." The Jewish teachers affected that title because they supposed that a teacher formed the man, or gave him real life, and they sought, therefore, to be called "father," as if they were the source of truth rather than God. Jesus Christ taught them that the source of all life and truth is God, and they ought not to seek or receive a title which properly belongs to Him. Elsewhere, Jesus said that the greatest in His kingdom is the servant. The most significant problem that mankind faces today is the hustle for superiority. It is passionately engraved on the hearts of many and its pursuits often skip steps which will always demand to be revisited...

****

Jesus said that unless a person is born again, he cannot see the kingdom of God (John 3:5). But some people have a problem with the born again experience or you may call it the second birth since we are born natural men after Adam and reborn spiritual men after Jesus Christ (the Second Adam). The Bible says concerning our bodies that "---it is sown a natural body, it is raised a spiritual body. If there is a natural body, there is also a spiritual body. So also, it is written, "The first man, Adam, BECAME A LIVING SOUL." The last Adam became a LIFE-GIVING SPIRIT" (1 Corinthians 15:44). Check out this biblical truth: "Blessing is the rule of the game in the kingdom of God but God blesses the second birth as opposed to the first birth. Cain was born first but God blessed Abel. Ismail was born first but God blessed Isaac. Esau was born first but God blessed Jacob. Manasseh was born first but God blessed Ephraim. You are born a natural man but the natural man is supposed to serve the spiritual man (our second birth)."

****

Jesus fulfilled the Law in three ways: 1) He lived the righteous life that is not in contradiction to the Law. His righteousness is imputed to us 2) He rightly interpreted the Law for us to implement. 3) He paid the wages of breaking the Law (sin), which is death, on our behalf.

The religious Jews observed the Moral Law, Ceremonial laws, civil laws and diet laws. All of these laws, apart from the Moral Law (Ten Commandments), are of no spiritual significance to us. Orthodox Jews don't speak of "Ten Commandments" and some would consider it misleading to do so. In their reading of the scriptures, there are 613 divine commandments (mitzvot) covering everything from diet, clothing, civil laws, morality and sexual behavior to the treatment of others. What Christians call the Ten Commandments, the Jews called them the ten sayings (Aseret ha-D'varim) of God; and for them, the most vital line of all is the opening one (not a commandment but a statement) which the Christian list sometimes excludes: "I am the Lord your God."

****

In biblical Hebrew, the Ten Commandments are called עשרת הדברים... deka logous, "ten words". The Ten Commandments (Moral Law) are the most important words spoken and written by God. The Moral Law was handed to the Jews on Mount Sinai but it was written on the hearts of all men at creation (Romans 2:12-16). The conscience is either accusing you or excusing you. The conscience of a believer is cleansed by the blood of Jesus (Hebrews 9:14).

****

Jeremiah 31:33 - "This is the covenant I will make with the people of Israel after that time," declares the LORD. "I will put my law in their minds and write it on their hearts. I will be their God, and they will be my people." When laws are written on our hearts our duty becomes our delight. Observing them becomes our pride.

****

"Therefore, the law is indeed holy, and the commandment holy and righteous and good . . . For I delight in the law of God" (Romans 7:12, 22). Also ""Are we, then, abolishing law through faith? MAY IT NEVER BE! Rather, we are establishing the law." (Romans 3:31).

The Moral Law (Ten Commandments) are binding. They work hand in hand with the grace. The Ten Commandments rightly diagnose our infirmities, and the grace heals them. The Ten Commandments define sin, and the grace saves us and teaches us obedience to God's commandments.

****

The fourth commandment is one of the most ignored law. Yet it is as relevant as the rest of the commandments. The word "sabbath" means to rest and to cease from work. "So long as the heavens and the earth endure, the Sabbath will continue as a sign of the Creator's power. And when Eden shall bloom on earth again, God's holy rest day will be honored by all beneath the sun." ~ Ellen G. White, The Desires of Ages, p.283

****

Genesis 39:7-10 – "Now Joseph was well-built and handsome, and after a while his master's wife took notice of Joseph and said, "Come to bed with me!" But he refused. "With me in charge," he told her, "my master does not concern himself with anything in the house; everything he owns he has entrusted to my care. No one is greater in this house than I am. My master has withheld nothing from me except you because you are his wife. How then could I do such a wicked thing and sin against God?" How did Joseph know that it was a sin to sleep with his master's wife when God had not yet given His Law to Moses? The Moral Law (Ten Commandments) were already in force long before they were officially given to Israel at Mount Sinai. Morality is God's image in us, although, it was blunted by sin. That is why even a man in the jungles who has never seen a Bible knows it is wrong to steal, to lie, to sleep with somebody's wife and etc. The Ten Commandments are God's spiritual laws (Romans 7:12, 14). They are just as active as the physical laws of gravity and inertia. Just as breaking physical laws results in physical consequences, breaking spiritual laws results in spiritual consequences.

****

Our priesthood is no longer external but internal. We are the temple of God. The Spirit of Christ sits on the throne of our hearts. We have access to the inner holy of holies whenever we liberate our thoughts from the corrupt nature by acquiring the minds of Christ.

****

We are priestThere is no freedom outside liberty to choose but the liberty to choose is annulled the moment it is exercised outside the will of God.

****

God's love is something every believer can celebrate today and every day. He loved us even when there is nothing worthy to love in us. Everyone is entitled to celebrate God's love and pass it on. Freely we are given and freely we are required to dispense it except in this one area where God is overprotective: The Bible restricts us to give affection to false teachers. "If anyone comes to you and does not bring this teaching, do not receive him into your house, and do not give him a greeting; for the one who gives him a greeting participates in his evil deeds" (2 John 1:10-11). Faith, hope, and love - the greatest of these is love (1 Corinthians 13:13). But the truth is greater than love!

****

Ephesians 2:4-5 - But God is so rich in mercy, and he loved us so much, that even though we were dead because of our sins, he gave us life when he raised Christ from the dead. (It is only by God's grace that you have been saved! God loves us as we are...not as we ought to be because in this earthly life we are never going to be as we ought to be. You are cared for and loved more than you know by the one and only, perfect, supreme God of the universe. "The maker of the stars would rather die for you than live without you. And that is a fact. So if you need to brag, brag about that." ~ Max Lucado

Ecclesiastes 12:13 – "Fear God, and keep his commandments: for this is the whole duty of man." There are two main heresies in Christianity. The first heresy involves the people preaching that we are saved because of our good works. The second heresy involves the people believing that we are saved by the grace, and after we are saved we don't have to obey the commandments of God. Salvation is a one-time event but a process as well. Justification is God declaring a sinner to be as righteous as God. It is absolutely what God does to your soul to save you without your works. We receive the gift of grace by faith (Ephesians 2:8). Simply defined, grace is God's unmerited favor. If you did anything to earn it or deserve it, it is not grace. Sanctification is a process of cleansing your mind (getting rid of sin). Sanctification involves your participation. "Like newborn babies, long for the pure milk of the word, so that by it you may grow in respect to salvation, if you have tasted the kindness of the Lord." (1 Peter 2:2-3). also, "I have been crucified with Christ; and it is no longer I who live, but Christ lives in me; and the life which I now live in the flesh I live by faith in the Son of God, who loved me and gave Himself up for me" (Galatians 2:20). Jesus lived the sinless life of obedience. "For sin is the transgression of the law" (1 John 3:4). The grace of God does not teach us to disobey the commandments of God but to obey. We grow into the grace by loving the things pertaining to God and serving Him with good attitude in spite of the pressure of life.

The Ten commands reveal to us the morality of God. We observe all of them without the fear of the consequences of breaking them because we were redeemed from the curse of breaking them (the Law). Obedient to the commandments of God is, therefore, the evidence (as opposed to the cause) of our salvation. All God's laws (the physical / spiritual laws) are there for our protection. We defy them at our peril. For example, you cannot jump from the roof without expecting to have fractured bones. The law of gravity is there for your own benefit. God's commandments do not restrict us but liberate us.

****

God does not justify the ungodly after he or she becomes godly but He justifies the ungodly so that he or she becomes godly. Grace works in cooperation with your positive response to it. In order for salvation to be yours, you must manifest the fruit of the Spirit (Galatians 5:22) in your life as evidence of your salvation. Grace, when disgraced, cannot bring salvation.

****

We were born dead and we live dead. The grace unmasks the human nature that the heart is deceitful and all our being is tainted by depravity. Faith is human cooperation with the divine intervention. It is an attitude of expectation from God and consistency trusting and patience.

****

The grace is Jesus Christ offering Himself to us. We offer ourselves to Jesus by our faith. The grace demands our response of faith. The Holy Spirit draws us to Jesus. There is no any other agent in between us and Jesus; not even the Church or the Virgin Mary.

****

If keeping the Law could save us then why did Jesus have to suffer and die to save us? Why is He called the Savior? Yes, Jesus showed us how to live by keeping the Law but such beneficiary is the reserve of only those who are saved by the grace. No sincere man can tell me that he keeps the Ten Commandments without ever breaking one of them! That is why Paul said that the Law condemned us. Not because there is something wrong with the Law but because no man can keep it as a whole without a possibility of breaking part of it in his or her lifetime. The Law is like a chain whereby breaking one means breaking all. The Law is good enough to guide us to the Savior. Paul calls the Law the schoolmaster that teaches us and proves us inadequate, directing us to the Savior (Galatians 3:24).

****

Matthew 5:20 – "For I tell you, unless your righteousness surpasses that of the scribes and Pharisees, you will never enter the kingdom of heaven." The Pharisees were a prominent sect of Jews in Christ's time. Their characteristic teachings included: belief in oral as well as written Law; resurrection of the human body; belief in the existence of a spirit world; immortality of the soul; predestination; future rewards and punishments based upon works. Matt 9:11-14; 12:1-8; 16:1-12; 23; Luke 11:37-44; Acts 15:5; 23:6-8. They were known for their strict observance of the laws of God based on their traditional interpretations. The looked for shortcuts to keep the Law because no man could observe it in its wholeness as it is given. Jesus condemned the self-righteousness of the scribes and Pharisees for rigidly adhering to their legalistic traditions in order to make themselves look better to others when in actual fact they were as corrupt as any other human being. They responded by opposing Him and plotting His death (Matt 12:14). They denounced Jesus (Matt 23) because He proclaimed that He is the way the truth and the life; the only means of salvation.

The dictionary definition of self-righteousness is "confidence in one's own righteousness, especially when smugly moralistic and intolerant of the opinions and behavior of others." Biblically speaking, self-righteousness, which is related to legalism, is the idea that we can somehow generate within ourselves a righteousness that will be acceptable to God (Romans 3:10). The Pharisees believed that they could be perfect by keeping the Law in accordance to their own traditions. Certainly, the Law could save but the problem is that no man could observe it as God intended. For this reason, the Law condemned man instead of saving man. Jesus warned His disciples that the saving faith goes beyond the attitude (yardstick) of the Pharisees.

Paul said that the Law is the schoolmaster (Galatians 3:24). The Law is, therefore, a teacher to show us our unholiness and to open our eyes to see the need of the Savior. Schoolmaster or guardian (or tutor) is not just someone who watched over the world until the Messiah came but teaches you and qualifies you to the next level of excellence. Tutors teach and prepare you for a final examination. This is exactly what the word "tutor" in Galatians 3:24 means. Unfortunately, like the Pharisees, the message of God's grace does not sound well in our ears. It is in our sinful nature (ego) to try to do something to merit our salvation. The costly freedom of grace bought to us by the blood of Jesus with no contribution from us is difficult for our prideful hearts to understand or to appreciate. Obedience begins by trusting in what God can do on our behalf (faith), and continues in yielding to His Word. 2 Peter 3:18 tells us to "grow in the grace and knowledge of the Lord Jesus Christ." Growing into grace is growing into obedience.

****

Psalms 18:2 - "Jehovah is my rock, and my fortress, and my deliverer; My God, my rock, in whom I will take refuge; my shield, and the horn of my salvation, and my high tower". "Rock" typifies something about the nature of God. He is solid as a rock. He is unchangeable in nature— immutable. The word "rock" is used about twenty-four times in the book of Psalms with reference to God. During the wilderness wandering, God caused water to flow from a rock. Moses reflected on this miraculous event with Israel on the shores of the Jordan as they prepared to enter Canaan (Deut. 8:15). Later, Moses was literally between a rock and a hard place in the wilderness — and for his own good, God hid him in the "cleft of the rock" and covered him with His hand for protection (Exodus 33:22). With these background experiences, Moses was the first in Scripture to use the word "rock" in a figurative sense in connection with God. "The

Rock, his work is perfect; For all his ways are justice" (Deut. 32:4; cf. vv. 13, 15, 18, 30, 31, 37). Others in Israel would speak of God in the same figurative way. Hannah prayed, "There is none holy as Jehovah; For there is none besides thee, Neither is there any rock like our God" (1 Sam. 2:2). The "rock" symbolism continues in the New Testament with reference to Christ. He is the foundation, the chief-corner stone. He is the rock of offense to those who reject Him, but the spiritual rock for those who obey Him (Eph. 2:20; Rom. 9:33; 1 Pet. 2:8; 1 Cor. 10:4). Jesus (the Rock) protects those who fall on Him, and He crushes those whom He falls on.

****

John 8:7-11 "Let him who is without sin among you be the first to throw a stone at her." And once more he bent down and wrote on the ground. When they heard it, they began to go out one by one, beginning with the older ones, and He was left alone, and the woman, where she was, in the center of the court. Straightening up, Jesus said to her, "Woman, where are they? Did no one condemn you?" She said, "No one, Lord." And Jesus said, "I do not condemn you, either. Go. From now on sin no more." All left because no one is without sin. All have sinned. Jesus alone (who is very God and very man) qualified to condemn this woman because He alone is without sin. But Jesus did not condemn her because He came not to condemn the world but to save it (John 3:17). Jesus instructed the woman not to continue in sin lest she meets Him in future as the Judge as opposed to the Savior. Jesus was calling her to salvation. The blood of Jesus discontinues the curse of sin. Jesus will preside on the White Throne to judge the world (Revelation 20:11-15). This is the ultimate judgment that cannot be escaped unless you are saved. "No one is too bad to be saved, and no one is too good to be saved. Everyone needs a Savior."

****

The Bible is not against religion but it is against religiosity and traditions of men that are in contradiction to the truth. Webster's

Collegiate Dictionary traces the word back to an old Latin word *religio* meaning "taboo, restraint." A deeper study discovers the word comes from the two words re and *ligare*. Re is a prefix meaning "return," and *ligare* means "to bind;" in other words, "return to bondage." Does the word religion appears in the Bible? The only non-deutero-canonical occurrence of the word is in Leviticus 16:31 (as rendered in the DR): "For it is a Sabbath of rest, and you shall afflict your souls by a perpetual religion." Also, James 1:26-27 - If anyone thinks he is religious, and does not bridle his tongue but deceives his heart, this man's religion is vain. Religion that is pure and undefiled before God and the Father is this: to visit orphans and widows in their affliction, and to keep oneself unstained from the world. Do you still want some of that "old-time religion"? "O foolish Galatians! Who has bewitched you! Having begun in the Spirit, are you now being made perfect by the flesh?" (Galatians 3:1).

****

There is a time you were not. If you are in Christ, there is no time you will never be!

****

Everything that comes from God is grace. Everything that comes from the world is corruption. Darkness is the absence of light. Evil is the absence of grace. Hell is the absolute and permanent absence of grace.

****

1 Timothy 2:5-6 - For there is one God and one mediator between God and mankind, the man Christ Jesus, who gave Himself as a ransom for all people.

****

Regardless of what the constitution and judges say, the Moral Law is God's standard of morality to all communities.

****

Proverbs 14:34 – "Righteousness exalted a nation: but sin is a reproach to any people." The word 'reproach' also means dismiss or terminate. The Bible says that "The wicked man has his soul forced from him; he dies in his sins, under the guilt and power of them. But the righteous has hope in his death" (Proverbs 14:32). The spiritual death is annihilation or separation of the soul from God. Without God, the world is sliding fast towards destruction. Often the people who are on the roadside have a better view of the speeding of the bus than those inside the bus. We (believers) who don't belong to the world can see well the terrific speed at which the bus of the world is racing towards destruction. We are whistleblower, called to warn those inside the bus of the world to come off in order to avert the imminent catastrophe; but they won't listen!

****

"When you are on the right side of history, the culture of the world will applaud you, but if you are not they will persecute you. Our primary objective is not to be on the right side of the history but to be on the right side of God."

****

Psalm 55:22 - "Cast your burden on the Lord...." You have been bearing it all on your weak shoulders, place them on the mighty shoulders of Jesus. Exchange your yoke with His yoke. Jesus said that "Take my yoke upon you and learn from me, for I am gentle and humble in heart, and you will find rest for your souls" (Matthew 11:29). We are unburdened by exchanging our lives with His life. His tender mercies and love continually yearn toward you. Your agonizing is the sensitive antennae by which He listens carefully and equips you with His Spirit for a breakthrough. A wicked looks inside himself and finds self but a Christian looks inside himself and finds the Holy Spirit. This is the comfort for the tried and afflicted soul; vexed with the tempest from within, looking for calm without!

****

Matthew 10:30 - "But the very hairs of your head are all numbered." God knows the hair that grows and that falls from your head. Imagine that He knows even the number of your hairs. He plants the hair on your head. He watches it grow. He notices when it falls off your head (die), and He attends its funeral. That is how close He watches over you. This is a figure of speech meaning that God knows the tiniest bits of your life. It is comforting to learn that God knows us more than we know ourselves. We are under severe divine surveillance. Today, electronic surveillance is increasingly used to keep tabs on law breakers. Surveillance of humans by humans is a rather new tool, the product of technology. But the practice is not new. Since creation, God has been the Eye-In-The-Sky from the beginning and without electronics! The Bible says that "From heaven the LORD looks down and sees all mankind; from his dwelling place he watches all who live on earth" (Psalm 33:13, 14). As for the believers, the divine surveillance is a blessing involving the divine protection.

****

Psalm 139:2 – "You know when I sit down and when I get up. You know my thoughts before I think them." The words of our mouth begin as the thoughts of our minds. It is not easy to know the unspoken thoughts of others. One writer said that you have to know someone a thousand days before you can glimpse his or her soul. There is an adage saying that "He who knows others is wise; he who knows himself is enlightened." The reality is that the heart of another is a dark forest always, to which we have limited access, no matter how close they have been to us, unless they open up to us. Only God and Him alone can know the thoughts and intents of the hearts of all men. Paul said that "For in him we live and move and have our being" (Acts 17:28).

****

God can reverse the irreversible. If He wants He can stop time like it happened in Joshua 12: 10 -14. He commanded the sun to stand still and don't set, and the sun stood still. The past, present and future coincide in Him (Isaiah 8: 7-8). Ezekiel 37:1-10 is a classical example of the Almighty God reversing the irreversible. "The hand of the LORD was upon me, and carried me out in the spirit of the LORD, and set me down in the midst of the valley, which was full of bones, of bones. And caused me to pass by them round about: and, behold, there were very many in the open valley; and, lo, they were very dry. And he said unto me, Son of man, can these bones live? And I answered, O Lord GOD, thou knowest. Again he said unto me, Prophesy upon these bones, and say unto them, O ye dry bones, hear the word of the LORD. Thus saith the Lord GOD unto these bones; Behold, I will cause breath to enter into you, and ye shall live: And I will lay sinews upon you, and will bring up flesh upon you, and cover you with skin, and put breath in you, and ye shall live; and ye shall know that I am the LORD." Receiving Jesus Christ is the only way to reverse the irreversible flow of the history of your corrupt nature. God is not asking you to do something for Him but He is asking you to allow Him to do something for you. All you have to do is to receive what He has done by repenting. "Today, if you hear his voice, do not harden your hearts as you did in the rebellion" (Hebrews 3:15). You have a divine appointment. Allow Jesus to reverse the irreversible, even your eternal destiny.

****

Joseph's brothers said "Here comes this dreamer! Now then, come and let us kill him" (Genesis 37:19-20). In a natural man, jealous and envy last longer than the happiness of those we envy, and will only end after destroying that what we envy. "In jealousy, there is more self-love than love." A virtuous person refrains from jealous and envy because his or her primary focus is to serve God by serving others. They are willful servants of Christ willing to bow down even serving those who hate them.

****

Genesis 22:2 – "Then God said, "Take your son, your only son, whom you love--Isaac--and go to the region of Moriah. Sacrifice him there as a burnt offering on a mountain I will show you." God tests our obedience by asking us to give up the very things we love most. The reason is because our will is closely attached to those things we love. Ironically, something you love more than God interferes with God's love for you. I mean that thing you are not willing to let go. The Bible instructs us to surrender everything including our very being to Christ. Surrender it to God then watch and see how life suddenly starts working for you rather than against you. The circumstances and the world will change when we change. The calling to change is a calling to repenting.

****

Hebrews 4:16 - "Let us therefore come boldly unto the throne of grace, that we may obtain mercy, and find grace to help in time of need." This is an invitation to come before the throne of God whenever there is a need. It is also a one-time invitation to those that are not saved to come boldly before the throne of grace without guilt. However, we are called to come and stay or settle there permanently. There is no time we can live without the presence of God. The grace is compared to oxygen, we cannot live a moment without it.

****

Romans 8:31-39 – "In Christ we are more than conquerors." The difference between conqueror and more than conqueror is that 'a conqueror' knows his victory only after the war is over but the 'more than conqueror' goes to war with victory already on his belt. Jesus Christ conquered on our behalf. By faith, at the snap of our fingers, we can now plunder the superabundant loot and pillage from our adversary, and repossess what was stolen from us.

****

John 11:21 – "Then said Martha unto Jesus, Lord, if you had been here, my brother had not died." During the earthly ministry of Jesus, He was in one place at one time. Jesus said that "Nevertheless I tell you the truth; It is expedient for you that I go away: for if I go not away, the Comforter will not come unto you; but if I depart, I will send him unto you" (John 16:7). The reason is because His Spirit (Holy Spirit) is omnipresent. We have no justified reason to complain that, "Lord, if you had been here" because He is everywhere. He indwells the believers wherever they are. He is invisible but visibly seen in us. We can now say that "See me, see Jesus" in the same way Jesus said, "You see me, you see the Father" (John 14:9).

****

1 Corinthians 1: 20 - 26 – "Brothers and sisters, think of what you were when you were called. Not many of you were wise by human standards; not many were influential; not many were of noble birth." The cream of the wisdom of man is considered to be foolishness when compared to the wisdom of God. The peak of the human wisdom is the base of the divine wisdom. God strategically excluded those who trust in their natural wisdom from salvation. Not because God does not respect wisdom. It is because by their wisdom, strength and nobility they saw the preaching of the cross as foolishness. God chose to use the despised and foolish people to speak wisdom to the wise. I am humbled to be one of the foolish people whom God changed from good for nothing to good for something. The sweetest words I expect to hear from God are: "Well done faithful servant" as opposed to "Well done great man of God."

****

James 4:6 - "God opposes the proud but shows favor to the humble." The Greek word "opposes" is to resists or to range in battle against. God is at war with the proud because the proud heart has no room for the grace. Pride views things from human prospective (self) as opposed from the divine prospective. The proud are so fleeting that they do not notice how they are deprived of true peace, and substituted it with sorrow, longing, despondency, and no comfort whatsoever. We are destroyed by the temporary comfort that we embrace with both hands. God never ceases to remind us that He is God, and we are not. The way up is the way down. The bearing of the cross is the wearing of the crown!

****

2 Samuel 23:5 - "For he has made with me an everlasting covenant." This is not an ordinary king but King of the kings of the earth, El -Shaddai, the Lord All-sufficient, the Jehovah of ages, the everlasting Elohim-" He has made with me an everlasting covenant to relate to Him. "For he who sanctifies and those who are sanctified all have one source. That is why he is not ashamed to call them brothers" (Hebrews 2:11).

****

Psalm 130:3 – "If you, LORD, kept a record of sins, Lord, who could stand?" If God kept records of my sins there would have been volumes of books. We know that God has ability to keep records of all people who ever lived on the universe. Today we have the technology whereby a computer has one or more disk drives—devices that store a vast amount of information on Hard disks. They have powerful magnetic memories called hard drives, which can remember things whether the power is on or off. Also, there are special chips called flash memories to store information permanently. The technology we have is nothing compared to God. But He keeps no record of the sins of the redeemed. The only condemnation we will ever know when we go to heaven is the condemnation of Jesus on our behalf.

****

Genuine peace is not the absence of war but the presence of Jesus Christ. Peace is neither a chance nor an accident; it is an act of will involving wise choices. "To say you have no choice is to relieve yourself of responsibility." We can choose our thoughts, our attitudes and our emotions in the same manner we choose friends. We are what we choose to be, so we must be careful about what we choose to be. The bad news is that we have no choices over the consequences of our choices.

Political Liberty / Political Statements:

Today, Friday June/ 12th/ 2015, we are celebrating the 240th birthday for the USA army. This being the most professional army in the world, I am privileged to add the following monograph on a stone tablet in recognition of our armed forces: "As the character of conflict in the 21st century evolves, the Army's strength will continue to rest on our values, our ethos, and our people. Our Soldiers and leaders must remain true to these values as they operate in increasingly complex environments where moral-ethical failures can have strategic implications. Most of our Soldiers do the right thing – and do it well – time and again under intense pressure. But we must stay vigilant in upholding our high professional standards". Happy Birthday!

****

4th July is America's Independence Day. Soon we shall go wild with fireworks, they will plunge into the sky and shatter the darkness. Colored lights representing our nation flag will blink on and off, racing across and lighting the sky, accompanied with thunderous explosions in defiance against colonial oppression and occupation. I suggest that this year's fireworks be in commemoration of the rebirth of the American dream. Let this day not be just a birthday to this great nation but a rebirth of consciousness to the virtues that make us a great country. Let it not be a celebration of the past but a realization of a new start, a fresh beginning, and a time to pursue new endeavors with ambitions glorifying to God. Let us resolve to move forward with confidence and courage in the liberty that was purchased by the blood of the fallen heroes. As Benjamin Franklin said that, "They who can give up essential liberty to obtain a little temporary safety deserve neither liberty nor safety." Let us be generous with the freedom we are celebrating by dispensing it evenly to all. As Abraham Lincoln insinuated, "Those who deny freedom to others deserve it not for themselves." "Life, Liberty and the pursuit of Happiness" is a well-known phrase in the United States Declaration of Independence. We have the right to resist the enemies of peace even when they pose as leaders. The US Declaration of Independence states that "when a long train of abuses and usurpations, pursuing invariably the same Object evinces a design to reduce them under absolute Despotism, it is their right, it is their duty, to throw off such Government" (emphasis added). "The history of liberty is a history of resistance." Happy Birthday America.

****

Today marks 239 years of America's independence. The 1620 establishment of Plymouth Bay Colony in Massachusetts by the religious immigrants known as the Pilgrims may be regarded as the beginning of large-scale migration from Europe to the territory that would eventually become the United States. They came to America in search of a country that is ruled by God (theocracy). America therefore is not just a name but an idea of freedom, liberty and pursuit of virtues. As Chuck Colson said that, "The doctrine of creation tells us the state is ordained by God; it is not a necessary evil but a good part of God's creation. Therefore, participation in political life is a moral obligation." Yes, Pastors should avoid getting involved in partisan politics but they should actively educate the masses regarding the good governance that embraces our Judeo-Christian values. The embrace of Judeo-Christian morality is an indispensable component of American life and conservative ideology. We have a belief in a transcendent order, or body of natural law, which rules society as well as conscience. "We recognize that political problems, at bottom, are religious and moral problems. Consequently, we do not reject moral certainties; we accommodate them." Although our first citizenship is in heaven, we are called to be the "best of citizens" of our earthly countries as well.

****

What is the difference between Liberals and Conservatives? Liberals stand for big government that can get involved in the lives of the people. Liberalism theoretically advocate the freedom of the people, individual rights and liberties. But practically they minimize the people's liberty. They mortgage the freedom of the people by making them depend on government handouts. Ironically, more free stuff means less freedom. The conservatives stand for small government and less government's involvement in the people's lives. The conservatives promote capitalism, whereby people are given opportunity to earn income and support themselves rather than depending on government handouts. Conservatism as a political and social philosophy promotes retaining traditional social institutions in the context of the culture and civilization.

****

"The Church is not the servant of the state, the Church is not the master of the state, the Church is the conscience of the state" ~ A Rogers

****

God assigns to the governments the duty of regulating evil but not to eliminate it. The government has the power to decree the values but the Church has the power to prescribe what the values should be. The Church has no power to impose but to propose her values. The Church must sound an alarm whenever the government oversteps to sanction immorality. In this case, the Church is the conscience of the government. God uses the Church rather than the government to revive the nation. Therefore, revivals do not begin in the White House but in the Church house and in your house (home).

****

He / She who plants the seed of democracy... plants the seed of freedom and justice ~ Ocholo Ottunu

****

Socialism works until you run out of all people's money. Secularism works until you run out of other people's faith.

****

"The easiest way to kill patriotism and nationalism is to foster impunity and hypocrisy for segments of society. And in Uganda we pretty well know who does what!"

****

Christians are called to turn the other cheek. But the government is called to protect its citizens even by means of wrath.

****

When the power of love overcomes the love of power…. The world will know peace.

****

Freedom is not free, must be demanded by oppressed.

****

Titles and accolades do not deliver anyone from the kingdom of darkness, God through a relationship with you does.

****

Billy Gram is one of the most respected evangelist of our century. Billy Graham had a rough beginning. He was conceived after his mother was raped. This means that unwanted pregnancy does not mean unwanted baby. In spite of the circumstances, he had the stamina to sprint to the finishing line with integrity. At the peak of his fame and popularity, Billy Graham was interviewed on CNN, if he considered running for the highest office in the country in next presidential race. Billy Graham gracefully answered that, "I consider it a demotion for me to abandon the highest calling by Christ in his kingdom, and serve in the highest office of this kingdom as president of USA". Child of God, it is not worthy to cut your conscience to fit this world's fashions.

****

Somebody asked "Are all leaders (bad/good) given to us by God?" True, no one can become a leader without God allowing them to be. However, the will of God is divided into three main categories. There is His precept or revealed will in Scriptures. Everything we consider to be of God must not contradict the will of God declared in the Scriptures. The perfect will of God must line up with the Scriptures. There is God's sovereign will revealed to people individually. Then there is the permissive will of God. At times God gives us the desires of our hearts even when they are not in His perfect will. For example God's perfect will is to save all; while it is clear that God takes no pleasure in the death of the wicked, it is also clear that He wills or decrees their death eternally. The Bible says that when the wickedness of Israel mounted, God gave them Saul the wicked king whom they deserved: "In those days there was no king in Israel: every man did that which was right in his eyes" (Judges 21). God was the ultimate King of Israel but it was the people's choice wanting an earthly king, and God honored their will. Therefore, when a person is elected in a political position it does not necessarily mean that it is the perfect will of God. Remember that there are by far more unbelievers in political leadership than believers.

****

In politics, it matters when somebody of significance status endorses a political candidate. Unlike politics, Jesus does not require any person's endorsement in order to qualify to be who He is. Therefore, your believing or not believing does not make a difference regarding who He is. Your believing is just good enough to earn you a place at His right hand, and you unbelief simply means separated from God forever.

****

Politicians are calling for reforms as means of improving the laws and constitutions in accordance with expectations of the public. God is calling for transformation as a means of restoration to the lost world, and the renewing of minds to those who are already restored. "Do not be conformed to this world, but be transformed by the renewing of your mind" (Romans 12:2). We must note that this is a command, not a suggestion. So, the objective is to be transformed, that is, have our lives changed further into the image of Jesus. It is a one-time transformation and a process of conversion. Conversely, the world pressures us to be conformed to its pattern, but we are called to be transformed. Politicians call for sweeping reforms but God transforms one soul at a time in order to change the world. The term 'conformed' is to be forced into a mold and the term, transformed, is a change from the inside to outside. The change of the heart is the true change that has impact on the character. It is change that flows from what is deposited inside of us, that is, the Spirit of God. The Spirit transforms us through the Word. Jesus said that "The words that I speak unto you, they are spirit" (John 6:63).

****

Politicians say that democracy is choosing between two evils but Christianity says that morality is choosing neither. Politicians agitate for reforms, Christians agitate for transformation. God's plan to change the world is in the Church. Revivals do not begin in the White House; revival begins in the Church house and in your house.

****

Politicians have no permanent friends, and no permanent foes, only selfish permanent interests. "No permanent enemies" means you'll always have the room to critique policy ideas and economic proposals that injure our interests." The nightmare is when the shiny things that you used to believe in begin to look rusty in your eyes!

****

In politics, there is no black and white. "There is, in philosophy, something called obscurantism, a phenomenon where ideas are deliberately obscured so that what is false appears to be true and vice versa."

****

To stand upright is to stand right up. It is to stand firm for the right cause. Unfortunately, most of the politicians today are allergic to the truth. No wonder many embrace the hoax of Global Warming. Promising to fix the climate is like promising to build a bridge where there is no water!

****

Rulers are like hills; when darkness falls, they all speak alike ~ Ugandan Proverb

****

Uganda's politics is a test of faith to all religious leaders. Fairness is not a concept. It's not something we should be striving for. It's a necessity because it is synonyms to justice. Religious leaders should fight for truth and justice irrespective of their political affiliation. Silence may be a tactical maneuver but staying silent forever is approving the wrong. Whenever we make a political statement, it must be in the best interest of our faith and the Lord whom we represent. The same God that commanded us not to lie, also, commanded us not to give false testimony against the neighbor (Exodus 20:16). A lie cannot be sugar-coated; at the end of the day, a beam of light will shine through the fog of lies eventually denting our characters. I believe that political leaders are sent by God for a season of time but they should faithfully embrace the democratic systems of the nations without fear and bias to prove that they are sent.

****

"The biggest weakness in Uganda is lack of principles and truth by people and trying to change history for selfish gains" ~ Kabaka Ronald Mutebi.

****

The army and police have different responsibilities. The army fights the enemies of the state, and the police serves and protects people.... But when the army and police become one, then the enemies of the state tend to become the people.

****

"In Uganda there are no bandits, but we are made bandits because we are denied our rights to be Ugandans" ~ Miria Matembe

****

Paul Kagame: "I don't want to be president for life". Kabindi responded to him: "Except Amin who called himself the life president (he probably still is) no autocrat or dictator ever says I want to be the life president. Why even waste time saying it?"

****

The people that enjoy the game best are those outside the pitch - on the sidelines; it is not different even in politics.

****

"Politics can be relatively fair in the breathing spaces of history; at its critical turning points there is no other rule possible than the old one, that the end justifies the means" ~ Artur Koestler

****

"Africa is a martyr of exploitation by the developed world who take its resources to enrich themselves" ~ Pope Francis

****

"America has no permanent friends or enemies, only interests". — Henry Kissinger.

****

Liberalism is the worst mental disorder in the history of Human Beings. Absolutely insane!

****

Hillary is the worst liar I think I have ever seen. She lied about laying ~ Breitbart

****

It is better for ten guilty people to go free than one innocent person to be wrongly convicted.

****

The civilization of a country consists in the quality of life that is lived there, and this quality shows plainest in the things that people choose to talk about when they talk together, and in the way they choose to talk about them.' ~ Albert J. Nock

****

Somebody asked that "Can a racist be a born again believer?" The racists believe that their races are inherently superior (physically, intellectually, or culturally) to others and, therefore, they have a right to dominate them. A person cannot claim to be a Christian and at the same time be a racist. Racism is a sect that wholly embraces prejudice. It is an attitude inclining to the fallen nature of humanity. A born again Christian is not identified by his past sinful lifestyle because he or she is a new creature with a new identity in Jesus Christ (2 Corinthians 5:17). Racism is not a skin problem, it is a sin problem. Yes, Christians can sin because they still have struggles with the old nature (flesh) and the corrupt world but they do not take pride in their sins. When they sin it is considered to be trespassing. In such a situation, they cry out to God in repentance, and grace is granted. The born again Christians see sin as God sees it - Sin is an abomination to God. Therefore, if somebody openly professes to be a racist, he or she is most probably not a Christian.

****

"In a world where technology is changing rapidly, development will bypass those who do not go to school----challenges such as HIV/AIDS prevalence, environment degradation, and others can be curbed through education and leads to a country's development." ~ Kabaka Mutebi

****

President Museveni wondered concerning death: 'if it is God who calls us, why does he tend to call Africans earlier?' Maybe God is not entirely responsible for this.

****

One of the greatest hindrances that have corroded the moral fiber of the leadership in Africa is the element of opportunism: It is the politics of the stomach that has characterized this continent since time immemorial!

****

In 1973, Kibedi fled Amin's brutality and went into exile in the United Kingdom. He returned to Uganda after NRM captured power. He lamented that "During Amin's regime, no one was safe. Not even his wives" ~ W. Kibedi

****

Somebody posted that, 'In 1975, sometime after the O.A.U conference in Kampala, I visited Rock Hotel in Tororo. Inside one of the public toilets, someone had scribbled the definition of O.A.U. on the wall: "Omusiru Afuga Uganda."'

****

Tanzania's Julius Nyerere did not come to the O.A.U conference in Kampala because he had issues with Amin. I recall him saying concerning Idi Amin that: "The problem with that brother of mine is that he thinks he has a direct telephone line to God."

****

Idi Amin did not do our economy a favor by expelling the Asians. He just switched the economy from the hands of the Asian colonialists to the hands of the Black colonialists of the Sudanese origin (Nubians/Anyanya). History has proven that African colonialists are worse than Asian and white colonialists.

****

Our seizure of power was not a "mere change of guards" but a "fundamental change". Under the NRM, human rights abuses, sectarianism, and mass poverty will come to an end ~ YKM Museveni

****

According to Prof. Luoga, successive governments after Idi Amin have grappled without success to bring under reign the hyperinflation that collapsed the Ugandan economy but it is Museveni's commitment and strong leadership that has salvaged the Uganda economy and today it is ready for integration within the East African Community.

"It cannot be denied that your excellence stands as a stabilizer of the nation and a champion of change," said Prof. Florens Luoga when President Museveni was awarded a certificate of Doctor of Literature Honoris Causa and decorated by Prof. Rwekaza Mukandala the University Vice Chancellor.

****

"Term limits are a very necessary check to the abuse of power and personalization of the state."

****

Professor Venansius Baryamureeba, presidential aspirant has said that term limit is one way of changing leadership at top in many African countries Uganda inclusive where it is very hard for incumbents to lose elections.

****

Supporters of no term limit: "Some scholars have actually argued that if the public wishes to re-elect their leader, it is undemocratic to prevent them from doing so no matter how long this leader has already served." They say that term limits result in a lack of experienced politicians since with experience, comes greater skill.

****

"I am not a prophet but I had a feeling long time before lifting term limits that M7 was not sincere about ceding power to anyone other than himself" ~ Ongunye

****

"Mbabazi had turned himself into a small god in the cabinet. Everyone feared him. He would walk as if the whole country belonged to him. All along we didn't know that he was a baby being supported by his mother. Now that the mother has dumped him, he cannot crawl," the minister remarked.

****

Jacqueline Mbabazi is beautiful! It could be the smile that illuminates her face, her fair skin or the full head of hair; something about her conjures images of a beautiful little girl twirling in her princess frock. Whatever it is, it makes you realize that none of the photos of her you have seen do her justice because they don't portray any of the warmth, or the relaxed and welcoming nature she gives off when you meet her. From the flamboyant elegant jackets she usually dons, to the dainty but lady-like energy with which she carries herself, there is little about her that tells of her 60 years.

****

"We paid a lot of sacrifice to get where we are now. I want you to know in your hearts that where you are standing is sacred ground for freedom fighters------ I assure you no one will destabilize Uganda. Anyone who tries to bring indiscipline here, we shall suppress him or her" ~ President Y. K. Museveni

****

Rev. Fr. Gaetano said that, any regime that tries to perpetuate itself in power; it has, with time, to lose its popularity. And as a result, it has to deploy undemocratic and unethical measures as some have already surfaced, to keep and sustain itself in power. These measures include corruption, patronage, nepotism, sectarianism, cronyism, intrigue, cliques (divide and rule), militarism, balkanization of the country into small and tribal districts for political gain, intimidation, arrogance, impunity, lies, etc.

****

"Uganda was one of the 'blessed' countries that were liberated by the rebels then, led by Gen Yoweri Museveni……. the 'messiah', who has consistently justified his option to fight the old regimes as opposed to engaging them politically has not behaved differently" - Sadam Gayila (The Observer, 25th May 2015).

****

Mbabazi cautioned the committee that he will continue embodying true purpose and identity of the party. He said that he is ashamed because the continuous use of state machinery in this competition and the use of Police for political objectives threaten to turn Uganda into a Police State. He said that he is ashamed of these recent actions because they confirm a long-held suspicion that we have deviated from our original vision, mission, character, aims, and objectives. "I will remain steadfast to our principles even if I find I stand alone. I will stay the course. Those who wish to veer off are free to do so but I will not be going with them".

****

"But what is making Museveni drunk? He is drunk on power. Excess unbridled power. The power is unbridled because the people who the constitution says are the sovereign power have been totally disconnected from all the levers of power" - Norbert Mao

****

Polls are like perfume - nice to smell but dangerous to swallow. Quit worrying about them - Samuel Nngira

****

If it is true that, "Politics is a dirty game", then Ugandan politics is a classic epitome of politics - Dick Kasolo

****

The only thing necessary for the triumph of evil is for good men to do nothing - Edmund Burke

****

"They can even shoot me if they want but they can't shoot the problem, the problem of 84% of youth languishing in unemployment, poverty, oppression etc." ~ Dr. Kizza Besigye

****

In Africa, a major split in a ruling party always results in political instability for the country and, often, a military coup or civil war ......
When the African and Indian elephants (no pun intended) start to fight, the grass that is Uganda is going to see what that means and it will be painful indeed. (Sunday Monitor).

****

South Sudan is too dependent on other systems some that are dependent on West too in many ways. "The notion that Kiir would resist for long was farfetched. Machar read between the lines and figured out pretty quickly the prudent thing to do while Kiir was still thinking of shooting his way out of the mess!"

****

Major General Muntu, who is also former Army commander in trying to justify his statement, said taking up arms is a "legitimate form of struggle". In any case, some people could have been frustrated by the futility of peaceful means to restore the rule of law and to make governments accountable to them. Maj Gen Muntu and his predecessor Dr. Kizza Besigye, however, said they would never participate in a military struggle. Military means would nurture a mind of entitlement, with some of the 'liberators' acting with impunity. Dr. Besigye added that "It is very difficult to deliver the objective of a democratic transition through the use of a violent struggle." (Daily Monitor May 11 2015).

****

"Dictators are not born; they are made. I pray that you don't reach a level of being autocratic and monocratic because once you qualify to it, you will create many enemies, both real and imaginary" ~ Rev. Fr. Gaetano

****

"To the strugglists, all gallant strugglists should remember that you don't kiss tyranny out of power, you kick out, you don't smile tyranny away, you smoke it out, you don't caress tyranny away, you crash it, you don't convince it away, you compel it out" ~ Sam Mugumya

****

"My position is very clear, I have thought about it. The time for my political journey to end has come now. God the Almighty created the world and heaven in six days, he rested on the seventh day; this is my seventh day" ~ Mukula

****

North Korean leader Kim Jong-Un has had his defense minister executed with anti-aircraft fire for insubordination and dozing off during formal military rallies. South Korean intelligence said Wednesday. "Hyon was seen as one of the three closest military officials to Kim Jong-Un," Yang told AFP. Please, North Koreans wake and get rid of mad men masquerading as leaders there is no room for nonsense and parochialism in this new world order. How can the world look the other side while the Irish potato shaped man reins over this great country and leads it to obliteration. "I think Koreans are living in real hell; like you freed yourselves from imperialism please do not stop free yourselves from state inspired terrorism" (Daniel).

****

Aha! Africa! When will those in power start to appreciate that some people have opinions that are different from theirs and that these people are perfectly entitled to those opinions under the freedom of rights? As long as African rulers fail to appreciate this, Africa will always remain backward because this is the root cause of state violence against defenseless citizens. Besigye, Lukwago and others of their ilk are Ugandans; they are entitled to present their agenda to the people of Uganda and let the people decide. This is what modern, civilized societies do; in such societies, one is not arrested for speaking his opinion or even abusing the president.

****

An insult on a tribe or a race is an insult to God who created the tribes and races; it's like telling Him He didn't know what He was doing when He created a particular tribe or race.

****

Tribalism is a failure of imagination ~ President Obama

****

"Racism will never end as long as white cars are still using black tires. Racism will never end if people still use black to symbolize bad luck and white for peace. Racism will never end if people still wear white clothes to weddings and black clothes to funerals. Racism will never end as long as those who don't pay their bills are blacklisted not white-listed." ~ Robert Mugabe

****

"There is no easy walk to freedom anywhere, and many of us will have to pass through the valley of the shadow of death again and again before we reach the mountaintop of our desires" ~ Nelson Mandela!

****

Everything has a price. Privileges come with costs: even the cost of sacrificing your comfort. Liberty precedes and would outlast our individual comforts. Without freedom humanity is doomed, degraded and depraved.

****

In his first address by a sitting US president to the African Union in the Ethiopian capital Addis Ababa, President Obama said Africa could not progress if its leaders refused to step aside when their terms ended. "I don't understand why people want to stay in power for so long especially when they have a lot of money. If a leader says he is the only one who can hold the country together, then that leader has failed to build their nation".

****

By definition, the dictator is responsible to no one, no organization, to no social institution. "You can't reform a dictatorship. You dismantle it; that is what some of us are focusing on" ~ General David Sejusa

****

In NRM there is only one teacher, only one lesson and one song. All easy to learn and rehearse. Failure to learn is indiscipline which can attract heavy punishment. (Weekly Observer).

****

"Are you sure Mbabazi didn't dig a hole there and put a carpet on top." My ex-late-father- in-law talked about life in the Ukraine. Potholes were fixed by putting branches over them. Covering up a problem seems to be a universal solution that solves nothing ~ Betty Long Cap

****

Any learned cadre of political science will tell you that all politicians the world over are pathological liars, liars who not only tamper with truth but also with canons of truth. Mbabazi therefore is no exception.

****

"Don't provoke me and take my patience for granted for I am like a glittering snake but full of venom inside" ~ A. Mbabazi

****

In more modern versions of dictatorship, the absolute ruler has to fabricate an elaborate cult of the personality to prove that he is more intelligent, more potent and generally superior to any other human being. Idi Amin fancied himself not only a physical giant but also as an intellectual giant. Besides, he boasted of a direct line to Allah his god.

****

When politicians are invited to the weddings they have a reputation of using the occasion to shine in the limelight. They end up stealing the people's focus from the brides to themselves. One critic made the following remarks: "The focus of the wedding should be on the bride and the bridegroom, not political juggernauts. You robbed this woman of her special day!!! Shame upon you!! Politics has its confines".

****

Gadaffi did not fall because of rivalry with another insider in his rule. The Libyan Youths did to him the damage. Unlike the Libyan Youth, the Ugandan Youths of today are made of softer hardware and their software are easily corruptible. They have no ideals to strive for.

****

Martin Luther King sacrificed his comfort for the sake of others. Generosity is a virtue. Our giving is a reflexive response to the grace of God in our lives. It doesn't come out of our altruism or philanthropy—it comes out of the transforming work of Christ in us. This grace is the action; our giving is the reaction. We give because He first gave to us. We love because He first loved us. When we are transformed God's measure of love becomes our measure of love. The greatest passage on giving in all Scripture ends not with "Congratulations for your generosity," but "Thanks be to God for his indescribable gift!" (2 Corinthians 9:15). The word "gift" is charisma: The root word (charis) means "grace" a gift of grace, a free gift. Freely we received, freely we give.

****

"I have just concluded – since President Obama endorses the same-sex marriage, advocates homosexual people and enjoys an attractive countenance – thus if it becomes necessary, I shall travel to Washington, DC, get down on my knee and ask his hand" ~ President Robert Mugabe

****

Response to Obama's visit to Kenya: "It is important for us as Kenyans to know that the US is not God, and thus we cannot follow them blindly," Kariuki said. Kenyan Lawmaker Charles Njagagua is persuading legislators to kick President Obama out of the parliament building the next time he mentions gay rights. Justin Muturi, speaker of Kenya's National Assembly has also said that the government would "sanction any advances perceived to encroach on our social fabric."

****

Obama's pledge to contribute to the economic recovery of Africa is applauded. We must not ignore the fact that it is the economic engine of the slave trade that helped to fuel America's prosperity.

The slave trade is not merely a footnote or a side story in the history of American slavery but was central to its modernization and continuation. Africa is naturally rich with human recourses and natural recourses. The secularists who believe that this universe is millions of years old say that Africa provides a comprehensive and contagious timeline of human development going back at least 7 million years. Africa, which developed the world's oldest human civilization, gave humanity the use of fire a million and a half to two million years ago. It is the home of the first tools, astronomy, jewelry, fishing, mathematics, crops, art, use of pigments, cutting and other pointed instruments and animal domestication. In short Africa gave the world human civilization. More important than tool making in human evolution is the mastery of fire.

Nearly 2 million years ago early East Africans had mastered the use of fire. This was a revolutionary step in the development of humanity. Today, we are no longer the Dark Continent but we have lost our ancient stamina and patriotism. While the developed countries are building space shuttles, disgusting as it may sound, we are busy figuring out if it is ok to eat gorillas! We are spoiled kids obsessed with handouts from developed countries instead of tapping into developing the amazing natural resources at our finger tips to enhance our industrial production. Africa has an amazing potential as the world's fastest growing youth population. Unemployment is really untapped potential and untapped intellect. We should blame ourselves for our woes.

What is it that is stopping us from developing? Dr. Ayittey writes devastatingly on the horrors of black neo-colonialism, arguing that it is naive for commentators to blame Africa's misery on external factors: African leaders have betrayed both the just aspirations of their countrymen and Africa's indigenous political systems, which in no way endorse tyranny. He argues that a second liberation struggle is beginning throughout the continent - one that will sweep away the kleptocracy and rediscover the African traditions that have endured throughout the horrors of both white colonialism and black neo-colonialism. So what we truly need to drive Africa forward is people to understand that there is no Negro Africans, no Bantu Africans, no Hamite Africans and no Bushman African but simply our Africa.

****

Donald Trump told a raucous New Hampshire crowd Friday that he'd make a smarter president than any of his competitors when it comes to the economy, the military and everything else. Given the fact, this guy is smart because it takes wisdom to become rich and to stay rich. One of the Great Rules of Economics According to John Green If you are rich, you have to be an idiot not to stay rich. And if you are poor, you have to be really smart to get rich. "The biggest challenge after success is shutting up about it."

****

John Oliver said concerning Donald Trump: "He's an open book, and that book doesn't have that many interesting words in it."

****

"It is easy to stand with the crowd; it takes courage to stand alone!
~ Donald Trump

****

Election fever is on. Christians are venting their frustration by strictly vetting and scrutinizing the morality of the desired candidate fit to occupy the highest office. As much as it is right, we must not hold our presidential candidates to a much higher standard as if we are electing a pastor of the Church. Let us acknowledge that the candidates are real people with flaws in the background. Morality is the main issue but it is not the only factor. We should put into consideration other factors like experience, charisma, economic robustness and capability to deliver what they promise.

****

We Caucasian Americans know few sub-Saharan, Black Africans welcome us with open arms, and those who do have their own hidden agenda, and can be even scarier than those who shun us. Months ago, a commentator suggested we Caucasian Americans speak through our narrow noses. That left me stunned and hurt that I would be regarded as a freak of nature. ~ Betty Long Cap

****

During his Talking Points Memo last night, Fox News commentator Bill O'Reilly offered an alternative suggestion on why violence seems to be on the rise in America – a lack of God in people's lives. "There is something else going on, a decline in spiritual belief coincides with a rise in violent crime. If you do not believe in anything, anything goes" ~ O'Reilly

****

One of the questions often directed to the aspiring presidential candidates is concerning raising the minimum wages. I am not an economist but I think raising the minimum wages is essentially the role of the marketing institution as opposed to the government. Most people that earn minimum wages are those unskilled workers who are just starting to work without required experiences. As soon as they acquire experience, they move on in search of green pastures. The jobs paying minimum wages are therefore a starting point or the first step for people to explore and catch the winds of adventures and discoveries in their sails. We should not forget that when the government raises minimum wages for unskilled workers there is a problem of taxes and prices going up. This is just my opinion.

****

"A revolution is not a dinner party, nor a painting, nor a piece of needlework. It cannot be so refined, so leisurely and gentle, so moderate, kind, restrained, polite and magnanimous. A revolution is an insurrection, an act of violence in which one system overthrows another" ~ Mao Tse Tung, February 1927.

****

Civilizations are tested with crises just as individuals are tried with adversity. Great civilizations measure up to their challenges and grow more resilient with each crisis, turning adversity into opportunity. It is much the same way with individuals. Critical moments in history test the mettle of humans. Great men and women bend history to their will, whereas weaker ones are swallowed up in the convulsions of time.

****

Great spirits have always encountered violent opposition from mediocre minds -Albert Einstein

****

"The tree of liberty must be refreshed from time to time with the blood of patriots and tyrants. It is its natural manure."

****

The supreme art of war is to subdue the enemy without fighting.

****

A wise man gets more input from his enemies than a fool from his friends!

****

Democracy cannot succeed unless those who express their choice are prepared to choose wisely. The real safeguard of democracy, therefore, is the massive education of the masses about democracy.

****

"The metrics by which God will assess our life are not in dollars or shillings, but will be in the individual people whose lives we have touched" ~ Emmanuel Tumusiime Mutebile

****

"You have one year to take the potential and turn it into a reality. One year to endure the monuments that will endure forever, not carved in granite or marble, but in the lives and hearts of the generation" ~ Ravindran

****

"In your mind, every day, you must accept that you cannot be a burden to be carried by others. That is part of self-worth" ~ Paul Kagame

****

Politicians are at large blackmailers. Blackmailers are dangerous. The moment you dare reveal yourself, you become vulnerable to their malicious propaganda. Pastors are victims of blackmailing because they are open epistle for the public to read. That leaves us wide open for blackmailing. "I am deeply convinced that the Christian leader of the future is called to be completely irrelevant and to stand in this world with nothing to offer but his or her own vulnerable self". On the other side of the coin, the word 'blackmailing' has often been applied by some worldly people, who are reluctant to own up their wrong doings, as smoke-covering to shield them from responsibility. When people commit havoc they think that nobody sees them. But when the atrocity is leaked, they begin to brag out of their mouth and call it a blackmail! I suggest that you better caution yourself before you find yourself exposed. If we are going to elude moral decay, there is an urgent need of behavior modification or cognitive behavioral change. Of course, genuine change that could change a person for real down to the bone comes from God.

****

A father asked his young son the following question: "How do you tell when a politician is lying?" The young boy answered that, "Whenever you see his lips moving". To most politicians there is no sin of lying. They partake of lying in the same way they drink water! So, the question is why do politicians so often lie, exaggerate, and distort the facts? The short answer is that it works! People are notoriously bad at detecting when others are lying, and there are several psychological reasons for this. In politics (and to some extent in social life), the more outlandish or audacious the lie, the more likely people are to believe it if the source is considered at least minimally credible. If a lie is repeated over and over, it is most likely to stick in the minds of people as truth.

****

One is often surprised, if not amused when people, especially those supposed to be the moral bearers and unity disciples brazenly entangle themselves with sentimental political ventures for whatever pecuniary benefits or for a mere show of irrational arrogance in the form of ungodly prophetic utterances. More painful is the obvious fact that such persons are not teachable, and cannot learn even from their ignoble personal experiences in the past. Not minding series of such, to say the least, far-from-God prophesies and utterances, such should-be-respected clergies still mount the pulpits to make such pronouncements that always hit the crossbar.

****

There is a philosophical saying that, "One thing we learn from history is that we don't from history".

****

Judge not the story's credibility on account of the words of the story but on account of the mouth that tells the story.

****

Of the many memories, she will carry with her from Uganda, four are permanently etched in her mind. These are: always have self-reservation about people (do not trash people easily), family and culture are important, slow down, life isn't a race and there is always a new spiritual dimension. "Everything about me is fast, including my golf-swing. I am the type of person who wants to do 100 things at once and very fast. But working in Uganda, I have learnt that life is not that fast and I have to slow down and smell the roses," Nokwanda Mngeni smilingly says.

****

Dr. Sella Nyanzi uses romantic language when it comes to expressing her admiration of Dr. Besigye: My admiration for his amazing wife kills any lustful desires that could have otherwise arisen in my adult loins. See? I don't do married men. I flee from adultery. But heh, supposing I were to make love with him, we would hump away like the bunny rabbits that advertise Energiser batteries. Haven't you observed his strong presidential back and big tender fingers created to play his lover's body like a string guitarist making fine music? Haven't you observed his expressive big eyes and his ample lips created to deliver a passionate lover's kisses? If I sexed Besigye, I would be honoured to take him to heaven and back. Now haters, hate!

****

The election fever is on. It is impossible to open the news front pages without a headline covering the character of one of those running for the highest office in the country. My advice is that don't make a decision by what other people deem important. Most of the editors of the American mass media are biased in their covering because they have candidates of their own choices whom they are trying to sell to us. This is true in particular with the Liberal Media. The leftwing bias of the American mass media is pervasive and quantifiable. It is not easy to know who the real hero is by reading news headlines. I want to end by affirming that heroism, after all, is not dead; but our ability to recognize it is sorely wounded. As Roberto Rivera likes to say, "Here's the cultural moment we're living in. We idolize the outrageous and mock true heroes, turning them into bobble-heads".

****

"A love for tradition has never weakened a nation, indeed it has strengthened nations in their hour of peril" ~ Winston S. Churchill

****

Many African Americans on social media are venting anger over the words uttered by one of the presidential candidates threatening to send them back to Africa. As far as I know, nobody, not even the president of the country has the constitution right to do this. What bothers me are not the words spoken but the attitude of some African American who consider it to be a grave insult. Personally, I see it as a compliment as opposed to an insult. It is a proud privilege to be linked to your roots. "Patriotism is the virtue of the vicious" In the spirit of patriotism it is sweet and fitting to die for one's roots. All of us (whites, blacks and brown), we can beat bigotry by feeling proud of our mother continents. We cannot change history but we can change our attitudes to accept history the way it is.

August: Evangelism

God is the creator and sustainer of everything. God is transcendent but also imminent. He is alone in His own class yet not far from us. Jesus bridged the gap between us and God. God is remaking and changing the broken world with the gospel. The gospel presents to us the works of Jesus Christ. They are proclaimed and then received by faith.

****

The gospel is the ultimate love of God that exposes our sins and cancels them forever upon repentance.

****

The Bible is God's story. The gospel is an invitation to us to be part of God's story. Jesus is the source of eternal life. The grace is God's decisive act and His commitment to make us alive in Christ. The grace is not self-improvement program. We are the sole recipient of Christ's works undeservingly. "Self-righteousness is much like a spiritual egocentricity. It constitutes a secular type of love that thrives under conditionality". The grace is in the past – We were justified. It is in the present – We are sanctified. It is in the future – We shall be glorified.

****

God works supernaturally through the Church in a natural manner. Every great work we do, it is not the mighty man of God at work but the mighty God of man. The book of Acts is the history of the personage called Jesus Christ working by His Spirit (Holy Spirit) through the early Church. We are an extension of the same church. Unfortunately, today we have lost the concept of the supernatural. As one preacher said that, "Take away 95% of the Holy Spirit from the book of Acts, and the church will cease to exist. But take away 95% of the Holy Spirit from the Church of today, and the church will flourish!"

****

Conviction is when the heart dictates to the minds what to do. Given the fact, not every conviction leads to salvation. For example, the court might convict you of wrong doing. In order for the conviction to lead to salvation, the Holy Spirit must be the agent that brings about conviction. Therefore, there cannot be salvation without the gospel.

****

Somebody asked that, "What is to blasphemy against the Holy Spirit?" Answer: In Matthew 12:31-32, Jesus, says to the Pharisees, "Therefore I say to you, every sin and blasphemy will be forgiven men, but the blasphemy against the Spirit will not be forgiven, men. Anyone who speaks a word against the Son of man, it will be forgiven him; but whoever speaks against the Holy Spirit, it will not be forgiven him, either in this age or in the age to come". The words of Jesus were directed to the Jewish religious leaders who rejected Jesus when trusting in their own self-righteousness by observing the Law. Jesus meant that it is ok to reject Him but there is one last chance extended to mankind. After He is gone to heaven He will send the Holy Spirit to convict people of their sins when the gospel is preached. Rejecting the conviction of the Holy Spirit to be born again is the blasphemy against the Holy Spirit. The Holy Spirit persuades and enables men to accept Christ and enjoy the saving benefits of the gospel (John 16:8; 1

Corinthians 2:12-14; Acts 7:51). It is unequivocally clear that the one unforgivable sin is permanently rejecting Christ (John 3:18; 3:36). Thus, speaking against the Holy Spirit is equivalent to rejecting Christ with such finality that no future repentance is possible. 'My spirit shall not always strive with man,' God said long ago (Genesis 6:3).

****

The depravity and corruption of our fallen nature diffused through the uttermost parts of our souls. The impact of our fallen nature is that we have desires, which as James 1:15 tells us, "gives birth to sin." We have the willingness to break the rules to get what we want even though we've been warned of the consequences. We have the predilection for rationalizing our actions, even when we've been caught. And finally, we have the elation that accompanies the sense that we've gotten away with something. Our depravity causes us not only to ignore God's commandments but also to challenge His grace! The true gospel will either transform your heart or harden it.

****

The glory (Shekinah) is the heaviness of the presence of God among us. Sin veils us from seeing the presence of God and separates us from God. The righteousness of Christ is the only antidote to sin. Jesus rips the veil preventing us from seeing God. Everything that comes from God to man is grace. Everything that comes from the world to man is corruption. Darkness is the absence of light. Evil is the absence of holiness. Holiness is the presence of Christ. Judgment is the absence of Christ. Hell is the absolute and permanent absence of grace.

****

Where is the easiest place to get a hardened heart? Perhaps there is no easy way to harden your heart than in the Bible. Satan has extensive powers to deceive people, and the deceived includes even the most learned and intellectual people of this world. Stand warned that the devil does not hang around cemeteries but hangs around places where people gather to seek God. Satan, the Devil is doing precisely what he is supposed to do – to steal and to kill. The easiest place to get a hardened heart is in the Scriptures. No wonder most of the world cults use the Bible, in particular, the book of Revelation as their point of reference! Satan is not afraid of somebody reading the Bible intellectually without the guidance of the Holy Spirit. The revelation is not necessarily finding something new, it is finding your problem spiritually addressed and solved by the promises of God in the Scriptures. Embracing Satan's deception is believing the twisted Scriptures as truth or being prejudice to some Scriptures. "Knowledge brings responsibility. And the same sun that softens the wax hardens the clay. The same message that transforms one's life can cause another to say, "I don't believe."

****

God spoke the universe into existence. By His Word, He made the world. Jesus builds His Church by His Word. Jesus told Peter that "Upon this rock (confession) I will build my Church" (Matthew 16:18). Jesus sends us to the uttermost ends of the world to preach His Word (the gospel). He builds His Church by His Word but delegates to us the responsibility to speak (preach/teach) His Word (Matthew 28:16-20). We are His mouth to speak; we are His feet to go; we are His hands to serve. We are called to do so without a possibility of retiring.

****

The baby camel asked his mother camel that "Why do we have large feet?" The mother replied so that we might not sink into the sand. Then he asked, "Why do we have big eyebrows?" The mother replied that to prevent sand going into our eyes. Then he asked, "Why do we have three big humps?" The mother replied so as to store water in the desert. Then he asked his mother this last question: "If that is so then what are we doing in the zoo?" Some Christians are in their comfort zones, in the zoo, when they are fully equipped to go to the uttermost ends of the world to preach the gospel.

****

Luke 9:5 - "If people do not welcome you, leave their town and shake the dust off your feet as a testimony against them." The word welcome in original Greek means to treat you with dignity as one of their own. Witnessing is successful as long as the people readily listen and attend with the ear of their heart to the gospel. Your success depends on this simple fact when people lend their ears to you to preach to them the gospel. Unfortunately, most believers consider the conversion of the soul to be the only success in evangelism. They end up getting frustrated whenever they preach the gospel, and there is no surrendering to Christ. We are sent to preach the gospel but not to save souls. Salvation is the absolute work of God and the response of the will of man. We sow the seed but God does the planting and the watering. Paul said that "I planted the seed, Apollos watered it, but God has been making it grow." (1 Corinthians 3:6).

****

Romans 9:3 - "For I could wish that I myself were accursed, separated from Christ for the sake of my brethren, my kinsmen according to the flesh, who are Israelites" The people whom Paul is willing to save even at the expense of his soul are the very people who want him dead. The uniqueness of Christianity is the commandment to love your enemies. Jesus died even for those people that crucified Him. Each of us is a unique strand in the resurrected life of Jesus Christ, and we are mandated to manifest His character. When the Spirit of God overshadows you, it is imperative to love all people unconditionally. You are constrained even to reach out to those people who naturally hate you. I call it the labor of love but our Lord calls it work well done.

****

Virtues are like a custom uniquely designed by God to fit all and tailored to lean on when the going gets tough. These are like a moral compass functioning as a guide for morally appropriate behaviors. Christianity demands that all people (regardless of their beliefs or lifestyles) be treated with dignity. A good example is when the scribes and Pharisees brought to Jesus a woman caught in adultery. Jesus first defended the woman from the aggressive characters: "He that is without sin among you, let him first cast a stone at her". After restoring her dignity, He went ahead to minister to her: "Go, and sin no more" (John 8:6-11). "It is easier to minister to the broken after we acknowledge that we are broken too!"

****

Satan attacked Adam and Eva from their point of strength by attacking the Word of God: "Did God say----" (Genesis 3:1). Satan's primary target is the gospel. Christians are persecuted because whenever there is an attack on the gospel, there is an attack to those who carry it too. The world can tolerate all kinds of hollow deceptions except the honest truth. Jesus warned that even our close relatives will turn against us: "And a person's enemies will be those of his own household" (Matthew 10:36). Jesus reserved His blessings for those who are persecuted for His name's sake (Matthew 5:10).

****

Christianity is not a spectator's sport. We are called to actively participate in establishing the kingdom of God on earth. We must be kingdom minded with a kingdom agenda in minds.

****

John 20:21 - "As the Father has sent Me, I also send you". Jesus came to be to us what the Father is to Him. He sends us into the world to be to the people what He came to be to us.

****

2 Corinthians 5:21 - "God made him who had no sin to be sin for us, so that in him we might become the righteousness of God." It is never wrong to do what God did, and it is never right to do what Satan did. God placed your sins on Jesus. Will you place your faith where God placed your sins?

****

According to a survey, the people of integrity who consider themselves to be the cream of the society are most likely to see no need of embracing the grace of God. They think that they are good enough to be accepted in the presence of God (heaven). Yet the Bible says that God accepts us only by His imputed righteousness of Jesus Christ. The reason is because even the best of our good works are tainted by our depravity. The person closest to the gates of hell is the person who looks in the mirror and says "Look at me I am a good person I need no Savior". The person closest to the gates of heaven is the person who looks in the mirror and says "What a wretched person I am, I need a Savior".

****

August 18th, 2015, in the USA, the school season begins today after a long summer holiday. I encourage students to take studying seriously knowing that your future job depends on what you do now. Studying is not limited to kids alone, adults can study too. Learning is a lifetime process. You can never be overeducated. As Gandhi insinuated, "Live as if you were to die tomorrow. Learn as if you were to live forever." Spiritually, the first step to backsliding is thinking that you know it all, and seeing no need to know more. We need to hear the gospel over and over.

****

John 20:21 - "As the Father has sent Me, I also send you". Jesus came to be to us what the Father is to Him. He sends us into the world to be to the people what He came to be to us.

****

A living, loving gospel sermon demonstrated by lifestyle however unlearned in matter and lacking in style, is better than the finest discourse devoid of action and power. A living dog keeps better watch than a dead lion and is of more service to his master, and so the poorest moral and spiritual preacher is infinitely to be preferred to the exquisite orator who has wisdom but that of words, energy but that of self, and no moral integrity to support his teaching.

****

Join me on a short term mission study trip to Africa from 28th December 2015 to 7th January 2016. Catch the vision that mission is the very essence of the Church. When Jesus called us to follow Him, it was a promise to make us fishers of men (Matthew 4:19). Charles Spurgeon said that "Every Christian is either a missionary or an impostor." It means that a calling to follow Him is a call to participate in preaching the gospel wherever and whenever He calls you. Please get out of your comfort zone and follow Him. For more information contact me at stephkyeyu@hotmail.com or inbox me. God bless.

****

The greatest story ever told is the biblical story of salvation. Christianity is unique such that people must be converted (after they reach the age of accountability) in order for them to become true believers. The vast majority of the people in other religions are born into their respective religions. They are members by virtue of their birth status because their parents belonged to the same religions. However, every Christian has the testimony of the transformed life and has an encounter with the living Christ.

****

Jonah 1:3 - Instead of going to Nineveh to preach the Word, as God told him, Jonah disliked the work and went down to Joppa to escape from it. There are occasions when God's servants shrink from duty. Christian, do not play the Jonah unless you wish to have all the waves and the billows rolling over your head. You will find in the long run that it is far harder to shun the work and will of God than to at once yield yourself to it. Jonah lost his time, for he had to go to Tarshish after all.

****

This weekend, make it a priority to go to Church. If you don't have a home Church shop for one, please. Never look for a perfect Church because there nothing like a perfect Church. The reason there are no perfect people. I want to point out that going to Church is not a smoke screen to conceal your sins. Jesus alone can save you from your sins. But we go to Church to fellowship and to grow into the grace of God. The Bible instructs us that, "Not forsaking the assembling of ourselves together, as the manner of some is; but exhorting one another: and so much the more, as you see the day approaching" (Hebrews 10:25). A Good Church is not judged by the fancy facilities or the mega congregation but on the right doctrine. The biblical preaching is likely to make you feel uncomfortable. But it makes the Bible your conscience. Have a blissful weekend!

****

2 Corinthians 5:19 – "That is, in Christ, God was reconciling the world to Himself, not counting their trespasses against them, and He has committed the message of reconciliation to us." We live in the period of restoration and glorification. God reconciled us to Himself and He sends us to reconcile others to Him. The gospel of the kingdom is the roadmap to your ultimate destiny. The gospel presents the person of Jesus Christ. Receiving Jesus is to accept His authority to do what He came to do and promised to do (to save you from your sins). It means you believe He has such authority and has exercised it on your behalf to change you into what God created you to be.

September: Resting in Christ

All the attributes of Christ, as truly God and truly man, are at our disposal. All the fullness of the Godhead, whatever that marvelous term may encompass, is ours to make us complete. He cannot endow us with the attributes of Deity; but He has done all that can be done, for He has made even His divine power and Godhead subservient to our salvation. His omnipotence, omniscience, omnipresence, immutability, and infallibility are all combined for our defense. The whole of Christ, in His adorable character as the Son of God, is by Himself made ours to most richly enjoy. His wisdom is our direction, His knowledge our instruction, His power our protection, His justice our guarantee, His love our comfort, His mercy our solace, and His immutability our trust. "He holds nothing back but opens the recesses of the Mount of God and bids us dig in its mines for the hidden treasure." ~ Alistair Begg

****

2 Timothy 1:7 – "For God hath not given us the spirit of fear". It does not mean we are not supposed to be afraid of Satan. It means that Satan is afraid of us because we are under the divine sovereign protection.

****

The glory belongs to God. We are not manufacturers of His glory but distributors. We are called to reflect His glory in everything we do for our own benefit. Manifesting the glory of God is our security on earth. God's man at the center of God's will is immortal as long as God is not done with him. The Psalmist said, "The LORD is on my side; I will not fear: what can man do unto me?" (Psalms 118:6). Paul said that "What, then, shall we say in response to these things? If God is for us, who can be against us?" (Romans 8:31).

****

Psalms 23:2 – "He makes me lie down in green pastures". The Psalmist meant that we find our resting in the finished works of Jesus Christ. We rest in Him and feed from His hands. The Word of God is the unchanging truth in the ever changing world where we find peace. Resting in Christ is resting in the peace that surpasses our natural understanding. When you seek God, the peace of God follows you. The Word of God is the unchanging truth in the ever changing world. Let God be your source of peace and encouragement.

****

Guide your minds with the truth. In order to walk in the truth, you must accept the truth, memorize the truth and act on the truth. Your thinking is the most important thing that must be protected from your enemy and not allowed to be conquered except for God. God conquers us when we surrender to Him our will. That is when His will becomes your will. We are free to do as we will but it takes the grace of God to do as He wills. God must conquer the man with whom He wants to share His ideas. He gives us His story then He sends us to share our story with somebody.

****

Luke 6:22 - "Blessed are you when people hate you, when they exclude you and insult you and reject your name as evil, because of the Son of Man." Elsewhere Jesus said that "If the world hate you, ye know that it hated me before it hated you" (John 15:18). The standard of the world hates the standard of heaven. If the world consistently applauds you, there must be something lacking in your spiritual walk. "We are followers of Christ because we hate what Satan loves and we love what Satan hates."

****

Luke 7:36-50 - When one of the Pharisees invited Jesus to have dinner with him, he went to the Pharisee's house and reclined at the table. A woman in that town who lived a sinful life learned that Jesus was eating at the Pharisee's house, so she came there with an alabaster jar of perfume. As she stood behind Him at His feet weeping, she began to wet His feet with her tears. Then she wiped them with her hair, kissed them and poured perfume on them. When the Pharisee who had invited Him saw this, he said to himself, "If this man were a prophet, he would know who is touching him and what kind of woman she is—that she is a sinner."

Jesus answered him, "Simon, I have something to tell you." "Tell me, teacher," he said. "Two people owed money to a certain moneylender. One owed him five hundred denarii, and the other fifty. Neither of them had the money to pay him back, so he forgave the debts of both. Now, which of them will love him more?" Simon replied, "I suppose the one who had the bigger debt forgiven." "You have judged correctly," Jesus said. Then he turned toward the woman and said to Simon, "Do you see this woman? I came into your house. You did not give me any water for my feet, but she wet my feet with her tears and wiped them with her hair. You did not give me a kiss, but this woman, from the time I entered, has not stopped kissing my feet. You did not put oil on my head, but she has poured perfume on my feet. Therefore, I tell you, her many sins have been forgiven—as her great love has shown. But whoever has been forgiven little loves little."

Luke 7:50 - Then Jesus said to her, "Your sins are forgiven." The other guests began to say among themselves, "Who is this who even forgives sins?" Jesus said to the woman, "Your faith has saved you; go in peace." Look at another parallel incidence "When Jesus saw their faith, he said to the paralyzed man, "Son, your sins are forgiven" (Mark 2:5). Observe, that the pardon of sin came in a single sentence. He spake, and it was done. Jesus said "Your sins are forgiven." Observe, also, that this sentence contains no conditions apart from the faith of the receiver. Jesus is appointed as High Priest on purpose that He may stand on God's behalf, and declare the remission of sin. What Jesus said was spoken with divine authority. The Bible says that only God can forgive sins. Jesus forgives sins because He is God. We go to Jesus (our High Priest) to sacrifice by repenting our sins to Him. We do not have to carry with us animal sacrifices because Jesus is both the sacrifice and the high priest. The moral lesson is that forgiveness is the greatest need of man because it restores our fellowship with God. God grants us forgiveness for his dear Son's sake!

****

John 11:21 – "Then said Martha unto Jesus, Lord, if you had been here, my brother had not died." During the earthly ministry of Jesus, He was in one place at one time. Jesus said that "Nevertheless I tell you the truth; It is expedient for you that I go away: for if I go not away, the Comforter will not come unto you; but if I depart, I will send him unto you" (John 16:7). The reason is because His Spirit (Holy Spirit) is omnipresent. We have no justified reason to complain that, "Lord, if you had been here", because He is everywhere. He indwells the believers wherever they are. He is invisible but visibly seen in us. We can now say that "See me, see Jesus" in the same way Jesus said, "You see me, you see the Father" (John 14:9).

****

Matthew 11:29 - "Take my yoke upon you, and learn of me; for I am meek and lowly in heart: and ye shall find rest unto your souls." The meek are often mistaken in our day as being weak. But meekness is actually great strength, under control – God's control. Great faith, great commitment, and great determination are needed on a daily basis to live a meek life before God. When He requires sacrifice, meekness trusts completely and gives willingly. When He demands obedience, meekness cancels out our selfish desires, crucifies personal ambition, and performs joyfully the good will of God. It is for this reason that the joy of the meek is continually increasing. Their pleasure is not found in personal circumstances; their happiness does not come about from worldly popularity; their fulfillment does not come from public success.

****

1 John 4:8 – "For God is love." God is self-existence. It means that there is no external force or agent that caused His existence. The life and love of God are within His very being. The love of God is not induced by our performances; it is unconditional love. The greatest expression of God's love is communicated to us in John 3:16: "For God so loved the world that he gave his one and only Son, that whoever believes in him shall not perish but have eternal life." The grace is His goodness toward those who have no claim on, nor reason to expect, divine favor. The grace is Christ's love at His expense. The grace projects that there is nothing you have done that can make God love you more or less. God has given those who receive His Son Jesus as their personal Savior the ability to love as He does, through the power of the Holy Spirit (John 1:12; 1 John 3:1, 23-24).

****

2 Corinthians 4:8 - "We are troubled on every side, yet not distressed; we are perplexed, but not in despair". The word 'perplexed' stands for a mystified situation that makes no sense to the natural minds. All of us occasionally face such tough times when the mind has perplexed itself with many hard questions. I mean in a situation when things do not make sense to us, and we are tempted to ask God: "Where are you in this situation?" In such a situation, never try to seek understanding or to make sense of the complicated situation. Pray for the comfort of the Holy Spirit, and continue to love and serve God till He reverses the situation. Remember that you have assured victory regardless of the turmoil because darkness cannot expel light. It is the light that expels darkness.

****

Stop feeling sorry for yourself. You're far better than what you think of yourself. You know what, the Enemy would want to judge you & convince you into believing you're nothing but a sinner, a weakling, a loser, a failure, an addict & a wimp. But you're not any of these. "You're what God says you're. And you ought to live like who God says you're. Quit every guilt, every inferiority complex, every poverty, failure & loser mentality and dare to be who God called you to be" ~ Prosper Igboke

****

Somebody asked that "Does the Epistle of James contradict the teaching of Paul on grace/faith?" The Bible has no contradiction at all. God revealed to Paul the doctrine of the saving grace - It is the gospel of justification by faith in the finished works of Jesus Christ (Eph 2:8-10). The grace is God's faithful act to fulfill His promise of salvation at the expense of Christ. Faith is our good work that connects us to the promise of God. The Epistle of James emphasizes the working faith (not grace plus works) that is proven by good works (James 2:17). Salvation is divided into three parts (Justification, sanctification & glorification. Justification is of God and by God alone. But sanctification involves our good works of obedience to the moral commandments of God. Our good works implicate our loyalty, trust, commitment and submission to God. Again, our good works are not the cause of our justification but the proof that we are justified. It is the inward transformation manifested to the outside (good works) that constitutes to faith. Look at the following teachings of Paul: "This is a faithful saying, and these things I want you to affirm constantly, that those who have believed in God should be careful to maintain good works." (Titus 3:8). ; "And let our people also learn to maintain good works, to meet urgent needs, that they may not be unfruitful" (Titus 3:14). ; "And let us consider one another in order to stir up love and good works" (Heb. 10:24).

September: Labor Day

My postings on labor / harvest

A laborer works with his hands, his head and his heart. Laboring was God's plan for humanity since creation. It is not a coincidence that before God created the perfect man (Adam), He planted for him a Garden (Eden). Adam delighted in plowing the dirt of Eden and taking care of all God's creations in the Garden. Laboring was not a curse; the curse of sin added sweating to labor: "Because you listened to your wife and ate fruit from the tree about which I commanded you, 'You must not eat from it,' "Cursed is the ground because of you; through painful toil you will eat food from it all the days of your life" (Genesis 3:17).

The infertile, ghoulish garden soil and the hostile environments we have today are due to the curse of sin. Christ came to save the people and the planet as well. Physical creation too will enter in the final synthesis of history, that is, heaven. The Bible says that "For we know that the whole creation groaneth and travaileth in pain together until now" (Romans 8:22).

The planet is not eternal but God is eternal. The planet belongs to God, and we are custodians. Meanwhile, we can enjoy the planet because this is our Father's universe. The current creation is fair and beautiful even in its present condition. We need to respect nature by refraining from our own asphyxiating pollution. We need to enjoy the fruits of our labor. I have no sort of sympathy with those who cannot enjoy the beauties of nature, and those who refuse to work. The Bible says that "He who does not work will not eat" (2 Thessalonians 3:10). Our labor preserves us from want. As much as it is good to share the wealth, it is not fair to legislate the poor into freedom by legislating the rich out of freedom! Happy Labor's Day.

****

God created Adam and placed him in the Garden of Eden to labor. The different between the garden and the wilderness is order. There is productivity where order flourishes.

****

John 5:17-18 - "My Father is working until now, and I Myself am working." For this reason, therefore, the Jews were seeking all the more to kill Him, because He not only was breaking the Sabbath, but also was calling God His own Father, making Himself equal with God." God ceased from His works of creation on the sixth day and said it is good. He declared the seventh day as a day to honor His benevolences of creation by resting. God resumed to work after Adam sinned. Jesus worked in honor of the Sabbath as opposed to dishonor it. He never broke any of the commandments of God because He was sinless. He maintained that the Sabbath was instituted for the wellbeing of man.

****

Time and space are bound to each other in the physical realm but the spiritual realm is not limited by time and space. God rested on the Sabbath because at creation He was operating in time and space. That is why creation is marked by days with limitation of time. The climax of God's physical creation was the Sabbath, the high mark of His creative power. God rested on the seventh day after completing creating everything. The number seven in the Bible represents divine perfection, totality or completion and is mentioned at least 490 times. God "rested" not in the sense of relieving exhaustion, as we normally do but to set aside a day for us to honor Him. Yes, we are called to honor Him at all times but on this particular day, when we rest and lay down our tools to honor Him, we all together declare His majesty. Also, we are separated from the rest of the world. The fourth commandment was given to Israel in the form of reminding: "Remember the Sabbath day, to keep it holy" (Exodus 20:8-11). The reason is because it did not begin on Mount Sinai but it goes all the way back to creation. The word Sabbath means resting. Jesus became our spiritual resting (Hebrews 4:4-11). We observe the Sabbath like all of the Ten Commandments not to earn favor from God but because we are highly favored of God (Hebrews 4:9).

****

Exodus 20:8 - "Remember the Sabbath day, to keep it holy" Sabbath was given in form of remembrance because the Sabbath predates the Mount Sinai occasion when God handed the Ten Commandments to Moses to serve as the moral code of behavior for the human race. The Fourth Commandment, to remember the Sabbath, concludes the section of the Ten Commandments that specifically helps define a proper relationship with God—how we are to love, worship and relate to Him. The other six commandments define how we relate to our neighbors. God instructed us to proclaim His day in His honor because this is how the world will know that there is the living God who created all things and who is the source of our provision and existence. Whenever we put down our tools and rest on the Sabbath day we are separated from the rest of the world. The early Church observed the Sabbath day (Saturday) as the resting day and the first day of the week (Sunday) as a resurrection day.

It is the Catholic Church that changed the Sabbath to Sunday in pursuit of their anti-semantic. The Catholic Mirror of September 23, 1894, puts it this way: "The Catholic Church for over one thousand years before the existence of a Protestant by virtue of her divine mission, changed the day from Saturday to Sunday." Around 364 AD, the Roman Catholic Church outlawed resting on the Sabbath in the Council of Laodicea when they decreed 59 Canon laws. Here is the final law. Canon XXIX: "Christians must not Judaize by resting on the Sabbath, but must work on that day, rather honoring the Lord's Day; and, if they can, resting then as Christians. But if any shall be found to be Judaizers, let them be anathema from Christ." (Percival Translation). While resting on the Sabbath was outlawed in favor of resting on Sunday as per Constantine's Sunday Law, Cannon law 16 was also issued by the Bishops in the Council of

Laodicea (A.D. 363-364) that confirms that Christians were in fact still worshiping on the Sabbath. Canon XVI: "The Gospels are to be read on the Sabbath [i.e. Saturday], with the other Scriptures." The fact that the council of Laodicea found it necessary to deal with this issue verifies that more than 330 years after the cross that there were many Christians who were still observing the Sabbath according to the Commandment.

****

Exodus 20:8 - "Remember the Sabbath day, to keep it holy" Sabbath was given in form of remembrance because the Sabbath predates the Mount Sinai occasion when God handed the Ten Commandments to Moses to serve as the moral code of behavior for the human race. The Fourth Commandment, to remember the Sabbath, concludes the section of the Ten Commandments that specifically helps define a proper relationship with God—how we are to love, worship and relate to Him. The other six commandments define how we relate to our neighbors. God instructed us to proclaim His day in His honor because this is how the world will know that there is the living God who created all things and who is the source of our provision and existence. Whenever we put down our tools and rest on the Sabbath day we are separated from the rest of the world. The early Church observed the Sabbath day (Saturday) as the resting day and the first day of the week (Sunday) as a resurrection day.

It is the Catholic Church that changed the Sabbath to Sunday in pursuit of their anti-semantic. The Catholic Mirror of September 23, 1894, puts it this way: "The Catholic Church for over one thousand years before the existence of a Protestant by virtue of her divine mission, changed the day from Saturday to Sunday." Around 364 AD, the Roman Catholic Church outlawed resting on the Sabbath in the Council of Laodicea when they decreed 59 Canon laws. Here is the final law. Canon XXIX: "Christians must not Judaize by resting on the Sabbath, but must work on that day, rather honoring the Lord's Day; and, if they can, resting then as Christians. But if any shall be found to be Judaizers, let them be anathema from Christ." (Percival Translation). While resting on the Sabbath was outlawed in favor of resting on Sunday as per Constantine's Sunday Law, Cannon law 16 was also issued by the Bishops in the Council of Laodicea (A.D. 363-364) that confirms that Christians were in fact still worshiping on the Sabbath. Canon XVI: "The Gospels are to be read on the Sabbath [i.e. Saturday], with the other Scriptures." The fact that the council of Laodicea found it necessary to deal with this issue verifies that more than 330 years after the cross that there were many Christians who were still observing the Sabbath according to the Commandment.

****

October: Halloween

What is Halloween really about? Is there something spiritual behind all the ghoulishness we see? To some, it is a day of having fun. Before you indulge in the profligacy remember that hedonism is the highest form of worshiping. To most Americans, Halloween is a satanic holiday. The heathens set a day aside to celebrate Satan and death. Originally, in the West, it was a day when Christians dressed up in costumes to mock Satan and his minions. The very name "Halloween" means "holy evening"—a throwback to when Catholic Christians prepared for the Feast of All Saints on November 1st. The Church of Antioch kept a commemoration of all holy martyrs on the first Sunday after Pentecost. The Protestants marked the same day as a Reformation Day. Satan strategically changed Halloween to be his day.

Today, in the USA, Halloween is the most celebrated day just next to Christmas. Skulls symbolic of death are littering the yards and the doors of most of the houses. The world is obsessed with a blatant exhibition of satanic symbolism and debauchery. Ironically, the real evil is not out there in the yards but it is within the hearts of men. People are more monstrous than the skeletons paraded in their compounds, and real death is lingering over their homes. It is for this reason Jesus came to save us by defeating evil in our hearts. We (the redeemed) can now mock death "O death, where is thy sting? O grave, where is thy victory?" (1 Corinthians 15:55).

****

Lucifer is a part of the demonic godhead. Remember, everything God has, the devil has a counterfeit. During Halloween, time-released curses are always loosed. A time-released curse is a period that has been set aside to release demonic activity and to ensnare souls in great measure. Mother Earth is highly celebrated during the fall demonic harvest. Witches praise Mother Earth by bringing her fruits, nuts and herbs. Demons are loosed during these acts of worship. Halloween is much more than a holiday filled with fun and tricks or treats. It is a time for the gathering of evil that masquerades behind the fictitious characters of Dracula, werewolves, mummies and witches on brooms. The truth is that these demons that have been presented as scary cartoons actually exist. I have prayed for witches who are addicted to drinking blood and howling at the moon. Christians should resist temptations to participate in Halloween rituals.

November: Praying

Prayer is a solemn request for help or expression of thanks addressed to God and is an act of worshiping. Prayer is conversation with God; the intercourse of the soul with God, not in contemplation but in direct address to Him. Prayer may be oral or silent, occasional or constant. It is "beseeching the Lord" "You may force your way through anything with the leverage of prayer. Thoughts and reasoning are like the steel wedges that give a hold upon truth; but prayer is the lever that pries open the iron chest of sacred mystery, that we may get the treasure hidden inside." (Colossians 1:9).

****

Prayer is seeking God (Ex. 32:11); "pouring out the soul before the Lord" (1 Sam. 1:15); "praying and crying to heaven" (2 Chr. 32:20); seeking unto God and making supplication" (Job 8:5); "drawing near to God" (Ps. 73:28); "bowing the knees" (Eph. 3:14).

****

Hebrews 4:16 - "Let us therefore come boldly unto the throne of grace, that we may obtain mercy, and find grace to help in time of need." This is an invitation for a sinner to come before the throne of the holy God. It is a onetime but continuous invitation to come boldly before the throne of grace without feeling guilt. This is not a place where we go and expect to leave. It is a place we go to in anticipation to embrace forever. The throne of grace is our shelter in a raging storm. God calls us to come before His throne and make it our home (settle there permanently) rather than occasionally approaching His throne in times of need. The grace is compared to oxygen; we cannot live a moment without it. We need God in the valley and at the mountain top.

****

Praying is not asking God to do what He didn't want to do. When praying becomes a demand it ceases to be praying. When praying becomes a ritual it becomes meaningless. When praying becomes our object instead of God it becomes an idol. Think about it!

****

This weekend pray for His will to be done in your life. Sometimes we pray for good things when God has already reserved the best for us. Prayer is putting oneself in the hands of God. Your prosperity depends on the unfailing beauty of God. "That which you create in beauty and goodness and truth lives on for all times to come." Real beauty is encountering the glory of God. A person guided by God walks uprightly. The discipline of the Christian living is that God directs your steps by directing your prayers. As precaution look where you walk and walk where you look.

****

James 5:16 - "The effective prayer of a righteous person has great power." Praying is effective when God is the initiator of our prayer. Praying in the Spirit is a conscious choice of faith to bring in line our praying with what the Spirit of God is saying through the Word of God. James' concern is not how prayer is made effective, but that prayer is effective. Prayer is effective, not because of great men who pray, but because of a great God who in Christ graciously hears His people.

****

Tomorrow, May 7 is a national Day of Prayer. Praying is our right that precedes the constitution; it is the right granted to man by God.

The National Day is intended to awaken us to pray. We enjoy a rich, dynamic and unbroken relationship with God through Jesus Christ but we must communicate to God in prayers. Whenever Jesus went to a place, He did not look for a motel but for a mountain, a lonely place to talk to the Father in prayers. He taught us how to cultivate and maintain the daily fellowship with our Father. "When we are in Christ, God is on our side. Therefore, prayer is not a means to get God on our side; prayer is a means to align ourselves with God's purposes, plans and will". You must pray.

****

Praying should not be a routine ritual made out of obligation and duty. It should be love-based out of conviction.

****

Praying is reporting on duty for instruction. It is praying for God's will to be done but not His will to be changed.

****

God is the origin and the object of our prayers. The prayer that goes to God begins from heaven and is directed by God. An effective prayer must be in the perfect will of God.

****

Delight thyself also in the LORD; and he shall give thee the desires of thine heart (Psalm 37:4). The desire of your heart must be the delight of God. This is possible when your conscience is cleansed by His blood; your heart is transformed by His Spirit; your mind is renewed by His Word. Then His attitude becomes your attitude, and your will does not contradict His will. This is how you can secure answered prayer.

****

"If there is something I could do different, I could pray more" ~ Billy Gram

****

Praying has brought me this far, praying will get me home.

****

Praying accomplishes the following purposes: 1) The blood of the Lamb on display. 2) The words of our testimony testifying His glory. 3) The love of God on display.

****

The law of prayer is the law of faith.

****

There is no such thing as too much praying. There is never a place, nor a time when prayer is inappropriate. God is never too far away or too busy, or too unconcerned to listen. Don't quit, don't cave in. It worth praying because the end result is promising. There is no condition that God cannot change when we pray. Be a survivor as opposed to a victim!

****

"When life is rough – Pray; When life is great - Pray" Praying is an all times thing, it is not a spare wheel that you pull out when you're in trouble BUT rather a steering wheel that directs the right path through life.

****

Never underestimated the power of darkness. Knowing your enemy well makes you stronger. Prayers penetrate the unknown zones of the enemy. Pray against secret oppression, secret counsels, secret conclusions, secret agendas, secret invasions and anything that the enemy is secretly planning against you. Do not pray for an easy life but pray for strength to overcome difficult times. Remember that when saints pray, opposition is inevitable but the grace of God helps us to go through tough times efficaciously.

****

Philippians 4:6 – "Worry about nothing; pray about everything." Whatever is going to happen will happen, whether we worry or not. Worry does not empty tomorrow of its sorrow, it empties today of its strength. "Worry is the most useless human activity on earth..... all it changes is your blood pressure. Use your energy to plan the future" ~ Myles Munroe

****

The measure of a man does not depend on how high he stands but on how low he kneels before God.

****

The law of prayer is the law of faith. Effective prayer requires fixed faith. I mean the faith of the mustard seed that has capacity to grow and move the mountain. Unfortunately, some of us look for the mountain faith without praying!

****

1 Samuel 3:10 – "Then Samuel answered, Speak; for your servant hears." Praying is listening to God rather than talking to God. It is saying to God, "Speak, your servant hears" rather than "I speak, Lord hear me."

****

Since conscience is a moral faculty, given by God, through which He speaks to us, our attitude towards it is of the utmost importance. The Puritans described conscience as "a mirror to catch the light of God's

Word and apply it to our own case". When we pray, God listens only to the words of our conscience. The whisper of the heart is louder than the voice of the mouth. Persecution may shut the mouth but it can't shut up the worship of the heart.

****

"When life is rough – Pray; when life is great - Pray". Praying is an all times thing. There is no such thing as too much praying. There is never a place, nor a time when prayer is inappropriate. God is never too far away or too busy, or too unconcerned to listen. Don't quit, don't cave in. Circumstantial faith looks at the surroundings; it is the kind of faith that goes up or down depending on the current set of circumstances. But objective faith focuses on what God can do. There is no condition that God cannot change when we pray. Decide to pray, and to be a survivor as opposed to a victim of circumstances!

****

For a believer, praying should be as natural as breathing. It should be cherished every moment we live. There should be no danger of doing what we were created to do.

****

When you whisper in prayers, God hears because the voice of the heart is louder than the whisper of the mouth.

****

Matthew 17:27 - "Go to the sea and throw in a hook. Take the first fish that you catch. Open its mouth, and you will find a coin. Give that coin to them for you and me." He is a God of precision and exactness. Pray with specifics and believe God for a definite miracle in your life.

****

True prayer is not something we make up ourselves for ourselves. It is God praying within us for Himself. The indwelling Spirit of the Son cries out from within us to the Father. The Father always responds to the cry of the Son within us. Answered prayer is when the Son prays on our behalf. He is sitting on the right hand of the Father interceding for us. His Spirit groans within us teaching us to pray. We have all that we need built into us by the presence of His Spirit- Christ in us the hope of all glory.

****

Two places are most valuable in the world: 1. The Nicest place is to be in someone's Thought. 2) The safest place is to be in someone's Prayers.

****

Do not face the day until you have faced God in prayer.

****

"Do not pray for an easy life, pray for the strength to endure a difficult one" ~ Bruce Lee

****

Never underestimated the power of darkness. Knowing your enemy well makes you stronger. Prayers penetrate the unknown tentacles and unfamiliar zones of the enemy. Pray against secret oppression, secret counsels, secret conclusions, secret agendas, secret invasions and anything that the enemy is secretly planning against you. Do not pray for an easy life but pray for strength to overcome the difficult times. Let the dark rain snivel continuously as long as you have the umbrella to walk through it. Remember that when saints pray, opposition is inevitable but the grace of God helps us to go through tough times efficaciously.

****

This weekend pray for His will to be done. God does not need you to pray but He wants you to pray. Remember that God has no need because He is self-sufficiency; He needs nothing outside of Himself. He is the sovereign God, and His will cannot be swatted by any natural means. God asks us to pray purposely to engage us in His divine plan on earth. Praying is volunteering to be one of the vessels that God can use to bring His will on the earth.

****

Knowledge changes with understanding. God knows us all the way, and He wants us to know Him all the way. Growing in grace is knowing Him and making Him known. Spiritual maturity always encounters opposition from mediocre minds. Our Identification with Christ does not mean knowing Him all the way. There is a need to know Him more every day. Avoid familiarity because it robs us of the required intimacy. Familiarity cherishes ritualism without sincerity. For example, it is possible to be caught up in routine circles of saying a few words of prayer before eating and before going to bed, and call that your prayer life. God needs value time with you. The length of prayer and the words used in prayer are not as important as the sincerity of heart desiring to fellowship with God. It is during that moment of quality time while waiting in silence in His presence that God whispers to our inner ears crystal clear so that we hear. Remember that when God speaks to us, He makes sure His message is clearly understood.

****

Praying begins with repentance: Jesus taught His disciples to pray to the Father that, "Forgive us our debts" (Matthew 6:12). We are all sinners that need to repent daily. Our sins affect God and our neighbors. "Do we realize that when we sin, we affect the entire family of believers? Read Nehemiah's example in Nehemiah 1. Or Ezra 9, which shows Ezra fasting and praying on behalf of the nation of Israel. In the Ezra and Nehemiah booklet, Mr. Flurry wrote, "Ezra prayed a deeply moving prayer of repentance for the nation. Ezra blushed and was greatly ashamed. The nation was all one family. Ezra set us an example in family repentance." Notice the Prophet Daniel's example: "And I set my face unto the Lord God, to seek by prayer and supplications, with fasting, and sackcloth, and ashes: And I prayed unto the Lord my God, and made my confession, and said, O Lord, the great and dreadful God, keeping the covenant and mercy to them that love him, and to them that keep his commandments; We have sinned, and have committed iniquity, and have done wickedly, and have rebelled, even by departing from thy precepts and from thy judgments" (Daniel 9:3-5). Do you see how Daniel approached God? He used the pronoun "We" that is inclusive. Although Daniel himself had not forsaken God, he knew his people had. Daniel loved his people (family) enough to cry out to God, 'We have sinned.' Such brokenness reflects the depth of love he had for God.

****

Praying involves confessing our sins to God and to one another (James 5:16). It is not going public into details of your past but it is the depth of confession involving sincerity. One of the most powerful Psalms on confession is David's great Psalm 32. David opens this Psalm with the words: "Blessed is the one whose transgression is forgiven, whose sin is covered." He speaks of keeping silent about his sin and then describes the drain on his life. Then, he states, he acknowledged his sin to God and did not hide his iniquity. Confession, then, is first and primarily to God. All sins ultimately are against God, and we need to acknowledge to Him that we have sinned, turn away from our sin, and seek His grace. If we do so, He has promised to forgive us and cleanse us from all unrighteousness (1 John 1:9). There are no other Biblical conditions to God's forgiveness. The throne of God is the throne of the grace where forgiveness multiplies and guilt vanishes.

****

All of us are called to be intercessors. Praying for yourself is not wrong because Jesus Christ instructed us to pray for ourselves. However, Christ prayed for Himself as well as for others. That is the mindset we must strive to emulate! Remember that picture of God's throne room. Jesus Christ is there, interceding for us yet today (Romans 8:34). This is one of His full-time jobs!

****

To intercede is to make petitions to God on behalf of others (Ruth 1:16; Jeremiah 7:16; 27:18; Job 21:15; Genesis 23:8; Isaiah 53:12; Jeremiah 36:25). Jesus set a tremendous example of intercessory prayer. Read John 17—the most complete prayer of His recorded in Scripture, spoken in the time of His own greatest need, the night before His crucifixion—and it is almost entirely a prayer FOR OTHERS! We are called to pray for others. At one point Samuel said he would be sinning against God if he ceased to pray for the people (1 Samuel 12:19-23). He knew that faithful intercessory prayer was his responsibility. We are called to pray for others with or without their permission. The power of intercession prayer overrides the free-will of the people whom we are praying for in such a way that they cannot resist our prayers. Intercessory praying is one of the ways whereby we can use our faith on behalf of the people who have no faith. God expects all believers to be involved in the intercessory ministry. But the responsibility for intercessory prayer doesn't end with the ministry. Intercessory prayer can help us conquer selfishness and vanity. It is a powerful antidote to our carnal selfishness.

****

Moses has three songs recorded in the Bible: the song sung after the destruction of Pharaoh's army (Exodus 15:1–18); a song recounting the faithfulness of God and the rebelliousness of Israel, which he sang before all the people just before his death (Deuteronomy 32:1–43); and a prayer recorded in Psalm 90. All of his songs are praising Yahweh (YHWH ("four letters") הוהי (Yod Heh Vav Heh) for His majesty works.

****

The first song recorded in the Bible was a song of redemption after God destroyed the Egyptian army and He miraculously allowed the children of Israel to cross the Red Sea (Exodus 15:1–18). The last song recorded in the Bible is the song of the Lamb; it is the song of redemption sung by the elects of God (Revelation 15:3). "Praise precedes victory; praise follows victory".

****

Praising is the "gate-pass" which allows us to enter the sacredness of God's glory. The psalmist writes, "Enter into his gates with thanksgiving, and into his courts with praise: be thankful unto him, and bless his name" (Psalms 100:4). The attitude of praising is an attitude of gratitude. We are called to praise God in good and bad times.

****

Praising is entering the pearly gates, treading along the streets of transparent gold. Entering the sapphire dome of the heavenly temple... grandest, crystalline stupendous splendor and orchestrated trumpet by heavenly hosts. Bowing and worshipping of the winged creatures that Glory to the Lord God and worthy is the Lamb that was slain. You are worthy of all worship, worthy of all praise. Hosanna in the Highest, Glory, Glory, Hallelujah Oh my King!

****

Psalm 122:1 - "I was glad when they said unto me, Let us go into the house of the Lord." Joy comes when we spend our lives praising God. God loves a cheerful giver even when it comes to praising. In good and bad times - just praise God and watch the joy of the Lord following you. David discovered the secret of Joyful praising. God put a new song in the hearts of the redeemed which the rest of the world cannot sing. "Let us be joyful now as we rehearse the song of eternal praise that will soon sound forth in full chorus from all the blood-washed host; let us copy David's exulting before the ark as a prelude to our ecstasies before the throne."

****

Praising involves melodies of joy to the Lord. We do not sing to be happy; we sing because we are happy!

****

I have seen the goodness of the Lord in the land of the living. This is enough for me to praise God!

****

James 5:13 - "Is anyone among you in trouble? Let them pray. Is anyone happy? Let them sing Psalms." The Psalms are songs of praising. Praise means "to commend or to extol", "to applaud or magnify." God treasured us with His Word. His desire is to draw out of us what He has invested in us. The Dunamis Power of Prayer is released in praising. The walls of Jericho collapsed, at the sound of the trumpet, when the men gave a loud shout or praise (Joshua 5:20). When Paul and Silas were in prison, at midnight, in spite of the throbbing pain in their bodies and the disheartening atmosphere, they were praying and singing hymns of praise to God. Then suddenly, there was an earthquake that shook the prison! The doors flung open, and amazingly, the bonds of Paul, Silas, and every other prisoner were released (Acts 16:25).

****

The Ark of the old covenant represented the Holy Temple of God in heaven. The temple is the dwelling place of God - symbolic of Jesus Christ the true temple. All believers make up the temple of God because each believer has a throne where Christ rules by His indwelling Spirit. Every soul filled to the brink is flooded with rivers of love for others to partake of. There is a fiery glow of the Holy Spirit, mapped in every corner of the universe. Like the stars shine and lights the heavens, we are the light lightening the whole earth with the righteousness of God. Indeed, God always gives His best to those who leave the choice with Him.

****

The Bible says that God inhabits in the praises of His people (Psalms 22:3). In other words, God "dwells" in the atmosphere of His praise. This means that praise is not merely a reaction initiated after coming into His presence - Praise is a vehicle of faith which brings us into His very presence! His presence is His power and glory. Praise and worship is the "gate-pass" which allows us to enter the sacredness of His glory. The psalmist writes, "Enter into his gates with thanksgiving, and into his courts with praise: be thankful unto him, and bless his name" (Psalms 100:4).

****

John 3:13 – "And no man has ascended up to heaven, but he that came down from heaven, even the Son of man who is in heaven." Paul said that "He who descended is Himself also He who ascended far above all the heavens, so that He might fill all things" (Ephesians 4:10). Jesus is God with us, and God revealed to us. Jesus revealed to us the mysteries hidden in the heart of the Father. He revealed to us the mystery of our destiny by His death and resurrection. He is the faithful witness of who God is. For this reason, God exalted Him to the highest place and gave Him the name that is above every name (Philippians 2:9). Go ahead and praise Him.

****

Christ's whole life is a mystery. A mystery is something true yet hard to understand by our finite minds. From the swaddling clothes of His birth to the vinegar of His Passion and the shroud of His Resurrection, everything in Jesus' life was a sign of His mystery. "By His Incarnation, He, the Son of God, has in a certain way united Himself with each man." We are sons of God by virtue of our fellowship with Holy Spirit (Ephesians 3:16). The begotten Son of God (Jesus) is God coming down to us when wrapped in human flesh. His humanity appeared as "sacrament", that is, the sign and instrument, of His divinity and of the salvation He brings: what was visible in His earthly life leads to the invisible mystery of His divine sonship and redemptive mission. Christ enables us to live in Him all that He Himself lived, and He lives it in us. We are called only to become one with him, for He enables us as the members of His Body to share in what He lived for us in His flesh as our model. Jesus Christ came down from heaven, and yet heaven was in Him: "And no man has ascended up to heaven, but he that came down from heaven, even the Son of man who is in heaven" (John 3:13). Heaven was in Him before He went to heaven. In the same manner, heaven must be in you before you go to heaven. Christ is God wrapped in human flesh coming down to us. A believer is the Holy Spirit (God) wrapped in human flesh going back to God the Father.

****

Since praise manifests God's presence, we should also realize that praise repels the presence of the enemy, Satan. An atmosphere which is filled with sincere worship and praise to God by the humble and contrite hearts is disgusting to the Devil. He fears the power in the name of Jesus, and flees from the Lord's habitation in praise. "Whoso offereth praise glorifieth me: and to him that ordereth his conversation aright will I show the salvation of God" (Psalms 50:23).

****

According to Luke, when Zacharias is in the temple he is greeted by an angel who promises him that he and Elisabeth will have a child. Zacharias replies: "Whereby shall I know this? For I am an old man, and my wife well stricken in years." The angel responds by making Zacharias dumb 'until the day that these things shall be performed, because thou believest not my words'. There are a few interesting things about this exchange: Zacharias' response to the angel is almost exactly the same as Abraham's response to the angel when he is told he will have a son. Luke is apparently drawing an explicit connection to this episode but the different outcome for Zacharias is striking. Abraham receives an assurance whereas Zacharias receives a very physical rebuke. Abraham may not have doubted like Zacharias but Sarah certainly did. She laughs when she and is even warned about mocking God but retains the ability to speak.

Mary also doubted the possibility of divine conception. The different is that Zachariah asks how he can know, and Mary asks how it will happen, even though she doesn't know (different connotation, but the same root verb). I take this to mean that Mary is more open to the mystery of it all. She immediately started praising God: "How will this be," Mary asked the angel, "since I am a virgin?" The angel answered, "The Holy Spirit will come on you, and the power of the Most High will overshadow you" (Luke 1:34-36). Mary responded by praising God (Luke 1:46-55). The power of God is able to pull you from a life of impossibility to a life of possibility. Get ready to praise because God is about to let your cup overflow.

****

Jesus is the object of our praising. This is the Son that has grown in favor with the Father. He obeyed all the way even to enduring the sufferings unto death at the cross. He has ascended to the right hand of the Father where He is exalted. The Father is devoted to Him. Praising is joining hands with the Father to rejoice for the victory of His Son.

****

At times, God speaks to us in times when we are stressed. A good example is that most of the hymns were written by men during times of great trials and sufferings. Hymns are intended to bring comfort and encouragement when we are faced with the pressures of life. Most hymns cannot be outdated because they were directly composed from the scriptures. Sing them and read them in form of

Scriptures for spiritual comforting and conviction. When we sing them together the positive energy spread to one will be felt by us all.

****

Meditation is chewing on the Word of God in the spirit.

****

Your grace still amazes me, your love still a mystery. Each day I fall on my knees... your grace still amazes me.....

****

Paul prayed to God to take the thorn from his flesh. God replied that "My grace is sufficient" (2 Corinthians 12:9). His grace is always sufficient to persevere you to the desired end. What more would I truly desire than the sufficiency of His grace?

****

Psalms 8:9 - "O LORD our Lord, how excellent is thy name in all the earth!" It means the impeccable (faultless) character and reputation of God. His splendor and majesty are above all creations. He alone is holy and immortal. Worshiping is part of praying. Biblical worshiping is sensitive seeking. God is seeking sincere worshipers. They are the ones acknowledging the awesomeness of God. Worshiping begins with our concept of God as infinitely great. Your worship is proportional to your understanding of the difference between God and you. "If we are going to worship in Spirit, we must develop a spirit of worship."

****

All times is worshiping time. We are worshipping as long as we are in the perfect will of God. Worship is not just an occasional feeling which "comes upon you," but it is rooted in a conscious act of the will, to serve and obey the Lord Jesus Christ. "As worship begins in holy expectancy, it ends in holy obedience. Holy obedience saves worship from becoming an opiate, an escape from the pressing needs of modern life" ~ Richard Foster

****

Worship is an aspect of covenant renewal. How you worship is related to who you worship. In business language, the customer is always right. In worship, God is the customer. He is our only audience that seeks faithful worshipers as opposed to entertainment. Worship is of the spirit but the whole person, with all his or her senses, with both mind and body, needs to be involved in genuine worship.

****

The book of Revelation contains 24 references in which the word "worship" appears, in most instances derived from the Greek *proskuneooe*, which means to prostrate oneself to pay homage or obeisance. The first reference to the concept of worship occurs in 1:17: "When I saw him, I fell at his feet as though dead. Then he placed his right hand on me and said: 'Do not be afraid, I am the First and the Last.'" Lofty and Majestic Worship: In chapters 4-5 worship is shown in its most lofty form. Humble Posture: In 4:10 the 24 elders "fall down before him who sits on the throne, and worship [proskuneooe] Him. . . ." In 5:14, following hymns of praise, the 24 elders "fell down and worshiped." A literal translation would be "fell down and prostrated themselves." The grand climax is reached when the whole universe worships God. The "Amen!" (Revelation 5:14) indicates the great controversy is ended, the work of the Church is finished, and the universe is once again at peace and in harmony with its Creator. A most majestic doxology!

****

Only God merits our worship. The disciples of Jesus worshiped Him. There is no indication that He objected to be worshiped (Matt 14:33; Matt 28:9, 17; Luke 24:52). Why did the Lord's disciples respond to Him in this way? They saw Him vested with the omnipotence of God. Overwhelmed by this proof of might, they fell down before him and carried out the *proskyneses*, exclaiming: 'Truly You are the son of God!' The adoration of the risen Lord has a similar background: Now the Lord stood before the disciples as the manifestly divine Lord. His disciples worshiped (Matthew 28:17; Luke 24:52).

****

Praise and Adoration: It is obvious that praise and submission are the most appropriate responses to the Gospel, the natural consequence of the Gospel. The Lord through Christ created us, and the Lord through the Lamb redeemed us, so we praise God, adore God, giving all glory to Him as we submit our lives to His lordship.

End of November for Thanksgiving

Thanksgiving is our national holiday that stems from the feast held in the autumn of 1621 by the Pilgrims to celebrate the colony's first successful harvest. The holiday is celebrated in the United States on the fourth Thursday in November. It is a tradition at this time for us to pause and thank God for His love, kindness and provision. Of course there is no greater gift than eternal life. We (believers) do not just hope but have assurance of eternal life (1 John 5:13). Believing is the ignition switch that gets us off the launching board to possess the promises of God.

Man was created to praise God because God deserves glory all the time (Isaiah 48:11). We exist not for ourselves but we were created to live for His glory. I appeal to you wherever you are to be saturated with an attitude of gratitude. Begin well with serenely and with too high a spirit to be cumbered with negative earthly worries. One of the giant killer of gratitude is comparing your blessings with other people's blessings. Certainly God does not bless us uniformly. We should therefore not indulge in lustful desires. Coveting is a sin. For example, some men lustfully desire to be women and women to be men, hence the blooming of homosexuality. Simply thank God for who you are in Christ.

****

"When we think back to that first Thanksgiving in 1621, and all that the Pilgrims endured, only half surviving the first brutal winter, we remember sacrifice upon which this land was built – and the sacrifice that continues to keep us free and safe."

****

Thursday is Thanksgiving Day. The Bible says, "Take delight in the LORD, and he will give you the desires of your heart" (Psalm 37:4). Even in times of sorrow, you will surely find the joy of the Lord in your heart. Don't focus on your monumental depressing situation but focus on Christ in you. Pour your tears at His feet with thanksgiving. They say that "A fear of weakness only strengthens the weakness." Turn your fears into strength by turning to the transcendent God. All sanity depends on acknowledging that nothing in this world is permanent but God is.

****

Philippians 4:6 – "Do not be anxious about anything, but in every situation, by prayer and petition, with thanksgiving, present your requests to God." The two important words often overlooked are, "WITH THANKSGIVING." Returning thanks for blessings already received increases our faith and enables us to approach God with the new boldness and the new assurance. God is deeply grieved by the thanklessness and ingratitude of which so many of us are guilty. When Jesus healed the ten lepers and only one came back to give Him thanks, in wonderment and pain He exclaimed, "Were not the ten cleansed? But where are the nine?" (Luke 17:17).

****

Go into praying with an attitude of thanksgiving. If you think it is not worthy to be thankful for the little you have received; be thankful for what you escaped. Thank God for what could have happened to you but didn't because of His swift grace. "The talent for being happy is appreciating and liking what you have, instead of what you don't have" ~ Woody Allen

****

Let gratitude be the pillow upon which you kneel to say your daily prayers. And let faith be the bridge you build to overcome evil and welcome good.

****

Loss is inevitable. Each one of us has ever experienced loss of something precious to us. For example lost opportunities, lost possibilities, and at times feelings, we can never get back again. That's part of what it means to be alive. How you respond to losses matters. Loss is devastating but it should never be allowed to define you. You are not a failure in God's economy. Remember the cliché: "You'll get over it…" Move on with hope and with a positive attitude. Begin well with serenely and with too high a spirit to be cumbered with negative worries.

****

"A rich man looked through his window and saw a man picking something from his dustbin, he said thank God I am not poor. The poor man looked and saw a naked man mischievous acting up on the street, he said thank God I am not mad. The mad man looked and saw an ambulance carrying a corpse to the mortuary, he said thank God I am not dead. In every situation give thanks to God".

****

What are you thankful for? John was thankful for this one thing: "I have no greater joy than this: to hear that my children are walking in the truth" (3 John 1:4).

****

Some things make you wonder whether its destiny, fate or coincidence... whatever it is I am grateful for the blessed opportunity! ~ Neoline Kirabo

****

I don't know about you, but I am already in the mood of praising God, for He has been good to me in spite of myself. Listening to God and praising are essential parts of praying. Waiting in the presence of God is saying to God, "Lord, speak I hear". Praising is God saying to you, "Speak I hear".

****

Waiting in the presence of God is part of praying. It is allowing God to minister to us. Prayer is two-way communication. God wants to speak to us when we meet with Him during praying. His desire to speak to us is far greater than our desire to speak to Him. He is as interested to speak to us as we are interested to hear from Him. Remember that faith comes by hearing and hearing from God. Our knees is the very place where faith is nurtured. Basically, praying is waiting in the presence of God to receive marching orders. In Proverbs, we read: "Blessed is the man who listens to me, watching daily at my doors, waiting at my doorway. For whoever finds me finds life and receives favor from the Lord" (Proverbs 8:34). Jesus said that "My sheep listen to my voice." (John 10:27).

****

I had a dream when I was being ridiculed and tormented by the people of the world. I was like an outcast in their eyes. In my dream, I was mentally and psychologically tormented, and I was forced to flee in search for a place of refuge or safe haven. After a long walk, I came across a very nice Church building. It was a relief to me as I entered it hurriedly. To my surprise, inside the sanctuary, there were no pews (benches). The only furniture inside was a well-constructed altar with a script above it saying "House of Prayer". This is a title that we rarely use in reference to our sanctuaries, yet it has deep spiritual meaning.

As soon as I woke up I pondered about what God was trying to say to me. I prayed in search for the interpretation of the dream. The following scriptures came to my mind: And he was teaching them and saying to them, "Is it not written, 'My house shall be called a house of prayer for all the nations'? But you have made it a den of robbers" (Mark 11:17). In order to understand what Jesus meant, we should read Isaiah 56:7- "On my altar; for my house shall be called a house of prayer for all peoples". The main reason we get together in our sanctuaries is to pray. Everything that takes place in the sanctuary must be in the context of praying. The total hour of praying includes: scripture reading, meditation, listening, singing, praising, worshiping, petition, interceding, fasting, repenting and giving. Using the Church or going to Church for other reasons other than praying is turning it into a den of robbers.

****

Tomorrow, May 7, is the National Day of Prayer. Praying is our right that precedes the constitution; it is the right granted to man by God. The National Day is intended to awaken us to pray. We enjoy a rich, dynamic and unbroken relationship with God through Jesus Christ but we must communicate to God in prayers. Whenever Jesus went to a place, He did not look for a motel but for a mountain, a lonely place to talk to the Father in prayers. He taught us how to cultivate and maintain the daily fellowship with our Father. "When we are in Christ, God is on our side. Therefore praying is not a means to get God on our side; praying is a means to align ourselves with God's purposes, plans and will". You must pray.

****

Worship is an aspect of covenant renewal. How you worship is related to who you worship. In the business language the customer is always right. In worship, God is the customer. He is our only audience. He seeks faithful worshipers as opposed to entertainment. Worship is of the spirit but the whole person, with all senses; with spirit, soul and body, needs to be actively involved in worshiping. Genuine worshiping acknowledges that God is worthy of all the glory.

****

John 4:22 – "You worship you know not: we know what we worship: for salvation is of the Jews". God reveals Himself to be worshiped. True worshipers have relationship with God. The Bible says that without faith it is impossible to please him: for he that cometh to God must believe that he is, and that he is a rewarder of them that diligently seek him (Hebrews 11:6). Worship is a dimension that cannot be unlocked unless you get to understand whom you are worshiping.

****

True worshiping begins by discovering the worthiness of God. We are not worthy but He makes us worthy. God is the reason for our worthiness. God is Spirit, and we worship Him in spirit and truth (John 4:23). Truth means the sincerity and integrity of the soul. Bodily exercise profiteth nothing. Our stresses, anxieties, pains, and problems expire after we step out of the physical into the spirit. Worries arise simply because we do not see God in His majesty worthiness or even ourselves worthy of His love. His worthiness can't be bartered over with the melancholies of this world. True worshiping is life changing; it is not contained in the church building but follows us outside the building to influence the lives of other people around us.

****

Paul said in Romans 3 that seeking God begins at conversion. We are called to structure our worship on seeking God. If we structure our worship with a view to seekers then our worship must be structured for only believers since they are the seekers of God.

****

Your most profound and intimate experiences of worship will likely be your darkest days - when your heart is broken, when you feel lonely and abandoned, when you are out of options, when the pain is great and you turn to God alone - Rick Warren

****

December: First / Second Coming of Christ

Luke 2:14 - "Glory to God in the highest heaven, and on earth peace to those on whom his favor rests." There can be no peace on earth unless there is a reconciliation between heaven and earth. In Christ, God came to establish the eternal covenant with us and save humanity. The Word was with God, and God was in the Word (John 1:1). The Word put on human flesh and dwelt (tabernacled) among us. Jesus paid for our sins and removed our guilt. We go back to God in His very righteousness. Now the curtain separating heaven from earth is ripped. His will is done on earth as it is done in heaven.

****

I pity people like Idris Kazibwe who ignorantly waste their time challenging and mocking the New Testament. Yet the same people have no problem with the Old Testament. The culprits are primarily critical of the deity of Jesus. They have no problem God revealing Himself to Moses in form of an insignificant thing like the burning bush but have problem with the revelation of God to us in human form! I want to say that man is the most treasured and unique creation on earth; man is above all creations. God spoke into existence all things but created man by His own hands, breathed into man His spirit and man became a living soul. God treasured man with His very breath (Spirit) (Genesis 2:7). Job said that, "The Spirit of God has made me; the breath of the Almighty gives me life" (Job 33:4).

There is a progressive revelation of God from the Old Testament to the New Testament. Progressive revelation does not mean the Old

Testament is somehow less true than the New Testament or vice versa. The Bible makes a distinction between the time before and after Christ. For the law was given through Moses, but grace and truth came through Jesus Christ (John 1:17). In the past, God spoke to us through images and prophets but in the present He has spoken to us directly through His Son (Hebrews 1:2; 1 John 2:23). The Law made it a necessity for us to have the grace in order for us to be saved.

The Scriptures testify to a progression of God's revelation of Himself to humanity. "The nativity mystery" conceived from the Holy Spirit and born of the Virgin Mary, means that God became human, truly human and truly God out of his own grace. Born of the Virgin Mary means a human origin for God, and conceived of the Holy Spirit means born from above. Likewise, God requires us to be born from above (of the Spirit). God did everything, emptied heaven, for the sake of the salvation of your soul. The choice is yours!

****

Jesus was born a little baby like any other person to relate to us. He became a Lamb to be the sacrifice for our sins. He rose from death so that we might become partakers of His resurrected life, the only kind of life that defeated death. He ascended to the heavenly throne so that the Holy Spirit can descend to the earth to sit at the throne of our hearts. This is not an ordinary king but El-Shaddai, the All-sufficient Lord, the Jehovah of ages, the everlasting Elohim!

****

There are over 400 prophecies in the Old Testament which point to the coming of the Messiah - His life and death. Jesus Christ perfectly fulfilled every single one of them. One of the most convincing evidence for the inspiration and validity of the Scriptures is the verified historical fulfillment of hundreds of specific predictions. The historical figure, Jesus of Nazareth, fulfilled over 300 precise detailed predictions. These ranged from the place of his birth, the method of his death, and even the amount of money he would be betrayed for.

The odds of someone doing that who was not the Messiah are too great to even figure. It is impossible. Look at some of the predictions about His birth: Isaiah 7:14 says, "Therefore the Lord himself shall give you a sign; Behold a virgin shall conceive and bear a son and shall call his name Immanuel." Jesus was born of the Virgin Mary. Micah 5:2: "But thou, Bethlehem Ephratah, though thou be little among the thousands of Judah, yet out of there shall he come forth unto me that is to be ruler in Israel; whose goings forth have been from of old; from everlasting." His being called Immanuel (Isaiah 7:14). "The virgin will conceive and give birth to a son, and they will call him Immanuel" (which means "God with us") (Matthew 1:23).

Prophecies about His death: The Messiah Will Be Betrayed By One Of His Followers. Psalm 41:9. Also, Psalm 55:12-13. Fulfilled in Matthew 26:47, 49-50. The Messiah Will Be Betrayed For 30 Pieces of Silver (Zechariah 11:12-13). Fulfilled in Matthew 26:14-16. The Messiah Will Be Tried And Condemned. Isaiah predicted the Messiah to be the Suffering Servant (Isaiah 53:1-8). Fulfilled in Matthew 27:1-2; Luke 23:1, 23. The Messiah Will Be Silent Before His Accusers (Isaiah 53:7-8). Fulfilled in Matthew 27:12-14. The Messiah Will Be Smitten And Spat Upon (Micah 5:1). Fulfilled in Matthew 26:67-68. The Messiah Will Be Mocked And Taunted (Psalm 22:7-8). The fulfillment in Matthew 27:39-40. The Messiah To Die By Crucifixion, With Pierced Hands And Feet (Psalm 22:14-16). The fulfillment in Matthew 27:31. The Messiah Will Suffer With Sinners (Isaiah 53:12). The fulfillment in (Matthew 27:38). The Messiah's Garments Will Be Divided By Casting Lots (Psalm 22:18). The fulfillment in (Matthew 27:35). The Messiah's Bones Will Not Be Broken (Numbers 9:12). The fulfillment in John 19:31-37. The Messiah Will Be Buried In A Rich Man's Tomb (Isaiah 53:9). The fulfillment in Matthew 27:57-60.

Jesus was born in Bethlehem. Jesus came as the Gracious Savior but He will return as the sovereign ruler to execute justice to all. You can escape condemnation by choosing Jesus the Savior as opposed to Jesus the Judge.

****

Luke 2:32 – "A light to lighten the Gentiles, and the glory of thy people Israel." The birth of Jesus was a fulfillment of Isaiah 49:6. In the Old Testament, God chose Israel and trusted her with His oracles to be a light to the nations that did not know God. Jesus is the promised faithful servant of Yahweh, who is the light to all nations (Jews/Gentiles), who honors the name of His Father. By the power of His death, Jesus liberates those who are bound by sin and live in darkness, in ignorance of the truth. He liberates us to liberate others. As we let our light shine, we unconsciously give other people permission to do the same. Let that little light of yours shine!

****

Every year, we take time to wonder at the kindness of a God who would descend from eternal bliss to live in squalor among us. His acts of kindness, and above all the gift of his own life for us, continue to work their way through history, inspiring countless acts of mercy throughout every land and age.

****

"Silent night, holy night! All is calm, all is bright." What made the silent night holy and bright is the glory of God that was born to light up the world. Jesus was born with the pivotal message that, "The darkness hovering around us does not have the final say." Lucifer (Satan), also called the light bearer, was the angel of light in heaven before he fell but he lost the light after the fall. He was cast down on earth, and his darkness hovered over the face of the earth. Adam was created with the light of God and placed in a special place called Eden but he lost it after he was corrupted by sin. The brightness of the light in Jesus is the very glory of God that Adam lost, and cannot be corrupted by sin. Thank God for His providential hand of grace that reached out to us in the fullness of time.

****

"'O Come Let Us Adore Him'" - A calling to worship Him on earth as it is done in heaven. His will is done on earth as it is done in heaven. Angels worshiping God in heaven descended to worship the Son born on the earth. On this day, every year, we take time to wonder at the kindness of the God that would descend from eternal bliss to live in squalor among us. His saving love, and above all the gift of His own life for us, continue to work their way through history, inspiring countless acts of mercy throughout every land and age.

****

Second Coming:

The return of our Lord is divided into two parts. The first part is when Jesus comes for His bride (Church). The second part is when Jesus returns to the earth with His bride.

****

The word 'rapture' does not appear on the pages of the Bible but its meaning is there. Just look at the life of Jesus. He came on earth by natural birth, and He left the earth by catching away in the cloud. "For the Lord Himself will descend from heaven with a shout, with the voice of an archangel, and with the trumpet of God. And the dead in Christ will rise first. Then, we who are alive and remain shall be caught up together with them in the clouds to meet the Lord in the air. And thus, we shall always be with the Lord. Therefore comfort one another with these words" (1 Thessalonians 4:16-18). Many Christians believe that Jesus will return in the clouds and take his church (Christians) up from the earth to meet him. They shall ascend into heaven with the Lord until Jesus is ready to return to earth for his second coming! The rapture is not the second coming of Christ. Jesus never touches down on earth but meets the believers in the clouds.

****

Anticipation is an important part of life. Enjoy the Christmas season in anticipation of the Second coming of our Lord. The story of Jesus has yet to be accomplished when He returns to establish His rule over all humanity. We are called to occupy till He returns. He will suddenly appear at such an hour when you think not! The Second coming is the perpetual light on the path which makes sense of the First Coming. "Apart from the Second Advent of our Lord, the world is more likely to sink into a pandemonium than to rise into a millennium."

****

The first miracle performed by Jesus was to restore joy on the wedding. The changing of water into wine projects the nature of His ministry. His ministry begins with the celebration of victory in joy and ends with the celebration of victory in judgment (cross). The ministry of Jesus began with Jesus changing water into wine (John 2:1-11) because the essence of His coming is to restore our lost joy. Wine represents the blood of Jesus and joy represents our new life in Christ (spirit). The ministry of Jesus begins in the Gospels with turning water into wine and ends the book of Revelation with turning water into blood (Revelation 8:8; 16:3).

His Second Coming is to judge the world. The wages of every sin that is not confessed and repented to Christ will be paid by individual people. The love of God brings salvation as opposed to judgment but the sovereign and sure judgment of God is coming to this world. Justice and holiness are attributes of God. It means we cannot escape His judgment unless we repent. The love of God extends to us a choice to make; an ultimate decision to judge ourselves unworthy by accepting the worthiness of God through Jesus Christ so that we might escape His judgment. Jesus partook of the bitter cup of the wrath of God so that you can partake of the sweet cup of salvation in celebration. Will you do that? The Bible says that today is the day of salvation. For he says, "In the time of my favor I heard you, and in the day of salvation I helped you." I tell you, now is the time of God's favor, now is the day of salvation" (2 Cor. 6:2).

****

It is ridiculous to celebrate the First Coming of Christ when you are not ready for His Second Coming because the two cannot be separated. "---instructing us to deny ungodliness and worldly desires and to live sensibly, righteously and godly in the present age, looking for the blessed hope and the appearing of the glory of our great God and Savior, Christ Jesus, who gave Himself for us to redeem us from every lawless deed, and to purify for Himself a people for His own possession, zealous for good deeds...." (Titus 2:12-13). And that holy life, just urged on the believer, of quiet self-restraint, of love to others, of piety towards God, must be lit up by a blessed hope, by a hope which is far more than a hope; that holy life of the faithful must be a continued waiting for a blessed hope—"the hope laid up for us in heaven". The acid test for a true believer is the coziness and readiness for His return. And so the preciousness of Christ is the evidence of your faith. And the anticipation of His coming is the evidence of His preciousness.

****

Somebody asked a question: "Why has Jesus delayed His return?" The mercies of God have delayed the return of our Lord; He is interceding for His Church. Suddenly, the judgment of God will overtake the mercies of God, and He will return to make the kingdom of this world the kingdom of heaven.

****

The believers are going to be judged by rewarding. God will reward our good work even though our good works are works of Christ through us. It is like crowning His gifts to us.

****

2 Cor.11 – "For I betrothed you to one husband, so that to Christ I might present you as a pure virgin. Christ, our bridegroom is coming for a pure bride." Virginity is the only gift that Christ bestows to His bride (Church). This is neither a natural quick fix nor an infantile superstition sense of self-worth. It is supernaturally motivated moral integrity bestowed to us. It is a virtue that separates us from the rest of the world that is in adultery. Jesus is not returning for a naked bride who is a practitioner of harlotry, poor and blind, but to a bride who has kept herself pure and without blemish, and who has clothed herself in faithful works (Revelation 19:7-8; Rev.3).

****

Revelation 20:3 – "He threw him into the Abyss, and locked and sealed it over him, to keep him from deceiving the nations anymore until the thousand years were ended. After that, he must be set free for a short time." Satan himself is shut up for a thousand years in the "abyss" (Greek for "bottomless pit"), the preparatory prison to the "lake of fire," his final doom. This is a place of confinement, Luke 8:31 for this is called a prison, Revelation 20:7 and is distinguished from the lake of fire, into which the devil is afterwards cast, Revelation 20:10.

****

Revelation 21:8 – "But the cowardly, the unbelieving, the vile, the murderers, the sexually immoral, those who practice magic arts, the idolaters and all liars1--their place will be in the fiery lake of burning sulfur. This is the second death." Sulfur contains compounds which smell bad will definitely turn people into social pariahs. The word theion translated "brimstone" is exactly the same word theion which means "divine". The ancients had used brimstone for religious purifications, such as in Homers Odyssey, which it is written; 'Bring hither fire, and hither sulphur bring To purge the palace' (Homer, Od. xxli. 481 f.).

The fumes from burning sulfur... are "toxic and dangerously irritating..." Olfactory fatigue, also known as odor fatigue or olfactory adaptation, is the temporary, normal inability to distinguish a particular odor after a prolonged exposure to that airborne compound. Whether it's roses, fresh cookies, or a skunk, when you get a whiff of something, molecules travel through your nose and to your odor receptors. This whole process is pretty intense for your brain. To keep your nervous system from exhausting itself with continuous stimuli, the receptors experience temporary sensory fatigue, or olfactory adaptation. Odor receptors stop sending messages to the brain about a lingering odor after a few minutes and instead focus on novel smells. That's why your nose adjusts to your coworker who wears too much cologne, but perks up again when he eats pad thai at his desk. However, the stench of Sulfur cannot be adjusted to human senses of smell.

****

Revelation 12:9 - "The great dragon was hurled down--that ancient serpent called the devil, or Satan, who leads the whole world astray. He was hurled to the earth, and his angels with him." Satan is the Dragon. The Antichrist is not Satan but he is Satan's answer to God's Son. The Antichrist is the "opposite Jesus"; he is the "instead of" Jesus. He is the counterfeit to Christ. He is the Beast (Revelation 19:20).

****

The scripture says that "All inhabitants of the earth will worship the beast--all whose names have not been written in the Lamb's book of life, the Lamb who was slain from the creation of the world" (Revelation 13:8).

Somebody sent me this comment: "I am an Atheist. I don't believe in anything. Therefore I will neither worship your God nor the antichrist as indicated in your Bible in the book of Revelation." Answer: I want to say that worship is somehow fundamental to human existence.

Even an atheist worships something. God created within us a space for Him to occupy. Without worshiping God, the emptiness within is filled with other lustful desires. We end up worshiping the false gods or idols in the form of material gains. The scripture says that "All inhabitants of the earth will worship the beast--all whose names have not been written in the Lamb's book of life, the Lamb who was slain from the creation of the world" (Revelation 13:8). Surely, if you are not among the redeemed of Christ, you will worship the beast. Satan will transform himself into an angel of light to deceive many (2 Corinthians 11:14). When the antichrist appears, it will be hard for a natural man to identify him as the beast. He will not be the ugly creature with horns as projected in our arts. He will look wonderful, and he will be charming and successful. He will be the ultimate winner, and will appear as an angel of light. He will appeal to the emotions of all people that are not regenerated spiritually, and they will surely worship him. Worshiping, in this case, is not going to church like we do; it is giving allegiance to the antichrist. The Bible gives a severe warning against worshiping the beast and receiving his mark: "If anyone worships the beast and his image and receives his mark on the forehead or on the hand, he, too, will drink of the wine of God's fury, which has been poured full strength into the cup of his wrath." (Revelation 14:9, 10).

****

13:4-5 - "And they worshiped the dragon which gave power unto the beast: and they worshiped the beast, saying, Who [is] like unto the beast? Who is able to make war with him?" "And there was given unto him a mouth speaking great things and blasphemies; and power was given unto him to continue forty [and] two months."

Eventually, the Beast turns this unbridled animosity toward all the people of God, as Rev. 13 v.5-7 makes clear: "And he was given a mouth speaking great things and blasphemies, and he was given authority to continue for forty-two months. The Little Horn: Then he opened his mouth in blasphemy against God, to blaspheme His name, His tabernacle, and those who dwell in heaven. And it was granted to him to make war with the saints and to overcome them." Earlier John makes it plain that the beast's power and authority and kingdom are given to him by Satan. (v.2). And John also tells us something revealed to no one else: The Bible gives a severe warning against worshiping the beast and receiving his mark: "If anyone worships the beast and his image and receives his mark on the forehead or on the hand, he, too, will drink of the wine of God's fury, which has been poured full strength into the cup of his wrath." (Revelation 14:9, 10). This is the beginning of the Great Tribulation which Daniel spoke about in when the sacrifice and the oblation ceases. This is called the Abomination of Desolation. Also, see Matthew 24 verse 15.

****

"At once I was in the Spirit, and there before me was a throne in heaven with someone sitting on it. And the one who sat there had the appearance of jasper and carnelian. A rainbow, resembling an emerald, encircled the throne." (Revelation 4:2-3).

Genesis 9:9-11– "Then God said to Noah and to his sons with him: "I now establish my covenant with you and with your descendants after you, and with every living creature that was with you—the birds, the livestock and all the wild animals, all those that came out of the ark with you—every living creature on earth. I establish my covenant with you: Never again will all life be destroyed by the waters of a flood; never again will there be a flood to destroy the earth." The floods destroyed every living thing on the face of the earth except those which entered the wooden box (Ark) built by Noah. Noah's Ark is symbolic of our salvation by Jesus Christ. God made a legal contract (covenant) with Noah, on behalf of all His creations on earth (man, animals and the physical features), never to destroy the universe with the flood again. God gave the rainbow as the visible sign to man to remind him of God's covenant.

The current world we live in will be destroyed by fire (2 Peter 3:10-11). This will be an end to the Old World that begun in sin (Gen. 2:16, 3:1-6). The end of our Present Kingdom Age of Grace will be marked by the physical end of the current heavens and earth. The Bible says that: "Looking for and hastening the coming of the day of God, because of which the heavens will be destroyed by burning, and the elements will melt with intense heat! But according to His promise we are looking for new heavens and a new earth, in which righteousness dwells" (2 Peter 3:12-13).

****

Seeking wisdom

Wisdom begins with God but there is such a thing as human wisdom and divine wisdom. The discipline to balancing the two is necessary. Human wisdom involves executing and application of the natural knowledge wisely. Practical wisdom involves human opinions, proper timing, prioritizing and experience (which are prerequisites to it). Human wisdom is limited in the physical realm but the divine wisdom works in both the heavenly (spiritual) and earthly (physical).

****

Knowledge is practically acquired by us but wisdom comes from God to us. We look for knowledge from around us but we look up in search for wisdom. When we possess wisdom, wisdom possess us. Wisdom is the beginning of knowing God. Wisdom is Jesus Christ.

****

It is true that we cannot use our brains to the maximum. Given the fact, our minds is the key to unlocking our potential. Your mind is a terrible thing to waste but a wonderful thing to invest in. Intelligence is determined by knowledge, creativity, and experience. Also, there is such a thing as emotional intelligence which is the cornerstone of mental sharpness. "Moments that test your mental toughness are ultimately testing your emotional intelligence. You can be intelligent but not educated or you can be educated but not intelligent, so embrace what you are good at and combine both formal and informal education." Spiritually, sanctification is to be set apart for the divine propose. Wisdom begins in knowing God. The gift of knowledge is reserved for those committed to the divine purpose - by surrendering wholeheartedly to God.

****

Both faith and wisdom come from God. The Bible says that faith comes to us by hearing and hearing (or reading) the Word of God (Romans 10:17). Faith is not mental, it is of the heart (spiritual). God gives each of us a measure of faith (Romans 12:3). God reaches out to us by His grace, and we are connected to Him by faith. The saving faith is the means of accepting the grace. Because each believer receives his measure of faith by God's allotment, we are prevented from thinking of ourselves "more highly" than we ought. The saving faith must be activated into the serving faith. Wisdom comes after the saving faith. Wisdom is acting on the truth in the sacred Word of God. This is a process intended to shape your life and bring you into conformity with Christ. The divine wisdom is actuated faith. Wisdom involves insight - the deepest level of knowing and the most meaningful to your life. Such as consecrated life to serve others by minimizing your own needs and desires. Also, not hesitate to face hardship, persecution and even death. Basically wisdom is staying true to your faith. We need the divine wisdom that surpasses human understanding to guard our hearts and to impact the world (Philippians 4:7).

****

The first step in the acquisition of wisdom is silence, the second listening, the third memory, the fourth practice, the fifth teaching others.

****

The school season begins today in the USA after a long summer holiday. I encourage students to take studying seriously knowing that your future job depends on what you do now. Studying is not limited to kids alone, adults can study too. Learning is a lifetime process. You can never be overeducated. As Gandhi insinuated, "Live as if you were to die tomorrow. Learn as if you were to live forever."

****

When God pushes you to the edge, trust Him fully, because only two things can happen: Either He will catch you when you fall or He will teach you how to fly - Unknown

****

"There are no disappointments to those whose wills are buried in the Will of God"

****

"Some things are better said when you say nothing at all" - Magode Ikuya

****

"I spent a long time trying to come to grips with my doubts when suddenly I realized I had better come to grips with what I believe" - Tom Skinner

****

The key to life is accepting challenges. Every blessing comes with a challenge. Being challenged in life is inevitable. Challenges are the causes of change; yet, change is not spared from challenges.

****

Life is a teacher, the more you live the more you learn.

****

For as Ecclesiastes 3 reminds us, there is a time for every matter under heaven, and those times and changing seasons are worth treasuring.

****

"Nature does not hurry, yet everything is accomplished" ~ Lao Tzu

****

Galatians 6:9 – "Let us not become weary in doing good, for at the proper time we will reap a harvest if we do not give up." Your responsibility is to continue to do good even when you do not see results because God alone knows the season of your harvesting.

****

The will of God will not take you where the grace of God cannot sustain you.

****

No one stays in a pothole forever. Tough times don't last but tough people do.

****

Sometimes the best way to know what your app should be is to know what it shouldn't be. Figure out your app's enemy and you'll shine a light on where you need to go.

****

Wisdom is more knowledge and intelligent. Wisdom is discernment and it includes the commitment to follow through the action.

****

Galatians 6:9 – "Let us not become weary in doing good, for at the proper time we will reap a harvest if we do not give up." Your responsibility is to continue to do good even when you do not see results because God alone knows the season of your harvesting.

****

The will of God will not take you where the grace of God cannot sustain you.

****

No one stays in a pothole forever. Tough times don't last but tough people do.

****

Sometimes the best way to know what your app should be is to know what it shouldn't be. Figure out your app's enemy and you'll shine a light on where you need to go.

****

Wisdom is more knowledge and intelligent. Wisdom is discernment and it includes the commitment to follow through the action.

****

Before you see the rainbow, you see the rain. If you want to reach your goals, you have to be able to put up with the pain.

****

Before your weaknesses are exposed to destroy your characters, attack them first. That is how we survive in the animal kingdom!

****

You are not in this world to live up to other people's expectations, nor should you feel the world should live up to yours.

****

The worst part about being strong is that nobody ever asks you if you are ok!

****

Never underestimate the impact you have on the lives of others. Even in your dark days, God uses you to light someone's path.

****

"Seven colors make a rainbow, seven chords make a music, seven days make a week, seven continents make the world and seven beautiful letters make us FRIENDS. Friends are priceless"

****

"It does not matter where there is a matter because you will matter where it matters" ~ Funke Adejumo.

****

Man's primary problem is ignorance. However, everybody is ignorant of certain things; nobody knows all things.

****

Strength isn't having muscles. It's having control of your own mind and making it capable of achieving anything ~ Alaso Alice

****

TIME decides who can be in your life.

HEART decides who you want in your life.

BEHAVIOR decides who will stay in your life.

****

Definition of stupid - knowing the truth; seeing the truth; but still believing the lies.

****

When someone hurts you; cry a river; build a bridge and get over it ~ Nyaiteera Victoria

****

"A life without fame can be a good life, but fame without a life is no life at all".

****

You have only one direction to move – That direction is forward.

****

The best way to predict your future is to create it.

****

"Each time we focus more on how a woman is dressed, rather than what is inside her head, we objectify women and that is to say they don't matter in society."

****

Opportunities and Chances favor those in motion.

****

The more arguments you win, the less friends you will have.

****

A psychologist is someone who takes a subject you understand and makes it sound confusing.

****

Life is better when you are happy. But life is the best when other people are happy because of you. Be inspired, give peace and share your smile with everyone.

****

Gratitude is my attitude.

****

Every blessing comes with a challenge.

****

It is equally important to get the proper diagnoses as it is to get the right prescription. Avoid putting bandages on headaches! "Truth is like surgery, it may hurt, but it cures. While a lie is like a painkiller, it gives temporary relief but has side effect later."

****

"It's better to be hated for what you are than to be loved for what you are not."

****

Failure is not the opposite of success, it is part of success...

****

Never ask for a lighter rain, just pray to God for a better umbrella. - That is the attitude!

****

I can do things you cannot. You can do things I cannot. Together we can do great things ~ Mother Teresa

****

Every bad situation has something positive... Even a Clock that has stopped is correct twice a day ~ Kimpur Seretion

****

Never underestimate the power of unity. "When spider webs combine, they can tie up a lion...." ~ (Ethiopian Proverb)

****

People are always going to throw stones in your path. It depends on what you make with them; a Wall or a Bridge? - Remember you are the architect of your life.

****

Belief is what we carry around... Passion is what carries us around...

****

Looking back makes you smart. Looking forward makes you mature. Looking down makes you wise. Looking up makes you strong - Amazing Grace!

****

Love is indescribable because God is Love.

****

Love is the pursuit of happiness but true love is tested in times of crisis.

****

"Love yourself for what you are, instead of hating yourself for what you are not."

****

Whereas some give to be loved others give to love!

****

A pen is mightier than the sword.

****

"To whom little is not enough, nothing is enough."

****

"If your expectation of others is a negative one, you never will never progress."

****

If you think that the world revolves on you, then your world must be really small!

****

Get your acts together, you never know who's watching...

****

Patience is not idle waiting, but responding while you're waiting.

****

"Attitudes are contagious. Are yours worth catching?" ~ Dennis and Wendy Mannering

****

The victory is not in changing the minds of your critics. The victory is in completing your assignment ~ Bishop Jakes

****

It's not important to hold all the good cards in life, but it's important how well you play with the cards you hold.

****

Every situation has an advantage. He that is down fears not to fall!

****

'Whatever you dream of becoming tomorrow, become now.' ~ Bishop Akintayo Sam Jolly

****

Only through the experience of trial and suffering can the soul be strengthened, ambitions inspired and success achieved.

****

To be ashamed of doing wrong is a virtue. When you truly don't care what anyone thinks of you, you have reached a dangerously awesome level of indiscipline.

****

When everything goes well stand warned that troubles are not far away stalking you. When you constantly do not experience any problem, it may be a signal that you are travelling the wrong path.

****

Walk over your trials because God's favor is with you. "Haters will see you walk on water and say it is because you can't swim."

****

Understanding the basis of every occurrence is what I call 'maturity'.

****

Great spirits have always encountered violent opposition from mediocre minds.

****

A little knowledge is dangerous. But nothing in the world is more dangerous than sincere ignorance and conscientious stupidity.

****

All of us need partnership; I mean somebody that will cheer us up in the life's journey. "If you want to travel fast go alone. If you want to travel far, go together" ~ African proverb

****

Toxic people will pollute everything around them. Don't hesitate. Fumigate.

****

"Life is a fight for territory, once you stop fighting for what you want what you don't want will automatically take over."

****

"Life becomes more meaningful when you realize the simple fact that you'll never get the same moment twice."

****

Having the sharp brain is not enough, the important thing is to know how we use it.

****

Never ruin an apology with an excuse!

****

My daily prayer: Oh Lord, I hustle in silence please let my success make noise.

****

"If you want to collect honey don't kick over the beehive because what might come out may not be honey!"

****

Ask yourself if what you are doing today is getting you closer to where you want to be tomorrow.

****

When things become tough, you should become tough. When trouble comes, run into it, you will find yourself running into the hands of Jesus. He shows up whenever we are in trouble.

****

Often when we lose hope and think this is the end, God smiles from above and says, "Relax, it is just a bend, not the end".

****

Music is comforting. When everything has changed, it's the lyrics that stay the same.

****

"In fiction: we find the predictable boring. In real life: we find the unpredictable terrifying" ~ Mokokoma Mokhonoana

****

"Love the life you live and live the life you love……. 'simple'" ~ Kal Harris

****

Sometimes you have to lose so that you can learn how to win.

****

No one can step on your back unless YOU bend it.

****

"If you can't be a pencil to write every person's happiness then be a rubber to erase everyone's sorrow!"

****

As long as you working towards your best, you need not worry. After all, nobody has ever been at his or her best!

****

Well done is better than well said.

****

If you want to fly, you have to give up the things that weigh you down.

****

The saddest thing in this life is to watch someone you love turn into everything you hate.

****

People need to understand that this world doesn't revolve around them. If you think that the world revolves around you, then your world must be really small!

****

Every person has a role to play in this universe. Some people make the world happen; some watch the world happen; some wonder what happened. It's your choice, which group you want to belong to. "The world dies over and over again, but the skeleton always gets up and walks."

****

The Happiness of your life depends upon the quality of your thoughts. So think positively....... Beauty does not depend on external details; Beauty reflects the inner disposition. External beauty should be the reflection of the internal cleanness.

****

"To me, the definition of family extends far beyond bloodlines. Family are those you choose to embrace with all the love and belonging and intimacy of blood lines" ~ Mama Thomas Winterburn

****

In places where child mortality is high and, parents depend on children especially in old age the more children they have the better. However, some consider having many children or migrating to distant places as signs of recklessness. They are calculations that having many children or risking your life on a dangerous journey to a new place has more benefits.

****

God defined love as loving neighbor as you love yourself. When someone else's happiness is your happiness, that's love.

****

Living is loving & loving is living one can't do without the other.

****

God is pleased by our faith because faith defiles the natural laws of the world.

****

Cowards never invest, and will never inherit the kingdom of prosperity.

****

Thank you, God not only for all of the blessings but for the frustrations which have helped me become a better person. "Everything that God allows to come our way is with a purpose. He uses even the greatest error & the deepest hurt to mold us into a person of worth & value" ~ Ssenyonjo Enock

****

When the Moon is full why looking for the Stars......

****

The bend in the road is not the end of the road unless you refuse to take the turn ~ Unknown

****

Oaks fall when reeds stand.

****

Our ability to express our emotions with tears is a gift, and God keeps track of every tear we cry (Psalm 56:8).

****

Your seed determines your harvest.

****

"The way of the righteous is like the first gleam of dawn, which shines ever brighter until the full light of day" (Proverbs 4:18).

****

One man's meat is another man's milk # maturity

****

A habit repeated becomes a behavior. A behavior repeated becomes a character. A character repeated becomes a personality.

****

"If you find an element of your interface requires instructions, then you need to redesign it." ~ Dan Rubin

****

Life begins when Jesus becomes the reason you live it.

****

"Truth never injures a cause that is just" ~ Mahatma Gandhi

****

"It is better to offer no excuse than a bad one" ~ George Washington

****

Pain warns you that something's wrong. Otherwise without it, you'd ignore what needs to be fixed in your life!

****

"Life is a challenge involving dealing with people, people, in particular, me".

****

Don't sell for less than the best.

****

The biggest risk is not taking any risk at all.

****

Respect people who carve time from their tight schedule to spend time with you. Such people never make an excuse of their tight schedule when you need them.

****

Discussing issues is the greatest weapon at our fingertips. It is what separates us from animals. A lot of problems in the world would disappear if we talked to each other instead of talking about each other.

****

Excuses don't construct monuments. Action does ~ Robin

****

Most people think that a good salesman is good at talking. But the most effective salesmen acknowledge that listening is the most important part of their job.

****

At times, people will notice the change in your attitude towards them but won't notice their behavior that made you change your attitude towards them ~ Kabahuma Desire

****

You can't reach for something new if your hands are still full of yesterday's junks.

****

Water finds its way where it flowed before. Money will come to those who had money before!

****

Do not regret growing older. It is a privilege denied to many that died young.

****

An over indulgence of anything, even something as pure as water, can intoxicate.

****

Never be afraid of errors. "Good ideas are the products of many bad ideas over time" ~ Dr. Wale Akiyemi.

****

He who marries beauty marries trouble ~ Nigerian Proverb

****

You can't fix yourself by breaking someone else!

****

If you are not talented then work hard; hard work can beat talents!

****

A society of paranoid people is what we've become. Too paranoid to show love and even more paranoid to receive it ~ Mfonobong Emerald

****

A wise man grabs concepts from the future and places them in now - This is considered to be the sense of creativity.

****

"Knowledge is no guarantee of good behavior, but ignorance and arrogance is a virtual guarantee of bad behavior."

****

Avoid multiplying words without knowledge.

****

Common sense is essentially necessary but not necessarily common!

****

The vision without action is daydreaming, action without vision is a nightmare!

****

You are confined only by the walls you build yourself.

****

97% of people who quit too soon are employed by the 3% that never gave up ~ Kamusime Sharon

****

Hurt me with the Truth but never comfort me with a Lie ~ Ssekkate Ivanovich

****

When you are wrong admit it. When you are right be quite.

****

The beautiful ones are not yet born.

****

Prepare for the worst in anticipation for the best. Live in the moment but invest in the future.

****

We live in a weird world whereby most people desire to be on the receiving end. Don't allow anybody or any situation to intimidate you or dictate your day & life.

****

"Love is not a place where we go and expect to leave. It is a house we go in anticipation to get embraced forever. Love is a shelter in a raging storm. Love is peace in the middle of war. Love will come and save us if we only call" ~ Okuyu Benard

****

Love has its source - God. Love comes to us from God but it is reserved for others. Love kills "self" and gives life to others.

****

Words have no wings but they can fly a thousand miles.

****

Blessed are they who don't know the why, but Trust in the character of the One who is supervising the process.

****

Discipline is just a choice between what you want now & what you want most ~ Luke De Gabriel

****

How people treat other people is a direct reflection of themselves.

****

Instead of walking in other people's shadows create your own shadow and walk in it.

****

"If your only tool is a hammer, all problems look like nails." Mark Twain.

****

Many people failed where I succeeded, simply because they were busy researching for impossibilities while I was researching for possibilities and solutions.

****

Don't do what others are doing; do what you are best at.

****

Acceptance is a very critical step in the journey towards healing. Denial seems sweet but only delays the journey.

****

When people lift you up, it is definitely not beyond the height of their hands, but when God lifts you up, it is limitless.

****

Life is a journey. Not everyone will understand your journey; you are here to travel the journey of your life even when nobody understand it. Sometimes you are going to make a decision about your own life that upsets others. Don't mind as long as you have the counseling of God.

****

What you make happen to others, God will make it happen to you!

****

Stop crossing oceans for people that won't even jump a puddle for you! ~ Chris Tusiime

****

God can do in a minute what we can't do in a lifetime! Let's learn to totally depend on God and to trust Him.

****

"At times, it is a serious risk not to take risk".

****

The struggle you are experiencing today is developing the muscles you need to move you forward tomorrow!

****

He has the most who is most content with the least.

****

This how much God cares: He attends a funeral of every hair that falls from your head!

****

Ridiculous things happen before a miraculous thing ~ Chris Tusiime

****

Love doesn't need to be perfect; it just needs to be true.

****

Never allow someone to be your priority while you are just their option! ~ Fidel Ojira

****

"He who stops being better stops being good" ~ Oliver Cromwell

****

Laughter and Love are priceless gifts, so live with passion, laugh and love as much as you breathe! ~ Steve Mbogo Ndigwa

****

Before you get mesmerized, maybe, you better first pinch that part you are looking at and see if the owners feel the pinch; then you can be sure what you see is what you get.

****

You remember your beauty when you feel ugly; your wholeness when you are broken; your innocence when you feel guilty; your purpose when you are confused, and hope when you are hopeless.

****

Better to make your absence felt than striving to make your presence noticed.

****

The deception of perversion is that it really thinks it can intermingle with purity and go undetected .... Never!

****

God does not only want your whole heart; He wants your heart wholly holy!

****

"If you really want to do something, you'll find a way. If you don't, you'll find an excuse." ~ Jim Rohn

****

God does not need your money; He is just testing your obedience!

****

Expression is saying what you wish to say; Impression is saying what others wish to listen.

****

Life is a people game... people helping & supporting other people.

****

Two things define you: The patience when you have nothing and the attitude when you have everything ~ Olga Were

****

It is only when it is dark enough that you can see the stars ~ Ed Kyeyune

****

You have not danced as yet as long as you can watch your steps. Real dancing is when every move you make does not involve conscious calculation. Dance like no one is watching. Work like you don't have to. Give like you don't have a need. Love like you've never been hurt. "A spiral with rhythms of progress and retrogressions are mighty and sublime".

****

"All blame is a waste of time. No matter how much fault you find with another, and regardless of how much you blame him, it will not change you." Wayne Dyer

****

Radical inner-honesty is the key to moral excellence. Honest people are first honest with themselves. Feeling good and doing good go hand in hand, but it must be the goodness that does not contradict the morality of God as portrayed in the Scriptures.

****

"Your faith is only as strong as the test it survives" ~ Myles Munroe

****

In order to stand up, you must know what it means to fall down.

****

The problem with closed-minded people is that their mouth is always open!

****

There is a thin line between confidence and arrogance, and there is a thin line between arrogance and stupidity!

****

"If you mess with the bull you're going to get the horns, sweetheart."

****

You cannot have the pearl without irritation, it is the friction that causes your pearl to shine.

****

"Faithless is he that says farewell when the road darkens." ~ J.R.R. Tolkien

****

High achievements are reserved for people with big plans. Aim high!

****

There is a way your past rears its ugly head especially when it's a nasty one.

****

God never sleeps, He never slumbers, He never tires from hearing our prayers. Believing is synonyms for optimistic.

****

It is not happy people who are thankful, it is thankful who are happy!

****

Volunteers are not paid, not because they are worthless but because they are priceless.

****

Sometimes the strongest people in the morning are those who cried all through the night.

****

You don't have to win every argument, agree to disagree.

****

A true friend never gets in your way unless you happen to be going down.

****

"Time management becomes an issue when your time is completely your own."

****

"Status quos are made to be broken." Inventions happen when a person is unsatisfied with the status quo. They are the ones who see things differently. They're not fond of traditional rules. And they have no respect for the status quo. Yet they are the epitome of development.

****

"He who fights with monsters should look to it that he himself does not become a monster because when you gaze long into the abyss, the abyss also gazes into you." ~ Friedrich Nietzsche

****

Psalm 139:2 – "You know when I sit down and when I get up. You know my thoughts before I think them." The words of our mouth begin as the thoughts of our minds. It is not easy to know the thoughts of others. One writer said that you have to know someone a thousand days before you can glimpse his or her soul. "He who knows others is wise; he who knows himself is enlightened." The reality is that the heart of another is a dark forest always, to which we have no access, no matter how close they have been to us unless they open up to us. Only God and Him alone can know the thoughts and intents of the hearts of all men. Paul said that "For in him we live and move and have our being" (Acts 17:28).

****

A dream is that thing you see when sleeping but the same thing that will not let you sleep.

****

Our greatest fear is inadequacy. The fear is not in some of us but in all of us. Yet, it is when we realize our inadequacy that we overcome fear because we see the need to depend on God.

****

If you stay ready you don't need to get ready!

****

The concept of the Christian life is in serving. The value in each human is the gift of serving others. The love of God in us is manifested in the love of the neighbor.

****

It is better to have been loved and lose it than never to have been not loved at all. Think about it whenever you lose a friend.

****

Real tears don't come when you miss a person; it comes when you don't want to miss her or him. Have a blissful weekend.

****

Who told you success comes on a silver plate. Success comes after repeated failing. It's about doing the right thing over and over again.

****

"You can never cross the ocean unless you have the courage to lose sight of the shore" ~ Christopher Columbus.

****

Favor is the divine partiality that qualifies the unqualified.

****

Experience is the best teacher but the tuition is high!

****

Confidence is not arrogance unless it is accompanied with pride.

****

Earthly life has a beginning but it is continuously changing with time. Everything has its place in time but no man is rich enough to buy back his past! Sometimes, the things we can't change end up changing us; our past is one of those things. Think about it.

****

There are two types of pain in this world: Pain that hurts you and, pain that changes you.

****

"The man who does more than he is paid for will soon be paid for more than he does" ~ Napuleun Hill

****

The ugly part about mediocrity is that it ruins many things; the beauty of it is that it always manifests itself!

****

There is nothing new to experience; experience comes by familiarizing that experience, if it has to acknowledge itself ~ Odeke Olira

****

Chance is a word void of sense; nothing can exist without a cause.

****

Never be afraid to take a stand even when it means standing alone because often times the one who soars solo has the strongest wings.

****

Any fool can drive in a straight line but it takes a real expert to handle the curves. I salute all the experts out there.

****

"The secret of happiness is not in doing what one likes, but in liking what one does" ~ James M. Barrie

****

"Dieting is the only game where you win when you lose!" ~ Karl Lagerfeld

****

Creativity is allowing yourself to make mistakes. Art is knowing which ones to keep.

****

Never make fun of someone who speaks broken English. It means they know another language.

****

A better tomorrow begins today.

****

"I have learned that faith means trusting in advance what will only make sense in reverse" ~ Philip Yancey

****

Opportunity is a moving target. The bigger the opportunity the faster it moves ~ Ed Kyeyune.

****

The good is the enemy of the best. A wise person aim for the best.

****

2 Corinthians 4:16 - "For which cause we faint not; but though our outward man perish, yet the inward man is renewed day by day". The character is renewed daily from inside.

****

Give all people "High five" with your eyes but not with your heart before verifying with scrutiny what they say. In ordinary life, if somebody consistently exaggerates or lies to you, you soon discount everything they say. It is called selective amnesia.

Humor:

"Everything men do, women can do it better." But the best chefs are said to be men.

****

Only a fool can say that he knows everything.

****

The fact that jerry fish have survived for 650 years despite lacking brains give hope to many people

****

If you want a religion to make you feel really comfortable, I certainly don't recommend Christianity" ~ CS Lewis.

****

Three thieves were taken to court and were found guilty. The first man stole a tin of sardine. The judge sentenced him to three years in prison because there were three fishes in the tin. The second man stole a tray of eggs, he got 30 years in prison because a tray of eggs contains 30 eggs. The third guy collapsed. He stole a bag of rice.

****

The boss asked his employee if he believes in life after death. The employee replied that certainly no, there is no proof. The boss replied well, there is now. After you left yesterday for your uncle's funeral, he came looking for you.

****

"So much of what we call management consists in making it difficult for people to work" ~ Peter Drucker

****

We live in the era of smart phones and stupid people!

****

So you lost your virginity for a Nokia 3310, now there's iPhone6plus. You should have waited. All is vanity!

****

"The more I understand people, the more I love my dog."

****

The two most beautiful words in the English language are "cheque enclosed" ~ Dorothy Parker

****

A drunkard man wondered: "So Jesus turned water into wine and forgot to turn it back into water!"

****

I am not competing with anybody........ if you get there before me..... congratulations. But remember life is an express road, overtaking is allowed....

****

Common sense is not a gift, it is a punishment because you have to deal with everyone who doesn't have it.

****

When a beautiful girl is stupid, it is not her head that suffers but her private parts ~ Tamale Mirundi

****

They say love is blind; I say to be in love is to be brain dead!

****

Love is like war, easy to start, hard to end and impossible to forget. So don't love.

****

"Having a female as a best friend is like having chicken for a pet; you will eat it someday." ~ Nigerian Proverb.

****

Never show up at your man's place un-announced, in the name of surprising him, you could end up surprising yourself!

****

You may have to renew your driver's license every year but not your marriage license.

****

The last time I was dumped I went to a random funeral and cried my heart out.

****

Don't let sex make you a mother before love makes you a wife.

****

Success is not sexually transmitted, so stop sleeping with successful men and work hard.

****

"We are living in a generation where people in love are free to touch each other's private parts but cannot touch each other's phones because they are private" ~ Tamale Mirundi

****

It's not that I'm afraid of falling in love, I am afraid of falling in love with the wrong person again

****

"All guys are the same. You better stick with me because that is all there is."

****

The Whitest man on earth has a black shadow.

****

He asked the mechanic if he repaired his car brakes. The mechanic replied that "I couldn't repair your brakes, so I made your horn louder."

****

A man who drives his dad's Mercedes has no moral authority to raise his voice at a man who rides his own bicycle!

****

Life is a dream for the wise, a game for the fool, a comedy for the rich, a tragedy for the poor!

****

"If Jesus had preached the same message that ministers preach today, He would never have been crucified."

****

"The Church used to be a lifeboat rescuing the perishing. Now she is a cruise ship recruiting the promising."

****

The only woman that knows where her husband is the widow. The rest of the women should just chill down.

****

Women say they don't understand me. It is not a surprise since my own mother has never understood me all these years, so I don't expect an alien to understand me either!

****

Abortion does not make you unpregnant, no! It just makes you a mother of a dead baby!

****

Don't be too honest in this world….. because straight trees are always chosen first for cutting!

****

The proof that man is the noblest of all creatures is that no other creature has ever denied it!

****

Never laugh at your wife's choices; you are one of them!

****

Unforgiveness is the sin unto death because even if we intercede for you, God cannot forgive you because you haven't forgiven others! (Matthew 6:15).

****

"If you want to change the world, do it when you are a bachelor. After marriage, you can't even change a TV channel!"

****

April 1st is Fools' Day. There are two ways to be fooled: One is to believe what isn't true; the other is to refuse to believe what is true. If you are victimized never consider yourself to be dumb. The humor is that you are a fool just this one day. This is the only day when the word 'fool' sounds with good tastes. The only day we allow to be fooled and we readily admit that we are fools with a bonus of a smile.

****

If you are thinking about sending me a gift today, please don't do it. The reason is because April 1st is not my day.

****

"Listening to your wife is like reading the terms and conditions of the website. You understand nothing, still you agree"

****

Stupidity is when you have a Land Rover plus a Land Cruiser and still have a Land Lord!

****

The longest route you can take is a Short-cut; avoid it if you can.

****

Ph.D. stands for Permanent Head Damage.

****

Stupidity is not a crime; it is the mistake that yields to crime.

****

"Marriage is neither heaven nor hell, it's simply purgatory" ~ Abraham Lincoln.

****

Half naked girls are hot, well -dressed girls are beautiful, hell is hot, heaven is beautiful.

****

I have come to understand that in the life of love there is no Mr. Right or Miss. Right. But what exists is Mr. Left and Miss. Left.

****

A successful man is one who makes more money than his wife can spend. A successful woman is one who can find such a man.

****

A man's devil is a woman and a woman's devil is another woman!

****

"They say you should never ask a woman her age & a man his salary..." The real reason is that most women do not know how many of their years they have actually lived & most men do not know how much of their income they have actually earned!

****

I don't understand banks. Why do they attach chains to their pens? If I'm trusting you with my money you should trust me with your pens!

****

The preacher began by saying, "I spent the very best of my years in the arms of another woman, not my wife." The church went silent until he said, "that woman was my mother."

****

Remember when people had diaries and got mad when someone read them? Now, they put everything online and get mad when people don't read them, then one wonders what do we want?

****

The best way for a wife to get a big birthday gift is when the husband forgets her birthday. He will end up buying something big in order to make up for the damage caused.

****

You aren't rich until you have something that money can't buy!

****

Your age does not define your maturity, your grades don't define your intellect.

****

If money can't buy you happiness, then you're not using it well.

****

Work hard in silence---- let success make the noise!

****

"Gaining weight while you still owe me money is a sign of disrespect!"

****

If you let a girl go and she comes back to you, it means no one likes her...

****

Men in suits look really successful until you find out that they work for men in T-shirts!

****

I walk through the rain so that nobody can see me crying because the rain washes away my tears!

****

"The most expensive liquid is "Tears" as it is made of 1% water and 99% feelings, so think twice before you hurt someone! ~ Negoga

****

"I am thankful for all of those who said NO to me. It's because of them I'm doing it myself." – Albert Einstein

****

"History does not repeat itself. Men repeat history, and then blame history for repeating itself" ~ Harry Truman

****

The woman who invented the phrase, "All guys are the same." was a Chinese woman who lost her husband in a crowd in China."

****

"I am not afraid of an army of lions led by a sheep; I am afraid of an army of sheep led by a lion" ~ Alexander the Great

****

Love is not what you say; love is what you do!

****

I don't seek attention: attention always finds me! ~ Zari Hassan

****

Being single doesn't mean you're available. Sometimes you have to put up a sign that says, "Do not disturb." ~ Ssenyojo Enock

****

A teacher was discussing with a parent concerning his son's performance at school. The teacher said, "Your child can not spell cow." The parent replied that, "The cow is too big, why don't you start with small things like mosquito?"

****

"In the military, they give medals to people who sacrifice their lives so that others can gain. In business, they give medals to people who sacrifice other people's lives so they can gain. We have it all backwards." ~ Simon Sinek

****

The lack of information was the problem of the past ages. The problem of the current age, the information age, is that we have too much information and too little time to absorb it. We are being bombarded with all kinds of needed and (mostly) un-needed information from all sides ~ Rwebishengye Rwabambali

****

A man asked his girlfriend what kind of gift she wants for Christmas, she replied "What about an ATM machine?"

****

He said it: President Robert Mugabe...

1. Racism will never end as long as white cars are still using black tyres.

2. Racism will never end as long we still wash first white clothes, then other colours later.

3. Racism will never end if people still use black to symbolize bad luck and white for peace!

4. Racism will never end if people still wear white clothes to weddings and black clothes to the funerals.

5. Racism will never end as long as those who don't pay their bills are blacklisted not White listed. Even when playing the pool (snooker), you haven't won until you sink the black ball, and the white ball must remain on the field.

6. But I don't care, so long as I'm still using the white toilet paper to wipe my black A*S, I' M STILL FINE! (Mugabe speech) LOL

Printed in the United States
By Bookmasters